Damp Squid

The English Language Laid Bare

Damp Squid

The English Language Laid Bare

Jeremy Butterfield

OXFORD
UNIVERSITY PRESS

OXFORD
UNIVERSITY PRESS

Great Clarendon Street, Oxford OX2 6DP

Oxford University Press is a department of the University of Oxford.
It furthers the University's objective of excellence in research, scholarship,
and education by publishing worldwide in

Oxford New York

Auckland Cape Town Dar es Salaam Hong Kong Karachi
Kuala Lumpur Madrid Melbourne Mexico City Nairobi
New Delhi Shanghai Taipei Toronto

With offices in

Argentina Austria Brazil Chile Czech Republic France Greece
Guatemala Hungary Italy Japan Poland Portugal Singapore
South Korea Switzerland Thailand Turkey Ukraine Vietnam

Oxford is a registered trade mark of Oxford University Press
in the UK and in certain other countries

Published in the United States
by Oxford University Press Inc., New York

© Jeremy Butterfield 2008

British Library Cataloguing in Publication Data
Data available

Library of Congress Cataloging in Publication Data
Data available

Typeset by Graphicraft Limited, Hong Kong
Printed in Great Britain
on acid-free paper by
Clays Ltd., St Ives plc

ISBN: 978-0-19-923906-1

3

Contents

A sea change
The Corpus

Those are pearls that were his eyes:
Nothing of him that doth fade
But doth suffer a sea-change
Into something rich and strange.
Shakespeare, *The Tempest*, Act I, Scene ii

Among the hundreds of words which Shakespeare bequeathed to English is *sea change*, and a sea change is exactly what the somewhat traditional world of dictionary-making has undergone.

Through advances in computer technology, and more recently the advent of the World Wide Web, it is now possible to amass previously inconceivable amounts of evidence about how English speakers around the world use English. Armed with this wealth of data, dictionary makers can now analyse English objectively to produce dictionaries describing it as it really is, rather than as it once was—or as some people feel it ought to be even now.

Traditionally dictionary makers have relied on three major sources of information:

- observing language in use—meaning written texts, often from an acknowledged literary canon

- their own, and other people's analyses, based on introspection about how language is used

- other dictionaries and reference books about language

While the second and third sources are easily available—if often unreliable—the first generally involved ploughing laboriously through hundreds or thousands of texts, to find examples of words used in all their different meanings. This in essence is how the *Oxford English Dictionary* (*OED*) was created, using the five million or so quotation slips that were filled in by armies of editors and volunteer readers.

The *OED* provides in ultra-scholarly detail the historical genealogies and biographies of all the meanings it covers. But most contemporary dictionaries aim to tell us how language is being used currently, relegating the 'when' and the 'where from' to the background. Where do the makers of such dictionaries go for their evidence? Traditionally, they, like the *OED*, have used reading programmes.

However, such programmes have two major defects: they are labour-intensive and arbitrary. Arbitrary, because it is humanly impossible to read all the written material on a given topic and therefore an arbitrary selection of sources has to be made. Arbitrary also because readers tend to comment on what's novel, unusual, or different about language, rather than on what's standard or typical (just as you or I when reading a book will linger over novel words, meanings, and phrases).

For most purposes, however, what people require dictionaries to tell them is the standard, typical meaning and usage of a word, not how it is used—possibly quite atypically—in literature. Defining and illustrating such central or typical use is important not only for mother-tongue speakers of English, but also for the hundreds of millions of people round the world learning and using English as a second language. And to illustrate that typical use a huge amount of evidence is required. Enter corpus.

What is a corpus?

corpus /kɔːpəs/ ▶ **noun** (pl. **corpora** or **corpuses**)

1 a collection of written texts, especially the entire works of a particular author or a body of writing on a particular subject: *the Darwinian corpus*.

■ a collection of written or spoken material in machine-readable form, assembled for the purpose of linguistic research.

2 *Anatomy* the main body or mass of a structure.

■ the central part of the stomach, between the fundus and the antrum.

– ORIGIN late Middle English (denoting a human or animal body): from Latin, literally 'body'. Sense 1 dates from the early 18th cent.

Oxford Dictionary of English (revised edition). Ed. Catherine Soanes and Angus Stevenson. Oxford University Press, 2005.

To create dictionaries of modern English, the enthusiastic and learned volunteers who sent in their quotations to the *OED* have been largely replaced by the computer—and by equally enthusiastic and learned IT specialists and computational linguists. Instead of getting people to read texts intensively, dictionary publishers now amass as many electronically held texts of different kinds as they can. They then data-process these oceans of words, adding linguistically relevant information, and creating special software programs to present the data in a meaningful way.

Such a collection of machine-readable texts is known as a '*corpus*'. By analysing the output of such corpora, lexicographers gather evidence about how words and phrases are used in authentic, natural contexts, and on this evidence they base their descriptions of language.

Nearly half a century has passed since the first electronic corpus of English appeared. The *Brown Corpus* became available in 1961. It contained one million words—considered a staggering amount of data at the time—but since then corpora have grown by orders of magnitude. The landmark of 100 million words was passed in the early nineties.

The *Oxford Corpus* used throughout this book (from now on referred to simply as 'the Corpus') was launched in 2006 and contains over two billion words. (1) (Just as there are 'generations' of computers and mobile phones, so there are generations of corpora, and some researchers refer to current corpora as 'third-generation'.) If you laid all the words in the Corpus end to end the line would stretch from the northern tip of Scotland to the Southern tip of New Zealand. If someone spoke all the words non-stop at moderate speaking speed— three per second—you would be listening from the day you were born until after your twenty-first birthday.

English in the noughties

The Corpus consists of texts from global English in the proportions shown below.

Canada 4%   S. Africa 1%

Australia 5%   **Britain 26%**

US 50%   Irish 6%

E. Asian 3%

India 2%   Caribbean 1%

N. Zealand 2%

To truly reflect 21st-century language, all data are from this millennium, and thus give a true picture of the language of the noughties—as well as providing overwhelming evidence that *noughties* really is the consensus name for this decade. Most of the material was collected from the World Wide Web, and some other online sources, supplemented by some printed texts such as academic journals. Using the Web has made it possible to create a corpus of unprecedented scale and balance.

The Corpus represents all types of English, from literary novels and specialist journals to everyday newspapers and magazines, and from Hansard to the language of chatrooms, emails, and weblogs. To help researchers explore how language use varies according to topic and style, texts are grouped into 40 subject areas, called '*domains*': for instance **Weblogs**, **Business**, **Religion**, **Science**, or **Sport**. Each domain is subdivided in turn into more specific themes, or '*subdomains*'. Of these, there are nineteen for **Life and Leisure**, ranging from gossip to gardening; sixteen for **Science**, and 40 for **Sport**, covering the whole gamut, from extreme sports to bowling, and from football to sumo wrestling.

All texts are coded to show whether they are informal, formal, standard, non-standard, or technical: this is known technically as their '*register*'. In addition, they are coded according to whether they were written by a man, a woman, or jointly. This coding is vital in keeping track of trends in language and how different groups of people use it. It probably comes as no surprise that the word *football* occurs twice as often in writing by men as in writing by women. What is more curious is that 'If I were you' is the only form used in the spoken data, in preference to the widespread 'If I was you'.

To analyse how a word or phrase is used, dictionary makers can look at all the lines of text containing the item in question.

These displays of lines are called '*concordances*', and a typical display format, called KWIC ('key word in context'), is shown below.

think of as cinema are on the verge of a	sea change	Whether that transformation occurs for
methods and school editions underwent a	sea change	much influenced by the research and development
66) . But by the mid - 1990s , a	sea change	had occurred in London theatre , making
more broadly , the novel illustrates the	sea change	between the immigrant dreams of the past
1960s and 1970s . They also precipitated a	sea change	in children 's literature in the late 1960s
aware that the controversy represented a	sea change	in English-Irish relations ; those more
the point . This record is a document of a	sea change	in Molina 's perspective as a songwriter
ambition , which group of achievers , which	sea change	was in play , and which chapter was being
regulation of labor " (15) . Now that is a	sea change	Mark Aldrich is Professor of Economics
Venezuela . Within the past few years , a	sea change	of opinion has forced heads of state from
landscape . We are in the beginning stages of a	sea change	A Radical Plan for Social Security
norm .</p> <p>But who will benefit from this	sea change	in the way that people get around ?</p>
consumers are prepared to pay for . This	sea change	in music distribution is already upon us

All examples in this book used to illustrate points about English are taken unedited from the Corpus. For online information about what the Corpus consists of, you can go to: www.askoxford.com.

What can the Corpus tell us?

The questions one can ask of these vast amounts of data are limited only by the powers of researchers' imaginations, the sophistication of software tools, and the processing power of computers. Because of its balanced coverage of so many different domains, the Corpus makes it possible to make verifiable claims about how people really use English. Some of the questions examined in this book with the aid of the Corpus are:

- Which words, phrases, and meanings are most frequent? How many words do we use in general language?

For example, does the Corpus support the idea that dogs are man's best friend? The answer is yes. The most frequent animal word in the Corpus, *dog* ranks 1,001[st] and appears on average once every 12,000 words. *Cat* ranks 1771st and appears only every 23,000 words. We look at how many—actually, how few—words we use, and how this works in texts, in **Chapter 1**.

- How are new words born? Which buzzwords are most productive?

Blog is extremely fertile, and the Corpus lists a staggering 214 derivatives. After *blog* (noun and verb) and *blogger*, the most common is *blogosphere*, denoting websites and weblogs collectively, with its adjectives *blogospheric* or, slightly tongue-in-cheek, *blogospherical*.

Blogrolls are the lists of other blogs which bloggers put on their sites, while big-cheese bloggers are *bloggerati*. English speakers' love of punning is obvious in the word *bloggocks*: '*Think I'm talking bloggocks?*', and in *blogstipation*, the blog equivalent of writer's block. The word to describe the English that bloggers use is *Bloglish*, based on the now established pattern of taking -*ish* and adding it on to the name of another language, for instance Spanish + English = *Spanglish*. **Chapter 2** looks in detail at how new words and phrases come into English.

- Which spelling variants (or mistakes, depending on whether you are a crotchety prescriptivist or a wishy-washy descriptivist) crop up most often?

Something tiny is now more often *miniscule* with an *i* (57 per cent of all cases) than the traditional *minuscule* with a *u*. When the bad guys get their *just desserts*, we may wonder why they deserve a pudding at all. Conversely, some people may draw comfort from the statistic that only 3 per cent of people writing about a debatable issue choose to call it a *mute point*, rather than a *moot* one. On a less contentious note, the Corpus can tell us whether people write *sea change* with or without a hyphen, or as one word: there is a very marked preference to write it as two. What the Corpus can tell us about spelling is the subject of **Chapter 3**.

• Which meanings are coming into the language?

Take the British use of *anorak* (in the US and elsewhere *nerd* and *geek* are the put-downs of choice), meaning 'someone obsessively and tediously interested in a subject that bores other people rigid', e.g. '*Political anoraks are spoilt for choice this Christmas with three political guides on sale to take them through the hectic events of the past year.*' First recorded in 1984, it has become a standard part of the language only in recent years. Nine out of ten Corpus examples are from the UK, with the 'nerd' meaning outnumbering the 'garment' meaning. So tainted is the word that even when clothing is meant, the context is generally unfavourable, as in: *'She was wearing tacky grey trousers and an unflattering blue anorak.'*

These themes of meaning in context, and meaning change, are explored in **Chapter 4**.

• Which recurring patterns predetermine what we write and say?

Words and phrases are used in highly predictable and routine patterns which can only be revealed by large amounts of data. In the quote at the start of this chapter, the verb that Shakespeare used with *sea change* was *suffer*. The Corpus shows us that the most common verb nowadays is *to undergo*. This is just a tiny example of the information about the 'personality profile' of words that we look at in **Chapter 5**.

Chapter 6 looks at some of the ready-made metaphors and idiomatic language we use in everyday language, and at how people creatively play with them, and **Chapter 7** examines exactly what people mean by *grammar*, and why it is such an emotive issue.

- Which words are being exported from their countries of origin?

The Corpus can show exactly how words and phrases are used in different types of writing, and in different regions. Indian English has a special word for 'classmate', *batchmate*: nine times out of ten it shows up in specifically Indian writing, so it does not yet appear to have spread far. But *maven*, for 'expert, aficionado', which the *OED* tells us is '*chiefly North American*', has been successfully exported to many other Englishes, while the *craic* for which Ireland is famous has found a home in Britain too. **Chapter 8** looks in passing at some British reactions to imported words, while examining other disputed usages.

A brief epilogue links modern dictionaries to their historical forebears, and looks at some of the landmarks on the way to their current approach to describing language.

In Shakespeare's time-honoured phrase (2), our ability to look at language through corpora constitutes a true sea change in the study of English. In a sort of human genome project for language, evidence from a corpus allows dictionary makers and linguists to look both at the whole genetic structure of English, and at the genetic make-up of each and every word. They can build up a picture of English as used and validated by the entire language community who speak it—for in the end it is speakers, not dictionaries, who decide how language is used. In Walt Whitman's poetic phrase:

Language is not an abstract construction of the learned or of dictionary makers, but something arising out of the work, needs, joys, tears, affections, tastes of long generations of humanity, and has its bases broad and low, close to the ground.

Walt Whitman, *Slang in America, 1892.* (3)

1 Size matters
How many words?

My, how they've grown!

The first corpus, in 1961, contained one million words. (1) The Oxford Corpus, at two billion words, is 2,000 times that size. Why does size matter so much where corpora are concerned, and why have they grown so phenomenally? For two major reasons: technological developments have made it easier, quicker, and above all cheaper to collect and process written material of all kinds. In addition, because dictionary makers and linguists need as much empirical evidence as possible about authentic language in use, bigger is definitely better. Investigating language in corpora is a scientific enterprise: findings from one set of data can be tested on other sets, and confirmed or challenged. The more data dictionary makers and researchers analyse, the more robust will be the hypotheses they put forward, and the sharper the picture of language they present. That's why the Corpus has two billion words, and will be enlarged by 350 million every year.

It is also necessary to have as much data as possible because words, meanings, and phrases are distributed very unevenly across the language we use: with smaller amounts of data less common items occur rarely, or not at all. For instance, a very common word such as *and* occurs over 46 million times in the Corpus. That means, on average it appears roughly every 44 words of text (and in this paragraph once every twenty words). A very uncommon word, such as *neurasthenically*—an old-fashioned, literary word meaning 'neurotically'—occurs just once in the two billion words of the Corpus. These are two extreme cases, but greater amounts of data provide a more accurate picture both of individual words and phrases, and of their relative frequency. Such information is particularly crucial for learners of English: broadly speaking, the more common words, meanings, and phrases they know, the better they will be able to understand, speak, and write English.

The figure of two billion may be hard to connect to our daily experience and use of language. How does it relate to the number of words we use every day? Or to the size of our vocabulary? How does it reflect the number of words in dictionaries? These are questions examined in this chapter, together with some key ideas which recur throughout the book.

How many words are there?

This is a question to which people unfailingly expect dictionary writers to know the answer—as if it is something that can be measured precisely, like the length of the Nile or the height of Mount Everest. There are many reasons why it's impossible to quantify English vocabulary with any precision. Let's examine them.

Imagine it's *your* task to calculate the figure: where would *you* look? For many people a word is only truly a 'word' if it appears in a dictionary, so a large dictionary would be a good starting point. You might begin with the second edition of the *Oxford English Dictionary* (from now on referred to as the *OED*) which contained getting on for 300,000 'entries' (the word you look up) when published in 1989, and is constantly growing. That sounds like an awful lot of words, but even so it would fall far short of the total.

First, there are all the different words people use in different countries of the English-speaking world (the 'Anglosphere'), or in different areas of a country. British and North American pairs such as *pavement/sidewalk, faucet/tap,* and *car/automobile* are well known and appear in most dictionaries. The Corpus is very useful for analysing which words are used in which countries, for national dialects, such as British or Australian English. But dialects still flourish within countries, particularly in Britain, and there are thousands of words that are only used in particular regions and communities. They will probably be recorded only in local or specialized literature and dictionaries; they may not even be written down at all.

You can refer to:

a female cat as

a betty cat   a ewe   a queen   a she   a sheeder   a tib

gooseberries as

goosebobs   goosegobs   goosegogs   goosers   grozers

a cross-eyed person as

boss-eyed   cock-eyed   glee-eyed   skelly-eyed   skend   squint-eyed

In Britain there are twelve words naming a pea pod, and 34 different ways of saying 'to throw', not to mention the 79 American ways of denoting a dragonfly. (2) Should you try to include them all in your tally, for completeness? There is no reason not to. They are as much 'real' words as the more generally used versions.

Even if you included all these local and dialect words, your trawl through the words of English would still not be over. What about rare terms? For instance, *ailurophobe,* which means a person afflicted with *ailurophobia,* a morbid fear of cats. Both are in the *OED,* but in the two billion words of the Corpus occur only once and three times respectively, which makes them exceedingly rare in actual use. But they are still English words, and should be added to your list.

What about scientific '*proper nouns*'—nouns referring to unique entities—such as E 330 (citric acid), or all the other E numbers? Or ABCA2, and all the other names for the thousands of genes identified in the human genome project? Are they 'real' words, and should they be included? You won't find them in ordinary dictionaries, only in specialist glossaries and lists. And what about abbreviations? One printed dictionary of abbreviations contains over 520,000 items. An online source boasts over 600,000. (3)

Gaspworthy

Another question you would need to ask yourself is: do I include only words in use as of now? That would make sense if you want to find out how people use English currently; but it could reduce your total, because words and meanings can die out—and often do. The *OED* contains thousands of rarely used or obscure words: *antidisestablishmentarianism* and *floccipaucinihilipilification*, often talked about as long words, but never otherwise used. Others seem to have been used only once, long ago, such as *brothelsome* (1624), meaning 'pertaining to a brothel, lewd, whorish'. Others never quite caught on, such as *attemptate* (1524), an inflated French-cum-Latin alternative to the noun *attempt*, Mary Queen of Scots being one of the privileged few to have used it—in a letter in the 1570s—before it too died a premature death. (4)

The accuracy of your total would depend on your sources being constantly up to date. Yet dictionaries inevitably exclude the very latest words: partly because dictionary makers wait to see if they will last the course, and partly because there is a gap between the end of editing and publication. As Dr Johnson said:

No dictionary of a living tongue can ever be perfect, since while it is hastening to publication, some words are budding, and some falling away. (5)

So, even supposing you somehow collected all words used by speakers of English round the globe within a defined period, you would never quite catch up: by the time you finished harvesting your words, new ones would have sprouted.

Your word count would be approximate because of the historical and geographical factors discussed. Another factor means that your count could never, ever include all the words of English, even in principle: that factor is creativity in language. Speakers are very inventive, and coin new words on the spur of the moment, usually by re-using existing words and word parts. If you see someone looking like a chav, or like Jennifer Lopez, you can call them *chavlike*, or *J. Lo-like*. Something appropriate to weblogs can be described as *blogtastic*. People can describe something that makes them gasp in wonder as *gaspworthy*, as the British gardening expert Monty Don did on radio. All these words are perfectly valid and understandable, but nobody can predict when a new one will emerge, and whether it will establish itself. None of them are to be found in dictionaries: they are just manifestations of the endless creative potential of English.

All these factors mean that any total for the vocabulary of English is very much a ballpark figure. The third edition of the *Merriam–Webster Unabridged* dictionary contains over 470,000 entries. If you add to that the 500,000 abbreviations available online the total approaches a million, which is a figure sometimes suggested. Two million is another figure given, including technical terms, but excluding scientific proper names. (6)

What is a word?

Let's assume you've extracted all the words from your sources and calculated your grand total. A crucial question still remains:

how exactly do you define a 'word'? This isn't just an idle, 'academic' question. It is extremely relevant when discussing fundamental questions such as: how many words do people use? How many words does a corpus contain? How many words do learners of English need to communicate adequately?

It also makes a great deal of difference when estimating the size of your vocabulary. For example, you and I know the 'word' *drive*, and probably think of it as a single vocabulary item. But *drive* can be a verb, a noun, and an adjective. As a **verb** we can use it in five different forms:

> *She's been learning to* drive
> *She* drives *a red Ferrari*
> *She uses satnav when she's* driving
> *Her partner* drove *her to the airport*
> *She's never* driven *so fast*

As a **noun** in two forms:

> *She parks her Ferrari on her* drive
> *It's wider than the* drives *on either side*

And as an **adjective** in two:

> *She's a* driven, *career-minded woman*
> *She travels onwards through the* driving *rain*

So is *drive* one word or nine? If we count it as nine, we'll marginally inflate the size of our vocabulary. But if we multiply all the nouns we know by two, and all the verbs by five, and most of the adjectives by three—*big, bigger, biggest*—what an impressively large vocabulary we shall have. But that is not the way vocabulary size is calculated, or how the Corpus is usually analysed. In those contexts it makes more sense to take *drive* as a single unit—technically, it's known as a '*lemma*', and is what you'd look up in a dictionary. Its individual variations are known as '*word-forms*'. Word-forms are linked computationally to lemmas in the Corpus, in a process known as '*lemmatization*',

such that a search for the lemma *drive* will retrieve concordance
lines showing its different word-forms.

thing shall be well ' . The artist	drove	her sports car at speed . Although moneyed
the twentieth century - the steam engine	driven	motor car . A number of important characters
they meet another cowboy who needs a car	driven	into Montana . Sal rides with the cowboy
of conversations between a Tehran woman	driving	a car and the passengers beside her .</p>
to correct the impression that everyone	driving	an expensive car does Yakumbuyo , but because
, " Forecasting is like trying to	drive	a car blindfolded , following directions

Like calculations of the number of words in English, estimates
of vocabulary size vary enormously. One estimate for an average
mother-tongue university student suggests a total of around
40,000 vocabulary items. Another, based on self-assessment,
is nearly 70,000. (7) In any estimate it is useful to distinguish
between words you use—your 'active' vocabulary—and words
you recognize from hearing or reading them, but wouldn't use—
your 'passive' vocabulary. Your passive vocabulary is likely to be
larger than your active one. Of the 70,000 just mentioned, only
around 30,000 were active, and only 16,000 were regularly used.
As we'll see, the Corpus may help us get an indication of how
many words people use 'actively'.

How many words do we use?

There's another way of looking at the question: 'How many
words are there?' and that is: how many 'lemmas', as we have
now defined them, do we use to communicate? The answer is:
rather fewer than you might think.

How can we find out which words people use most often?
Corpus data gives us the answer with relative ease—if we first
make the reasonable assumption that it is large and varied
enough to be a representative sample of writing in English.
A ranking can be produced showing how often each lemma is
used. This ranking shows how unequal the division of labour
among lemmas is: a mere ten make up a quarter of everything
written. They are:

- *the, be, to, and, of, a, in, that, have, I*

In other words, averaging across the whole Corpus, one of the top ten appears every four words. If to these ten you add the next 90 most frequent lemmas in English, you cover half of everything people ever write. Here is the list of the most common 100 English lemmas in the Corpus.

Half of all writing consists of . . .

1 the	26 from	51 when	76 come
2 is	27 we	52 more	77 now
3 to	28 say	53 make	78 then
4 and	29 they	54 me	79 over
5 of	30 her	55 can	80 its
6 a	31 she	56 like	81 only
7 in	32 will	57 people/person	82 also
8 that	33 an	58 time	83 back
9 have	34 or	59 just	84 after
10 I	35 my	60 know	85 use
11 it	36 one	61 no	86 us
12 for	37 all	62 take	87 two
13 be	38 would	63 him	88 work
14 not	39 there	64 year	89 well
15 on	40 their	65 into	90 our
16 with	41 what	66 see	91 how
17 he	42 so	67 some	92 first
18 as	43 up	68 good	93 because
19 you	44 go	69 could	94 want
20 do	45 out	70 them	95 way
21 at	46 who	71 your	96 even
22 this	47 about	72 think	97 these
23 but	48 if	73 look	98 very
24 his	49 get	74 other	99 any
25 by	50 which	75 than	100 give

Empty words, full words

Many of these top 100 seem not very interesting: *a, as, not,* and so forth don't convey much meaning compared with meatier words like *people, child, good.* They don't point to anything in the real world, or suggest ideas, but act as the glue holding together other words which have greater information content. Because they are devoid of conventional meaning content, the eminent Victorian grammarian Henry Sweet christened them '*empty words*', and also '*form words*': they are words in form only. 'Empty words' are also called '*grammatical*' or '*function*' words—their function being to hold conversation or writing together grammatically. Their opposite numbers are '*full words*', '*content words*', or '*lexical words*'.

These 100 lemmas, many of which are 'empty', then, make up half of everything we write. To illustrate this, the previous paragraph is repeated below: word-forms in the top 100 are in bold, while those outside the top 100 are in *italic*. It becomes immediately clear that the italic items are often the most meaning-laden, the most lexically rich.

Bold = within top 100; *italic* = outside top 100

Many of these *top 100 words seem* **not very** *interesting:* **a, as, not, and so** *forth* **don't** *convey much meaning compared* **with** *meatier words* **like** *people, child, good.* **They don't point to** *anything* **in the** *real world,* **or** *suggest ideas,* **but** *act* **as the** *glue holding together* **other** *words* **which have** *greater information content.* **Because they are** *devoid* **of** *conventional meaning content,* **the** *eminent Victorian grammarian Henry Sweet christened* **them** *'empty words',* **and also** *'form words',* **because they are** *words* **in** *form* **only.** *'Empty words'* **are also** *called 'grammatical'* **or** *'function' words*—**their** *function* **being to** *hold conversation* **or** *writing together grammatically.* **Their** *opposite numbers* **are** *'full words', 'content words',* **or** *'lexical words'.*

But if 50 per cent of what we write consists of a mere 100 lemmas, what does the other 50 per cent consist of? Why does our writing not descend into a sort of troglodytic telegraphese, and why do we need so many words in English? This is how it works. Like all languages, English consists of a small number of very common words, a larger number of intermediate ones, and an indefinitely long 'tail' of rarer terms. More than half the Corpus consists of lemmas which are found only once, rarities or one-offs, such as *unpollarded* referring to willows, and *cross-phyletic*, for crossovers between zoological phyla. (Words which occur only once in a text or corpus are sometimes known as '*hapaxes*', from the Greek for 'once', or '*nonce-words*', a term coined by the editor of the *OED*, James Murray.)

1,000 lemmas cover 75 per cent of the Corpus and 7,000 cover 90 per cent. But to get to 95 per cent, you need 50,000 lemmas, and to get to 99 per cent you need more than a million. The more Corpus you wish to account for, the more lemmas you need, and the more unusual, technical, or obscure they become, as the table below shows.

Vocabulary size: how many lemmas?	Percentage of Corpus	Examples
10	25%	the, be, to, and, of, a, in
100	50%	you, from, she, will, go, first
1000	75%	girl, kind, decide, huge, football
7000	90%	imagine, tragic, crude, purely
50,000	95%	saboteur, autocracy, conformist
> 1,000,000	99%	laggardly, nephritic

In everyday writing, we can probably get by with using a limited number of lemmas—between the 7,000 and the 50,000 mark. (Interestingly, the 50,000 figure is quite close to the estimates of around 40,000 given earlier for vocabulary size.) If we take the figure of 7,000 lemmas, or 90 per cent of the Corpus, it should account for 90 per cent of an average text—nine out of every ten words. Does it seem feasible that we can communicate using so few lemmas? It certainly appears so. To give you an idea of how much vocabulary falls within this range of 7,000, all the words in this paragraph do—except for some of the numbers, and the word *lemma* itself. I also checked the first 1,000 words of this chapter: only 26 words, or 2.6 per cent, fell outside the 7,000. They included:

- less common adverbs: *phenomenally, exceedingly, unevenly*
- specialist words: *linguists, corpus, dialect, quantify*
- rarer adjectives: *inflated, empirical*

Meanings are distributed in a similar way to lemmas. The commoner meanings are often much more frequent than the less common ones: for instance, *rich country* occurs fourteen times more often than *rich sauce*, and *poor country* 35 times oftener than *poor soil*.

Clearly, how often a lemma or meaning occurs depends on the kind of text. In a medical article on kidney disease you wouldn't be surprised to see *nephritic*, but you might never encounter it elsewhere. Words and phrases such as *drizzled with* and *liberally* are hugely more frequent in the Food and Drink subdomain of the Corpus than in other subdomains. The relative frequency of words and meanings would be very different if the Corpus consisted entirely of romantic fiction, for example, or of sports reports. Instead, its great variety, as well as its size, means it provides Oxford dictionary makers with an incomparable resource for describing contemporary English.

2 Your Roman-Saxon-Danish-Norman English
Where do words come from?

So now they have made our English tongue a gallimaufray, or hodgepodge of all other speches.

Dedication to Spenser's Shepheardes Calender, *1579.*

As both title and quotation suggest, the vocabulary of English is decidedly mongrel and downright messy: a *gallimaufry*—the more standard spelling than Spenser's *gallimaufray*—and *hodgepodge* indeed. (In the context, it's doubly appropriate that both words come from French.) Defoe satirized the motley origins of Englishmen in a phrase which applies just as well to the language: '*Your Roman-Saxon-Danish-Norman English*'. (1)

The story of *gallimaufry* and *hodgepodge* aptly illustrates the tortuous paths by which so many words have taken root in English (and, in the case of *gallimaufry*, all but withered away again). Both mean 'a confused jumble', and were originally cooking terms, *gallimaufry* having once meant—in English—a ragout, and *hotchpotch* a mutton stew. *Gallimaufry* combines the Old French verb *galer*, 'to have a good time', with the dialect *mafrer*, 'to eat a lot', which in turn comes from Dutch *moffelen*, 'to chew'. *Hodgepodge* is a variant of *hotchpotch*, a word first recorded in Chaucer in the 'jumble' meaning. It comes from the French *hochepot* and means literally 'shake the pot'.

English's mongrel nature may enhance its charm for those who grow up speaking it, but it often makes it hard for speakers of other languages to master. Its mixed pedigree means that words which are cousins in meaning have no family resemblance. Take the scientific adjective for dog: *canine*; or the common-or-garden adjectives for tooth and law: *dental* and *legal*. What's the word for what you eat? *Food*. What do you do in a kitchen? *Cook*. And so on. And on.

Some languages are much tidier. German systematically uses existing words to create others ('*compounds*'), which are the sum of their parts, in a sort of linguistic simple addition. Knowing that *Arzt* means 'doctor' and *Zahn* means 'tooth', when you come across *Zahnarzt* you understand that it means . . . 'dentist'. *Tier* is an animal, so a *Tierarzt* is a vet. While English has this facility too—*curtain rod, earring, fireplace, toothbrush*, and so forth—its chequered history means that thousands of words such as doctor, dentist, and vet wouldn't recognize each other across a crowded room.

But the other side of this coin is that its mixed origins have made English incomparably rich in synonyms. The money you earn from your job can be your *wages, salary, pay, fees,* or *allowance*, all from Anglo-Norman or Old French; your *remuneration* or *stipend,* from Old French or Latin; your *emoluments,* from Latin; or, from humble English roots, *earnings, income,* and *handout.*

If you want to use less formal language, your options increase still further:

- *shekels* from Hebrew
- *dinero* from Spanish
- *wonga* from Romany
- *loot* from Hindi

- *dough* from Old English
- *oscar* Australian rhyming slang ('Oscar Asche' = cash)

This chapter will look at the main ways in which modern English creates words, and some of what the Corpus can tell us about them. To help, we'll also cast a backward glance at how English vocabulary grew, and at what English was once like.

The past: a West Germanic language

Modern English is part of the great family of Indo-European languages. That family covers modern languages as diverse as Icelandic and Greek, Russian and Albanian, Hindi and Welsh. Specifically, English belongs to the West Germanic group, from which have come modern German, Dutch, Flemish, and Frisian. (Frisian, spoken in parts of northern Holland, is the closest surviving relative of English.)

Modern English vocabulary can be seen as the result of the interplay of five major linguistic influences:

- **Old English**, sometimes known as Anglo-Saxon
- **French**, including the varieties used in England after 1066
- **Norse** words, introduced by the Vikings
- Words taken directly from **Latin** (and **Greek**) at different periods of British history, but mostly from the late Middle Ages onwards
- Words **borrowed** from over 350 languages around the world

To take the first of these influences, Old English developed from the interrelated dialects brought by the Angles, Saxons, and Jutes, whose home was just across the North Sea. Unlike modern English, with its hybrid vocabulary, most of the lexicon of Old English was Germanic. This makes it impossible for modern-day speakers of English to read Old English without a dictionary.

In addition, Old English grammar combined all those
bewildering features which have put generations of British
schoolchildren completely off learning foreign languages. In
fact, it was quite similar to modern German grammar. Nouns
had grammatical gender, and cases; verbs not only had masses
of different inflections, and a subjunctive, they could also pop
up in the most unexpected places; and adjectives had two
different forms, according to whether or not they were used
with words such as *the* and *a*. (2)

If we were still speaking Old English, Mark Twain's diatribe
against German grammar would completely lose its point.
He famously professed to find German infuriating and
illogical because the word for a young girl—*das Mädchen*—
was neuter:

*In German, a young lady has no sex, while a turnip has. Think
what overwrought reverence that shows for the turnip, and
what callous disrespect for the girl.*

The word for 'girl' in Old English looked and sounded
very similar, and was also neuter: *mægden*, our modern
maiden. (3)

Just like modern English, Old English created new words
by using '*prefixes*' and '*suffixes*'. Some of them still survive,
such as the *-dom* in *kingdom*, the *-ship* in *kingship*, and
the *with-* in *withstand*, but others have dropped out of
use altogether. Though a disenchanted Ella Fitzgerald once
sang about being '*bewitched, bothered, and bewildered*', we
don't usually make up new verbs and adjectives by putting
be- in front of other words. (Remarkably, the form *bebothered*
also exists, though probably only ever used once. It is recorded
in the *OED* from 1866 in the phrase '. . . *in this bebothered
state*'.)

Then and now: The Lord's Prayer

The Lord's Prayer in Old English is sometimes taken as a yardstick of how much English has changed. Below is the Old English text, followed by the version from *The Book of Common Prayer*. To make resemblances to modern English clearer, word parts which complicate matters have been crossed out, and can be ignored. There is a word-for-word translation in the right-hand column, which also highlights that word order is often very different.

Many of the words are spelled differently from today, but can be recognized without too much hard work: *fæder* for 'father' and *heofon* for 'heaven'. Apart from these spelling differences, a couple of unfamiliar letters are used. They both represent the two 'th' sounds in modern *this* and *thick*: þ, 'thorn', and ð, 'eth'. At the beginning of words they are pronounced like the 'th' of *thick*.

The Lord's Prayer in Old English

Fæder ure, *(father our)*
Our Father,

þu þe eart on heofon~~um~~, *(thou that are in heaven)*
Which art in heaven,

si þin nama ~~ge~~halgod. *(be thy name hallowed)*
Hallowed be thy Name.

~~To~~becume þin rice. *(may your kingdom come)*
Thy kingdom come.

Gewurþe ðin willa on eor~~ðan~~ *(may happen your will on earth)*
swa swa on heofon~~um~~. *(just as in heaven)*
Thy will be done, in earth as it is in heaven.

Urne ~~gedæghwamlican~~ hlaf syle us to dæg. *(our daily bread give us today)*
Give us this day our daily bread.

And forgyf us ure gyltas, *(and forgive us our sins)*

> *And forgive us our trespasses,*
> **swa swa we forgyfað urum gyltendum.**   *(as we forgive our sinners)*
> *As we forgive them that trespass against us.*
> **And ne ~~gelæd~~ þu us on costnunge,**   *(and lead thou us not into*
> *And lead us not into temptation,*   *temptation)*
> **Ac alys us of yfele. Soþlice.**   *(but free us from evil. Amen)*
> *But deliver us from evil. Amen.*

Possibly not the easiest of reads, it must be admitted. Yet, making allowances for how the look of these words has been altered by pronunciation and spelling, most of them have survived into modern English. There are 34 basic word types, or '*lemmas*', in the text, and we still regularly use 28. Fourteen of those are among the top 100 lemmas of current English. In total, these 28 make up over a **tenth of everything** we ever write. (4)

Of course, selecting this text makes it look as if English has changed rather less than it really has. The illusion is created because many of the words are the 'grammatical' or 'function' words, such as *to, of, and*, etc., which tend to change very little. One estimate suggests that about 85 per cent of Old English vocabulary is no longer used. (5)

A language sandwich

English has three main layers: at the bottom, chronologically, Anglo-Saxon or Old English; in the middle, varieties of French; as the top layer, Latin and Greek. These three ingredients are still apparent in just about any stretch of text you care to look at, as can be seen in the following extract from the first page of *The Lord of the Rings*:

The Lord of the Rings: words from Old English, French, Latin

[Bilbo] was very rich and very *peculiar*, and had been the wonder of the Shire for sixty years, ever since his **remarkable disappearance** and *unexpected* **return**. The **riches** he had brought back from his **travels** had now become a *local* **legend**, and it was *popularly* believed, whatever the old folk might say, that the Hill at Bag End was full of **tunnels stuffed** with **treasure**.

Roman type = Old English origin; **bold = French origin**; *italic = Latin origin*

As a result of these three key influences, English has hundreds of 'triplets': groups of three words, one from each ancestral strand, which describe related actions and concepts, but with rather different nuances. Three words in the *Lord of the Rings* passage illustrate this perfectly:

Old English	Old French, Norman French	Latin
to come back	***to return***	*to regress*
folk	*people*	*population*
weird	*strange*	***peculiar***

Though very visible, these three strands do not explain where all the words of English came from. First, there is a Scandinavian ingredient, from the Vikings.

Slaughterous wolves

Though the period of Viking incursions into Britain lasted only a little over two centuries, the mark of the feared Norsemen— 'slaughterous wolves' as they were called in a poem of the time—is still very evident today. Some of the words they brought were incorporated into late Old English: *call*, and *fellow*, for example; others, such as *awkward* and *beaker*, into Middle English. Some, such as *freckle* and *gormless*, bubbled under in dialects, sometimes for centuries, before entering mainstream English. There are estimated to be up to 900 words of Viking origin, and many of them are ones we would sorely miss. (6)

Common Viking words in English

The body: *ankle, calf, fang, freckle, gill, leg, scab, skin, wing, die*
Eating and drinking: *beaker, cake, egg, knife, steak, tang*
Names for people: *fellow, husband, lass, sister, swain, tyke*
Fish and animals: *bull, crake, filly, fry* (fish), *gelding, gosling, kid, reindeer, skate*
Basic words: *both, get, give, same, take, they, their, them, till, though, until, want*

The figures below show the relative proportions of words from the strands that we have been looking at, as reflected by the words in a desk-size Oxford dictionary.

Norse 2%   Old French 21%

Latin 46%

Greek 18%   Old English 13%

A nation of shopkeepers turned foodies

The final element in the lexical make-up of English consists of the thousands of '*loanwords*' imported from over 350 languages. (7) In this section we'll look particularly at food 'loanwords', ancient and modern.

Napoleon famously dismissed the British as 'a nation of shopkeepers', but into those shops he despised came goods from all over the world. With them they brought thousands of exotic names which have enriched English: from *damask* (named after Damascus, in Syria, *c*.1430) to *pashminas* (Urdu, 1989), and from *coffee* (Arabic, possibly via Turkish, 1598) to *wasabi*, Japanese horseradish (Japanese, 1903).

Nowadays the British are more a nation of foodies (1982) than shopkeepers, and this shows up in the lashings (Anglo-Irish, 1829) of words the food and drink industry feeds into the language. For example, our rediscovered coffee mania has brought in or revived a mini-lexicon of Italian:

Coffee words

1945 – *espresso*	1982 – *barista, crema*
1948 – *cappuccino*	1989 – *latte, macchiato*

As a sign of how well embedded in English these coffee terms are, they can now be 'blended' to produce beverages such as *mochaccino*.

So eclectic have we become in our eating habits, that a trip to the *deli* (originally US, from German, 1954) or the *supermarket* (US, 1933) could easily involve borrowing from well over twenty languages, not counting French, from which in any case so many of our food words come.

Multilingual food shopping

>   Italian – *risotto*, any kind of pasta
>   Dutch – *gherkin*
>   Spanish – *tapas*
>   German – *Sauerkraut*
>   Greek – *pitta*
>   Swiss–German – *rosti*
>   Russian – *blini*
>   Portuguese – *piri-piri*
>   Arabic – *couscous*
>   Thai – *nam pla* (fish sauce)
>   Japanese – *sushi*
>   Cantonese – *bok choy* (Chinese leaves)
>   Mandarin – *chow mein*
>   Malay – *nasi goreng*
>   Tamil – *curry, poppadom*
>   Bengali – *bhoona*
>   Urdu – *tandoori, nan*
>   Hindi – *basmati, chutney*
>   Punjabi – *tikka, gobi* (cauliflower)
>   Persian – *aubergine, paneer, spinach*
>   Nahuatl (the language of the Aztecs) – *avocado, tomato*
>   Narragansett (a Native American language) – *squash*
>   Taino (a Caribbean language) – *maize, potato*

The present: where do words come from?

As W.H. Auden wrote: '*The winds must come from somewhere when they blow | There must be reasons why the leaves decay . . .*' (8) Words too must blow in from somewhere—and they decay too, like *gallimaufry*—and later on we'll be looking at how exactly they take root in the language.

How many new words blossom each year? The honest answer is that nobody knows for sure. As with words in general, it depends what you count and where you look. Perfectly 'valid' words can be invented on the spur of the moment, and then are never used again. Assuming they are recorded anywhere, are they to be classed as 'proper' new words? Or a social or professional group may use a word or term which never spreads to another group. The only concrete figures to go by are the words that dictionary makers add to new editions of their dictionaries. The 2007 edition of the *Shorter Oxford English Dictionary* added about 2,500 new words to the previous edition of five years earlier. So that means dictionary makers selected about 500 words per year to include. Another indicative figure is the average of 900 words per year throughout the twentieth century for words added to the *OED*. In principle, no single organization or person can or ever could monitor all uses of English. In practice, the Corpus takes us a step closer to comprehensive information on how language is developing.

Irrespective of the overall numbers, some areas of activity produce words in abundance. Among those areas are:

- computing and telecommunications
- science, health and medicine
- lifestyle
- media
- sports
- ecology and travel
- eating and drinking
- politics and government
- fashion.

Let's look at a couple of them: computing and telecommunications, and lifestyle.

Online

Every year our lives are supposedly made easier, more efficient, and more pleasurable by new technology. That gadgetry has names and, assuming the gadget concerned catches on, those names enter the language: *digital TV, Blackberry®, iPod®, flatscreen, broadband, Skype, digibox, webcam* . . . Thanks to the internet, we can track down long-lost friends, reveal our innermost thoughts to the whole world, share photos and videos, and even create a completely new identity for ourselves in a fantasy world.

As the introduction to this book showed, one of the most productive words in the internet age is *blog*, which has more than 200 derivatives. *Cyber*, too, has produced scores of derivatives, including the sinister *cyberbullying*, *cyberstalking*, and *cyberterrorism*. Fashioned by the love of wordplay which shapes many new words, *cyberchondria* is the readiness to believe that you have a disease whose symptoms you've read about on a website. Other recent computing and internet terms equally notable for their wit include:

- *cobwebsite* – a site which hasn't been updated for a long time, so that figuratively it has cobwebs hanging off it
- *data smog* – the overwhelming excess of information that the internet provides
- *doppelgoogler* – modelled on *doppelganger*, a *doppelgoogler* is someone with the same name as you whose existence you find out about through the internet. (Try doing it, and the results may surprise you.)
- *egosurfing* – seeing how many hits your name gets when you search for it on the web
- *linkrot* – the morbid condition that occurs when hyptertext links on a website lead nowhere
- *404* – a person who you consider is not the fizziest lemonade in the fridge, derived from the error message you get when you can't access a web page.

Lifestyle gurus

Caught as we are in the *hedonic treadmill*—which dictates that the more goods and possessions we have, the more we want—we turn for help to *lifecoaches* or *lifestyle gurus*, to help us *declutter* or *dejunk* our lives. Sometimes it can seem that we're expected to change lifestyle as often as we change cars. Roll up, roll up, roll up: there's a new way of getting in touch with our real selves, a different way of looking more attractive, a novel means of feeling that we're saving the planet.

Some lifestyle words bubble under for years and then break through on the back of media exposure. Consider *unibrow*, a single, uninterrupted eyebrow, à la Frida Kahlo—popularized in *Queer Eye for the Straight Guy* (2003), but first recorded sixteen years earlier. Similarly, *metrosexual* was in the limelight in the early noughties (the first decade of this century) thanks to that archetypal metrosexual, David Beckham, but it had been first coined by cultural commentator Mark Simpson at the start of the previous decade. Other words are concocted by journalist or marketers on the look-out for good copy, but are as short-lived as dragonflies: *Brad Jones*, the male version of Bridget Jones, to describe men living alone, and *contrasexual*, describing women who are the polar opposites of Bridget (both from 2004).

Male grooming is a major growth industry—and a major growth area, it would seem, for knowing puns. Would-be *metrosexuals* get their body and lower-body hair removed through *manscaping*, also known as a *back, sac, and crack*. Equipped with the indispensable *manbag*, and possibly wearing *guyliner*, they venture out in search of a mate. The more sensitive souls avoid the horrors of *vertical drinking* and *speed dating*, and plump instead for *read dating*—dating events in libraries and bookshops where attendees put the title of their favourite book next to their name to give would-be partners an opening gambit.

If all this sounds a bit narcissistic and self-obsessed, that's because it is. And with all this self-obsession, it's no surprise that people who don't get what they want when they want it fly into temper tantrums or hissy fits. People don't only rage against the machine, they rage against anything that doesn't suit. Here are some popular rages from the Corpus:

A glossary of rage

road rage – the anger induced by other motorists selfishly and deliberately doing all they can to slow you down

'roid rage – short for steroid rage, the abnormal aggressiveness sometimes experienced by body-builders and athletes taking steroids

air rage – aggressive behaviour to fellow passengers and cabin crew, usually caused by those in-flight miniatures

trolley rage – the ire caused by dithery shoppers, and those who barricade with their trolleys precisely the shelf you most urgently need

spam rage – the incandescent anger caused by dozens of emails offering to enhance parts of your anatomy you were perfectly happy with

surf rage – fury at another surfer who has the gall to ride **your** wave

pavement rage – you thought motorists were dawdlers till you started walking

office rage – throwing all your toys out of the pram, but in the office

golf rage – induced by your own miserable handicap, or by other golfers just 'not playing the game'

Other rages include *tube rage* on the underground or subway, *parking rage*, and *phone rage*, when you can't get through to a call centre, or when a mobile phone user gets your goat for whatever reason. At one stage, coinages with *rage* were used so wantonly by journalists in search of a headline that one distinguished lexicographer (9) coined *rage rage*: 'the anger felt by dictionary makers as journalists invent yet another non-existent social malaise.'

Something old, something new, something borrowed, something blue

As the rhyme has it, there are four things a bride needs to wear on her wedding day. They are also useful shorthands to describe how new words come about.

Where words come from

Something old
Existing words:
come together to create new ones
change meaning
are pruned back

Something new
New words:
cannibalize existing words
are named after people and places
use the first letters and syllables of other words
join up existing word parts in novel ways

Something borrowed
English absorbs words from other languages.

'Something blue' is also part of the story. Some words become 'blue' and taboo for social, political, or ethical reasons, and alternatives have to be found, usually from the existing word-stock.

'Something old . . .'

A + B = C

English has an endless capacity for creating new words, such as *extraordinary rendition*, *activewear*, *bedmate*, *mouse potato*, and *carbon footprint*, simply by yoking together words that already exist. The results of such yokings are '*compounds*'.

In theory, any number of nouns can be joined, and journalists routinely join as many as is feasible in headlines such as: '*3 million Brits in vomit virus agony*' or '*Toddler cleaning fluid drink horror*'. (Fortunately, because such compounds refer to passing events they tend not to become enshrined in the language.) Coupling two words is the most common way of neologizing: about half of all new items entering English are of this kind. Most of the words created through compounding are nouns, but compounding also creates adjectives such as *streetwise* and verbs such as *to cybershop* and *to comparison-shop*.

We've already seen how many different angers can be described by compounds with *rage*. In the light of concern over global warming, *carbon* seems set to become just as prolific:

Carbon + sequestration, assimilation, sink, tax, credit, reduction, trading, offset, footprint

Another fertile breeding ground for new words is—as it has always been—insult. Take *brigade*, as a disparaging way of referring to a group of people of whom you don't approve. The Corpus suggests that it is strongly associated with the way people dress, and with colours. We have the *blue-rinse brigade*, for conservative ladies of a certain age, and the *green-ink brigade*, to denote the people who write cranky letters, supposedly in green ink, to public—especially media—figures. The *green-wellie brigade*—after the green wellington boots popular in country circles in Britain—and the *Barbour*™ *brigade* are natural allies of the *blazer brigade*, and possibly of the *old-school-tie brigade*. The *saffron brigade* is a term used by their opponents to disparage the ultra-Hindu BJP (Bharatiya Janata

Party) in India. Referring to people as the *tinfoil hat brigade* suggests that their beliefs are beyond the merely wacky: the tinfoil is there to stop them being affected by mind-reading rays and the like.

Evolution: changes in meaning and function

It's easy to overlook how much new language is created simply from old words changing meaning, and having a makeover. About 15 per cent of new words emerge this way. The textbook example of how meaning changes over time is *nice*. At various times in its 700-year career it has meant 'foolish', 'lascivious', 'ostentatious', 'scrupulous', 'dainty', 'refined', 'respectable', 'in good taste', and 'pleasant'.

Some striking examples of meaning change in our current everyday language which it's easy to take for granted are: *mouse*, as on a computer (1965); *wireless* referring to computers rather than radios (1997); *browser* meaning 'web browser' rather than someone in a bookshop (1993); and *challenged* used, seriously or jokingly, as a euphemism for 'handicapped' (1985).

Some changes in meaning involve using words in a different grammatical function (a process known as '*conversion*'). We now use *remotely* to describe how we *log in* as often as we use it in sentences like: '*Nobody seemed remotely interested*'. How many of us still do a double take, as I do, at cars and doors being 'alarmed'? English is strikingly flexible in the way that nouns can assume entirely new grammatical personalities by behaving like verbs: *to interface, to contact, to benchmark, to author, to eBay, to google*. This particular tendency—called '*verbing*'—is often despised by language purists. Yet many of our verbs came via this route. We do not object to *salting* our food or *peppering* our conversation, so it might seem illogical to reject other verbs created in the same way.

Hard pruning: abbreviations and back-formations

Another way of creating new words from old is by pruning back excess growth. The process and the result are known as '*clipping*'. Economy of means seems to be a driving force in language change: why use the four syllables of *advertisement* when *ad* conveys the same information in one? And why take five syllables to say *administration* when *admin* says the same in two? *Aggro, bi, bike, blog, bus, goss* all exist for similar reasons of economy, and Australians seems to have honed clipping to a fine art: *arvo, barbie, blowie* ('afternoon', 'barbecue', 'blowfly/blowjob'), and so forth.

There's another important aspect of verbal pruning: through a process known as '*back-formation*', an existing word is trimmed into a new shape. Take *edit*, which was back-formed from *editor*. There is no written record of it in use before 1791, but *editor* in its current meaning had come into English nearly a century earlier, being first recorded in 1712, according to the *OED*.

Back-formation has given us such common words as the ones listed below. Sometimes it has taken less than a decade, sometimes two centuries or more. (10)

Common back-formations

pre-existing word		back-formed word		time-lag
injury	(1430)	*injure*	(1586)	156 yrs
emotion	(1660)	*emote*	(1917)	257 yrs
diagnosis	(1681)	*diagnose*	(1861)	180 yrs
enthusiasm	(1716)	*enthuse*	(1827)	111 yrs
reminiscence	(1811)	*reminisce*	(1882)	71 yrs
bulldozer	(1930)	*bulldoze*	(1942)	12 yrs
sleazy	(1941)	*sleaze*	(1967)	26 yrs
nitpicking	(1953)	*nit-pick*	(1956)	3 yrs
grotty	(1964)	*grot*	(1971)	7 yrs

'. . . something new . . .'

As we've seen, most 'new' English words are not strictly new at all. So, what 'new' means in this context needs clarification. A word can be new in one of two ways. First, by not including any meaningful word part ever used before. Under this heading come:

- unique creations such as James Joyce's *quarks*, J.K. Rowling's *quidditch*, Lewis Carroll's *vorpal*—but such words are really rather rare
- names of people—real or imaginary— put to new uses: *sandwich, cardigan, knickers* (shortened from Diedrich Knickerbocker, a fictional character created by Washington Irving)
- occasionally, names of places mutate into dictionary words: *denim*, from *de + Nîmes*, the town in France; *marathon* from the site of the Greek battle; *paisley*, from the mill town in Scotland where material with that particular pattern was produced; *Mecca* for anywhere which is a centre of attraction.

The second way in which new words are formed is by drawing on pre-existing material:

- words are run together, or one is inserted in another: *breakfast + lunch = brunch; chuckle + snort = chortle* ('*portmanteau words*', or '*blends*')
- the first letters or syllables of words are used to create '*acronyms*' such as *Aids, radar, laser, DVD*
- recyclable word parts are joined in novel ways: *Europhile, Sinophobic, commitment-phobic, chatterati*.

People and places

It's surprising how many words that we take for granted enshrine the names of people and places, real or fictional. Words commemorating people are '*eponyms*', and '*toponyms*'

come from places. There are some obvious ones, such as
sandwich after the disreputable fourth Earl of Sandwich, who
needed a snack during a gambling marathon; *Alice band* after
Lewis Carroll's Alice; or *Bunsen burners*, after the German
chemist who invented them.

Inventors, such as the Hungarian *László Bíró* and the
Italo-American *Candido Jacuzzi*, and dozens of others, are
immortalized in the names of their inventions and discoveries.

- **Molotov cocktail** – after the twentieth-century Russian
  statesman *Vyacheslav Mikhailovich Molotov* (1890–1986)
- **Leotard** – after the inventor of the garment, French trapeze
  artist and acrobat *Jules Léotard* (*c.*1842–1870), who inspired
  the song '*That Daring Young Man on the Flying Trapeze*'
- **Gallup poll** – after the American statistician *George Harris
  Gallup* (1901–1984), who predicted the outcome of the 1936
  US presidential election
- **Mount Everest** – in honour of the Surveyor-General of
  India, *Sir George Everest* (1790–1866) who first mapped the
  Himalayas
- **Jack Russell** – after the man who first bred them, *John
  Russell* (1795–1883), clergyman and master of foxhounds

But sometimes history or events disguise words so that the
original connection is lost: *tawdry* comes from St Audrey,
venereal from Venus, *denim* from Nîmes, *calico* from the
former Calcutta, and *dunce* from the medieval philosopher
and theologian Duns Scotus.

The publicly available software *Linux™* is a mixture of *Linus*,
its inventor's first name, and *Unix*. *Bluetooth* technology is
named after King Harald Bluetooth of Denmark and Norway.
At other times the original surname is disguised by a prefix or
suffix. *Poinsettia* is named after J.R. Poinsett, the American who
introduced it to the United States in 1825, and *greengage* after

Sir William Gage, the botanist who introduced it to Britain around 1725.

Word collisions: portmanteau words and blends

In the motor trade, the front of one car can be welded to the back of another to produce highly dangerous *cut-and-shuts*. Certainly safer, but to some people nearly as controversial, are the contraptions produced by welding two words together: *brunch* (*breakfast* + *lunch*), *podcast* (*iPod®* + *broadcast*), or *webinar* (*web* + *seminar*).

They are often known as '*portmanteau words*'—a whimsical term we owe to Lewis Carroll—or, more prosaically, as '*blends*'. (*Portmanteau* previously referred to a type of travelling case, hinged so that it opened into two parts, whence the analogy.) In Chapter 6 of *Through the Looking Glass*, Alice asks Humpty Dumpty the meaning of *slithy*, as in *slithy toves* from the *Jabberwocky* poem in Chapter 1, and he explains:

'Well, "slithy" means "lithe and slimy" . . . You see it's like a portmanteau – there are two meanings packed up into one word.'

Carroll coined not only the term but also some portmanteaux which have stood the test of time. Relatively common is *chortle* (*chuckle* + *snort*). Much less often used are *galumph* (possibly from *gallop* + *triumph*), and *mimsy*. (11)

Portmanteaux are an extremely versatile and creative way of coining new words. A recent Australian portmanteau will strike a chord with people who have teenage children: *floordrobe*, 'the use of the floor as a sort of horizontal clothes storage system'.

Beginnings and endings: acronyms

Professionals love jargon, and lexicographers are no exception. Things that most people would normally just lump under the

heading of 'abbreviations' they often classify more precisely. An
'*acronym*' is a word formed from the first letters of other words:
Aids, Anzac, AWOL, Ernie, laser, and so forth. In the case of *Ernie*
and *laser* we'd probably be hard pressed to remember the words
that fathered the acronym—which is why acronyms are so
useful. (The words are: **e**lectronic **r**andom **n**umber **i**ndicator
equipment for *Ernie*, and **l**ight **a**mplification by **s**timulated
emission of **r**adiation for *laser*.)

The acronyms just mentioned can be pronounced as
spelled. But many abbreviations, such as *ICI* and *ITV*, can't.
An abbreviation which uses the first letters of other words
pronounced individually is sometimes called an '*initialism*'.
Most of the major TV stations in the Anglosphere are
initialisms: *BBC, NBC, CBC, ABC, TVNZ.*

Recycling: derivation

English has a hoard of word parts it can recycle endlessly.
There are scores of these '*prefixes*'—added to the beginning of
words—and '*suffixes*'—added to the end of words. Traditionally
these prefixes and suffixes have come from the three main layers
of the language: Old English, French, and Latin or Greek. They
range from the millennial Old English *friend***ship**, *star***dom**,
and *together***ness**, through French *amuse***ment** and *employ***ee**,
to Latin *liber***ation**, and Greek **para***normal* and **photo***synthesis*.
It is interesting to see how these traditional suppliers of
prefixes and suffixes are being supplemented by other
languages.

Spanish *-ista*: defined by the *Oxford Dictionary of English* as
'*denoting a person associated with a particular activity, often
with a derogatory force*', this suffix arrived in English in the
1980s from the *Sandinistas*, the Nicaraguan political movement.
Since then it has been fully naturalized in two uses: first, in

words denoting what people do, but with heavy overtones: *puppetistas* are puppet artists with a radical political agenda; *opinionistas* are people who volunteer or are paid to give opinions, but the people who describe them thus feel they shouldn't be: '. . . *laziness is endemic in Australia's opinionista elite*'. Its second use is to describe people's affiliations and allegiances. It can refer to supporters of specific politicians— *Blairista, Clintonista*; or more broadly to a set of beliefs, as in *Guardianista* to describe the typical reader of the British *Guardian* newspaper; or *trendinista*, which is self-explanatory.

German *-fest* has spawned a motley brood. Some words, usually written with a capital letter, have a neutral meaning equivalent to 'festival' in celebration of something: *Summerfest, Beerfest, Bookfest*. Others are rather ironic: *-fest* connotes self-indulgence in *talkfest* and *gabfest*, both of which dismiss conventions and organizations as mere talking shops: '*It will be just another talkfest which will not do anything for families.*' More dismissive still are *wankfest, crapfest*, and *bitchfest*: '*I don't like the wankfest that constitutes the Turner prize.*'

Italian has been one of the major contributors over the centuries to the riches of English. The suffix *-ati* has long existed in words such as *literati* (perceived as Italian, though actually from Latin) and *castrati*. It is now added to a bewildering variety of words to denote members of groups, usually negatively. *Glitterati*, meaning 'celebrities', puns on the well-established *literati*, as does *cliterati* for feminist writers. But the Corpus suggests *-ati* has become a free agent and can attach itself at will: *blazerati* for those who wear blazers; *chatterati* for the 'chattering classes'; *digerati* (from *digital* + *-ati*) for the technologically clued up; and *bloggerati* for the big cheeses of the blogging world.

Mutant morphemes

English plays fast and loose, in a way that many languages can't and don't, when it recycles word parts. Speakers don't care whether the word part they cannibalize is meaningful in its own right—as in *-ista* and *-ati*—or not. Take the *-thon* element in *marathon*. On its own it didn't actually **mean** anything; it's just part of the original Greek place name from which *marathon* came. But it has become a '*morpheme*' (the smallest meaningful part of a word) in its own right, and a very prolific one too. People use it to describe sporting events held for charity, such as 5,000-metre *swimathons* and *walkathons*. It has expanded from there to cover activities such as TV events—*telethons*—, sponsored reading events—*readathons*—, and sponsored dieting—*slimathons*. Speakers have taken these four 'meaningless' letters to their hearts and given them the meaning of 'charitable event'.

Top ten *-thons* in the Corpus

1 *telethon*	6 *walkathon*
2 *blogathon*	7 *skipathon*
3 *slimathon*	8 *bikeathon*
4 *swimathon*	9 *boobiethon* (for breast-cancer research)
5 *readathon*	10 *danceathon*

The suffix *-tastic* is also a very versatile 'morpheme'. Historically, like *-thon* it has no independent meaning, but people have commandeered it: *geektastic, poptastic, Abbatastic, craptastic*. Describing a film about the Tudors, the adjective *tudortastic* fell effortlessly from the lips of Kirsty Wark, the British broadcaster.

But the mother of all morphemes must be *-gate*. Described sibilantly as '*a suffix in search of a scandal in search of a name*' (12), it can be slotted on to any proper name: *Andrewgate,*

Bingogate, Blobbygate, Bradgate, Bruneigate, to name just a few forgotten scandals from letters *a* and *b*. The coinages are often wryly humorous, as with *Zippergate* as a synonym of *Monicagate*.

'. . . something borrowed . . .'

English has borrowed from over 350 languages, and continues to do so. Borrowings have come from all round the world, and to do them justice would require a book in itself. (13) Just looking at some of the languages on the American continent from which English has borrowed gives some idea of the riches.

North America:
moose, skunk Abnaki
moccasin, persimmon, tomahawk Algonquian
sequoia Cherokee
bayou Choctaw
toboggan Micmac
powwow, squash, squaw Narragansett
chipmunk, totem, wigwam Ojibwa

Caribbean & Central America:
barbecue, canoe, iguana Arawak
avocado, chilli, chocolate, guacamole, ocelot, tomato Nahuatl
cassava, hammock, hurricane, maize, potato, savannah Taino

South America:
poncho, gaucho Araucanian
coca, alpaca Aymara
jaguar, petunia Guaraní;
cocaine, guano, llama, pampas, puma, quinine Quechua (the Inca language)
cashew, cayenne, jacaranda, piranha, tapioca Tupi

The figures overleaf show the relative proportions of some languages which have been very generous to English.

Spanish 13%
Arabic 8%
French 41% German 12%
Italian 20%
Hindi 6%

'. . . something blue . . .'

In the past euphemism has often been a way of deferring to
sexual or religious sensitivities. In Victorian times referring
to trousers was taboo, and they were variously called
indescribables, *unmentionables*, and *inexpressibles*. (14, 15) To
avoid mentioning the name of God or Christ, there is a long and
inventive tradition, ranging from the obsolete *zounds* (from 'by
God's wounds') (1600) and *egad* (1673) to the jolly-hockey-sticks
crikey (1838), *Christmas* (1898), and *crumbs* (1918).

Nowadays euphemism tends to rewrite social situation rather
than sex, race rather than religion—though the examples in
the Corpus of *horizontal jogging* and *a bit of how's your father*
might suggest that the grand tradition of comic prurience isn't
altogether dead. And if we don't want certain taboo words to
sully our lips, we can refer to the *f-word*, the *c-word*, and the
n-word.

As regards social situation, take *solo parent*, a compound
that some people in that position prefer, as an example from
the Corpus suggests: '*She's very specific that she's a solo parent
and not a single mom.*' With its positive connotations of
independence and determination derived from the artistic
and sporting worlds—*solo album, solo exhibition, solo*

flight—and its lack of gender reference, it's easy to see why it's preferable to *single mom/mum*, with its baggage of failure and irresponsibility. However, the Corpus also suggests it has a long way to go before ousting *single mum*. On the ethnic front, *dual heritage* fulfils a similar role of being more positive than *mixed race*, and it avoids 'race', one of the great taboos of our time. Just like *solo parent*, however, the Corpus suggests it has a huge amount of catching up to do.

I began this chapter by applying to the English language Defoe's satire of Englishmen as mongrels. There is a strong argument that its mongrelism is in fact one of its virtues. Its ability to scoop up words from other languages is phenomenal, and is a habit it shows no signs of kicking. A look at a mere fraction of all the words added to the 2007 edition of the *Shorter Oxford English Dictionary* shows borrowings from eleven languages: from Portuguese to Arabic, and from Italian to Hawaiian. There may, after all, be a lot to be said for mongrelism.

3 Beware of heard
Why spelling wobbles

'My spelling is Wobbly. It's good spelling but it Wobbles, and letters get in the wrong place.'

A. A. Milne, *Winnie-the-Pooh*, 1926.

Like Winnie-the-Pooh, most of us have probably experienced our spelling wobbling, and getting our letters in the wrong place. Given how motley English spelling is, wobbling is forgivable (and you're a better speller than me if you didn't wonder whether forgivable needs an *e*. It doesn't). The man who gave the world the phrase '*conspicuous consumption*' also lambasted English spelling as '*archaic, cumbrous, and ineffective*', a judgement with which it's hard to disagree. (1) Certainly, it is often old-fashioned, for it retains spellings like 'knight' and 'would', reflecting the way words sounded several centuries ago. It is cumbrous, because mastering its intricacies is complicated, time-consuming—and possibly never-ending. Calling it 'ineffective' might be overstating the case, as it is, despite the quirkiness of its orthography, the world's most used language, but inefficient it certainly is. If people were inventing it from scratch, as some spelling reformers have suggested, they wouldn't do it this way.

But if our spelling occasionally wobbles, we might draw some comfort from being in good company. Collins dictionaries once surveyed 100 leading politicians and media figures on some difficult-to-spell words: a meagre four, including the egregious Ann Widdecombe, managed to get them all right. Why not see how you measure up? Which is the correct version of these four words? (The original survey consisted of ten words, so this is easier.)

A spelling survey

a) miniscule b) minuscule c) miniscool d) minniscule
a) mocassin b) moccasin c) moccassin d) mocassine
a) supersede b) supercede c) superseed d) superceed
a) sacreligious b) sacriligious c) sacrilegious d) sacrelegious

---

The correct spellings are: b), b), a), and c).

Even one of the most revered lexicographers of the twentieth century, Robert Burchfield, wobbled occasionally, as in his succinct definition of language conservatives: '*Prescriptivists by and large regard innovation as dangerous or at any rate resistable . . .*' For *resistable* read *resistible*, at least according to modern conventions. (2)

Shaky spelling, or orthographic wobbliness, is something that understandably upsets employers when they recruit. Periodically they panic about applicants' writing skills, as this quotation from *The Times* suggests:

Employers have claimed that they face a 'nightmare' scenario as they try to deal with teenagers who are unable to read or write properly. (3)

Supporters of spelling reform even go so far as to make the connection between illogical English spelling and crime: '*Our odd spelling retains words like cough, bough, through and though. This increases illiteracy and crime.*' (4) Learning to write English fluently is not a skill that can be taken for granted, and in this chapter we'll analyse some of the most common mistakes

people make, and look at how a major aspect of spelling—
joining words together—is changing.

Europeans do it better

In a European context, some British conventions, such as
driving on the left and sticking to a different currency, can
seem perverse or eccentric. Just as perverse and wayward in
comparison with most European languages is the spelling
system of English. It is notoriously irregular, as this well-known
(at least in spelling circles) rhyme highlights:

> Beware of heard, a dreadful word,
> That looks like beard and sounds like bird.
> And dead: it's said like bed and not like bead,
> For goodness sakes don't call it deed!

But if English is so irregular, what would a 'regular' spelling
system look like? The principle is simple: there would be a
one-to-one relationship between letters and sounds. Every
letter or combination of letters would invariably represent one
sound; and each sound would invariably be written the same
way. Some European languages, such as Finnish, Spanish, and
Basque, come close to this one-to-one relationship, and many
others, such as Italian, German, and Greek, are much more
regular than English.

In Spanish, for instance, there are precisely five pure vowel
sounds, which map perfectly onto the five vowel letters—*a, e, i,
o, u*—of the Roman alphabet. So, wherever and whenever one
sees a Spanish *a, e, i, o,* or *u*, one can be confident that it stands
for the same sound. (5, 6) The same goes for nearly all Spanish
consonants as well. Because of this regularity, once you have
learned a few simple rules you know how every Spanish word
sounds purely from its look on the page. The welcoming phrase
Mi casa es su casa (= 'make yourself at home', word for word 'my

house is your house') contains four *a* sounds, and they are all the same—always. All this makes Spanish a largely 'phonetic' language, in the *OED* meaning: '*Of the spelling of a word or of the written form of a language: closely corresponding to the current pronunciation.*'

Compare this efficient situation with the lamentable state of English. At school they may have taught us that '*a* stands for *apple*'; what they forgot to tell us is that it also stands for several other sounds. (You may want to read these aloud, so that your mouth can prove to your brain that the 'a' sound in each pair really is different from the next.)

A is for *apple*? and also . . .

car, arm	any, many	late, to delegate	wasp, quality
talk, all, walk	above, miracle	climate, senate	compare, dare

Another oft-quoted example of the inefficiency of English spelling is the combination *ough*:

> Though the rough cough
> And hiccough plough me through,
> O'er life's dark lough
> My course I still pursue. *(Anon)*

Though only a handful of words contain the sequence *ough*, there are nine different ways to pronounce it. (7) But the conundrum of English spelling doesn't stop there. Not only do the same letters stand, confusingly, for several different sounds; the same sound can appear in a bewildering variety of guises and disguises. The 'ee' sound in *feet*, for instance, can be spelled: d*ea*l, amn*e*sia, n*ie*ce, rec*ei*ve, p*eo*ple, mach*i*ne, k*ey*, qu*ay*, f*oe*tus, C*æ*sar. In fact, the mismatch from sound to spelling is much greater than the other way round. It has been calculated that on average there are 13.7 spellings per sound, but only 3.5 sounds per letter. (8)

Although English is so clearly not a 'phonetic' language, in the sense mentioned previously, there is a lot of regularity. Examples like the ones we've been looking at are extreme, if intriguing, cases. Studies suggest that between roughly 75 and 85 per cent of words follow regular, predictable rules. Even so, such figures don't necessarily reflect the overall impact that irregular words have, because some of the rogue words are also the most common ones. As we've seen in previous chapters, the commonest words in the language make up a huge amount of text. If anybody misspelled *the*, that single mistake would affect a disproportionate amount of what they wrote: about 5 per cent. It also depends which rule you take as being 'regular'.

But the impact of spelling mistakes in the real world isn't statistical. If a job candidate writes 500 words in their CV, and only five of them are wrong, that's a 1 per cent mistake rate; but the candidate might not be called for interview. If a medic writes *hypotension* (low blood pressure) instead of *hypertension* (high blood pressure), the consequences could be quite dramatic.

English spelling is not 'phonetic' and there is an obvious reason for that. While the alphabet we use contains 26 letters, our language has upwards of 44 meaningful sounds. Consonants are just about manageable, but major problems arise with vowels: the twenty vowels and diphthongs of Received Pronunciation have to be shoehorned into five letters. As will presently be seen in more detail, this shortfall is the root of many spelling problems.

A very sumpshous house

There is a Victorian classic called *The Young Visiters* [*sic*], written by Daisy Ashford at the age of 9. The charm of her child's-eye-view of an adult world is greatly enhanced by her unorthodox but phonetic spelling. The book opens with the immortal words: '*Mr Salteena was an elderly man of 42 and was fond of inviting peaple* [sic] *to stay with him.*' Early in the narrative Mr Salteena receives: '. . . *a top hat wraped up in tishu paper*' from his friend Bernard. When he goes to stay at Bernard's he compliments him like this: '*Well said Mr Salteena lapping up his turtle soup you have a very sumpshous house Bernard.*' We can larf or smial at the spelling, but it's a reminder that speech comes first, and writing second. Speech came to us naturally as children, but we had to struggle and practise so much to learn the shapes of those letters that we fall into the trap of believing they really represent how we speak. We're so used to seeing, say, these six symbols—t-i-s-s-u-e—to convey these four sounds—tɪʃuː —that we forget how disconnected the two systems often are. The mistakes revealed as common by the Corpus all boil down to this one truism: our writing system doesn't really convey the way we speak, while 9-year-old Daisy Ashford's *tishu* does.

This disconnection reveals itself constantly in the most frequent spelling errors. It has various guises: the sound known as schwa, of which more later; double letters, and silent letters; and words like *peddle* and *pedal* which sound identical (technically, '*homophones*'). The divorce between spelling and sound is aggravated by several other factors. Spelling rules for adding elements to the end of words—'*suffixes*'—can be complicated: why *pitiful*, not *pityful*, *appealing*, not *appealling*, and *benefited*, not *benefitted*?

Second, the history of English means that many derived words alter the spelling of their root words: *humour* loses its *u* when it became *humorous*; the *c* in *space* turns to *t* in *spatial*; the -*tain* of *maintain* and *retain* becomes -*ten* in *maintenance* and *retention*. Third, to confuse matters even more, there are variants. Some words have different forms dictated by context:

practice is a noun and *practise* is a verb (in Britain). Others, borrowed from overseas, can vary wildly: is it *yoghurt, yoghourt,* or *yogurt*? For 'Chinese leaves', is it *bok choy, pak choi, bok tsoi,* or which of the 32 different spellings found in the *OED*?

Whispering schwat nothings

The most common letter in English is *e*. But which is the most common vowel sound? You might be surprised. It doesn't have its own letter, and you might not even think of it as a 'proper' vowel sound at all. It's the murmur we make when we're unsure of something, and has been unattractively described thus: *'it often sounds like a very faint and stifled grunt or a half-suppressed short clearing of the throat'*. How can such an unmelodious sound be so pervasive? (9)

To appreciate its particular quality, I invite you to say *banana*, at normal speed. How many **different** vowel sounds does it contain? Only two. The middle one is the same as in *far*. The first and last are the same as each other, and like the 'a' sound of *above*.

Here's a longer example, which suggests how common this sound is. Say the following phrase as quickly as you can (like rapid speech, not as if you're auditioning for drama school): *I ordered an avocado and a banana*. How many times does the sound occur? Five, six, seven, or eight? Here it is again, with the relevant letters in italic: I ord*e*r*e*d *a*n av*o*cado *a*nd *a* ban*a*n*a*. It occurs seven times.

There are two things to notice about this sound. First, it only applies to syllables which are not stressed, such as the ones in italic in av*o*cado and b*a*nan*a*. Second, many short vowel sounds can be pronounced this way when they're not stressed. Why not test yourself: which of the following words does not contain this sound?

Beware of schwa

Letter	Word
a	above, miracle, extra
e	after, number, the
o	obey, occur, commit
u	success, cupboard, picture

They all do. Apologies for the trick question, but it was to make you aware of just how pervasive this sound is. (And the list does not cover all its manifestations.) And what is this sound called? Well, with one of those ironies so typical of English, its spelling and pronunciation are at variance: write it *schwa*, but say it 'shwah' to rhyme with 'grand**ma**'. The name is from ancient Hebrew, and is an alteration of a word meaning 'emptiness' —very appropriate in view of the schwa's unobtrusiveness.

So, how exactly does all this affect spelling? Like this. Mistakes often happen when people spell vowels that are pronounced as schwa. Let's take a concrete example: *relevant* is often spelt *relevent*, *relavent*, and *relavant*. It's easy to see how it happens. Both the last syllables are pronounced schwa, as shown by the upside down 'e' in this phonetic notation: reləvənt. The schwa sound can be as easily represented by a letter *a* as by an *e*, so all of those spellings mirror the pronunciation, yet are still incorrect. The treacherous murmur of the schwa is behind hundreds of common mistakes such as *seperate*, *corollory*, *accessary*, *availible*, and *accessable*.

Double consonants are another spelling banana skin. They're very common in Italian: *al-legro*, *ar-rivederci*, *piz-za*, *Boc-cac-cio*, and they can carry meaning: *nono* = 'ninth', *nonno* = 'grandfather'. If we pronounced English in the same way we might avoid consonants which don't double up when they should, such as *acomodate* and *milenium*; and wrong double consonants which hedge their bets, such as *dissappoint* and *exaggerrate*.

Daisy Ashford's phonetic writing produced dozens of spellings based on speech, such as *sumpshous, monagram,* and *grammer*. The last two are often found nowadays, together with *sumptious* for *sumptuous*. Other common examples of speech affecting how people write are: *Febuary, contempory, mischievious,* and *definately*. The influence can work the other way too, with people pronouncing words exactly as they're written, but differently from the traditional pronunciation. For instance, in British English the *th* in *Anthony* is now sometimes sounded, in line with the traditional American pronunciation, but contrary to the previous British norm.

You say choritho, I say choritso

When it comes to spelling imported words, English is sometimes conservationist, sometimes cavalier. Many languages smooth the *ph* in Greek words such as *philosophy* and *Europhile* down to an *f,* but English hangs on to it. Similarly, the seemingly impossible run of letters in -*phth*- is preserved in *diphtheria,* even though ar-ti-cu-la-ting it as dif-thee-ree-uh could sound ra-ther pre-cious.

But some other words which don't fit into the standard patterns of English are tinkered with until they do. The *longue* element of the French import *chaise longue* is an example: how to pronounce and write it Englishly? Only *tongue* resembles it, but people seem to have thought it perverse to write *longue* that way. So, the letters of Gallic *longue* are reshuffled into the more homely *chaise lounge,* through the process known as 'folk etymology' (discussed further in Chapter 6). (10)

Food terms have flooded into English, and several of them cause problems. How we pronounce them can affect their spelling in unexpected ways. One that tends to flummox English speakers is *bruschetta*, with its -*sch*- in the middle, a sequence found only in such un-household words as *Aeschylus* and *eschatology*, or in *discharge*, where the *dis*- is clearly a prefix. Pronouncing *bruschetta* as 'broo-sket-ta' can sound like a bit of one-upmanship, so 'broo-she-tuh' is what you tend to hear, reflected in the spelling *brushetta*. Another example is the spicy Spanish sausage, *chorizo*. In Spanish the -*izo* part can be pronounced 'ee-so' or 'ee-tho'. But very often in English what you hear is the Italianate 'cho-reet-so', with the *z* pronounced like the double *z* of *pizza*. As you'd expect, you find spellings based on that pronunciation: *choritso* and *chorizzo*. Pronouncing a Spanish loanword in an Italian way is one of the many quirks of English.

Apart from food words, plant names can be tongue-twisting spelling traps. Where else can you find the tongue-spraining combination -*schsch*- but in the botanical name of the California poppy, *eschscholzia*? Though *fuchsias* immortalize the sixteenth-century botanist Leonhard Fuchs, we tend to write him out of history by rhyming it with Confucius, and putting the *s* before the *c*.

Mighty oaks from little eggcorns grow

Other changes are the result of people torturing alien word shapes to extract a confession of meaning. *Chaise lounge* is one example, and another is *in one foul swoop*. The reasoning seems understandable. *Fell* no longer exists as an adjective in its own right, and is therefore not meaningful. It makes great sense to reinterpret it as a more common word which seems to convey the meaning of the phrase: something cruel and underhand. The many variations on *fell* revealed by the Corpus show people struggling to make the phrase meaningful for them: *full, foul, fall, fatal, fallow, flail, fowl, felled, feel.*

Inventions like *foul swoop* are known as '*eggcorns*', and often affect words or meanings used only in stock phrases. Eggcorns are the result of people using analogy and logic—which in language are often fallible guides—to literally rewrite a word's history. Invented in 2003 by the linguist Professor Geoffrey Pullum, the name came from the chance sighting of the spelling *eggcorn* when 'acorn' was meant. The change was not arbitrary: it made some kind of semantic and conceptual sense. The difference between eggcorns and folk etymologies is that they are individual, rather than collective.

Linguists and word buffs can get very excited about eggcorns because they show language changing before our very eyes, and often throw light on how and why. They can also illuminate how it has changed in the past—apart from which many eggcorns have a folksy charm all their own. Here are the frequencies of some eggcorns in the Corpus, compared to their original versions. As can be seen, some of them are due to '*homophony*', that is, to words with different spellings being pronounced the same; many of them affect idioms. As the percentages show, some, such as *just desserts*, are now used more often than the original, but others, such as *no love loss*, are still in the minority. Only time will tell if they eventually become the majority.

Eggcorns in the Corpus

Eggcorn		Original	
Eggcorn more common than original			
just desserts	60.8%	just deserts	39.2%
straight-laced	52.6%	strait-laced	47.4%
miniscule	52.1%	minuscule	47.9%

Eggcorn less common than original			
free rein	42.67%	free reign	57.3%
with baited breath	33.7%	with bated breath	66.3%
preying mantis	14%	praying mantis	86%
slight of hand	13%	sleight of hand	87%
foul etc. swoop	8.1%	fell swoop	91.9%
hammer and thongs	4.5%	hammer and tongs	95.6%
no love loss	3.5%	no love lost	96.5%

Some interesting ones which crop up less often are *beknighted* and *at somebody's beckoned call. Beknighted* is puzzling, because it replaces the common word *night* with the much less common *knight*, whereas eggcorns usually do the opposite. One suggestion is that it derives from the idea of people being held in higher esteem than they deserve. With *beckoned call* there is a kind of logic in operation. *Beck* is unknown (11) outside this phrase, so 'beck and' is re-analysed as 'beckoned'. Sound helps here, because the unstressed 'and' is pronounced as our universal mumble, the schwa. The reinterpretation also makes semantic sense, because it's easy to imagine somebody imperiously beckoning someone else to do their bidding. (Quite coincidentally, the home-grown reinterpretation fits the etymology: *beck* is in fact a variant of *beckon*.)

A blemish to be avoided

'*A blemish to be avoided wherever possible,*' was Winston Churchill's opinion of the hyphen, and modern dictionary writers seem to agree. The 2007 edition of the *Shorter Oxford English Dictionary* consigned 16,000 hyphens to the lexicographical lumber room, on the basis that hyphen usage had declined by 5 per cent in the previous 30 years. '*If you take hyphens seriously, you will undoubtedly go mad,*' was the view of the anonymous writer of an Oxford University Press style guide/

styleguide/style-guide (leaving one to wonder if this turned out to be a self-fulfilling prophecy). What we're talking about here is the use of the hyphen to join words, known as the '*hard hyphen*', rather than at line endings, the Daliesque '*soft hyphen*'.

As an example of the confusion caused by this innocuous-looking symbol, let's take a phrase that Shakespeare gave the language: *wild goose chase*. Is it three words, two words, or one? If two, which two? And does it require hyphens? You can indulge in a hyphenfest and write *wild-goose-chase*; you can go to the opposite extreme and make a clean break between each word; or you can create any permutation in between. In theory, there are nine ways to write it; in practice, there are six different versions, between the *Oxford English Dictionary* and the Corpus. As it happens, the most popular version in both sources is the one in tune with meaning and modern hyphenation: *wild-goose chase*. It makes sense because it unambiguously answers the question: 'What kind of chase is it?' It's a chase which has to do with wild geese, not a chase which is wild. Without the hyphen it is unclear whether *wild* refers to the chase or the geese.

You could say, 'So what?' Everybody knows what the phrase means, and getting uptight about a little line is, arguably, a trifle pedantic. It is true that using hyphens in compound nouns, such as *website*, is generally unnecessary. Winston Churchill's view was that you could either run words together or leave them apart, except when '*nature revolts*'. But that leaves a lot of room for subjectivity: you and I may have very different views of nature's breaking point. Let's see. The *Shorter Oxford* has removed hyphens from these words.

One word or two?

Which ones would you personally write as shown?
fig leaf, pot belly, pigeonhole, bumblebee, chickpea, crybaby, logjam, ice cream, hobby horse, test tube

So, is the hyphen ever useful? Well, Oxford University Press suggest the example of *twenty odd men* versus *twenty-odd men*. Without the hyphen it refers to a score of male eccentrics; with one, it denotes about twenty normal blokes. The oft-quoted *extra marital sex* should be good news for both parties in the marriage, whereas *extra-marital sex* probably isn't. And in Lynne Truss's example, a *pickled-herring merchant* is eminently respectable, while a *pickled herring merchant* has had one too many. (12) Hyphens can avoid ambiguity in compound expressions in front of nouns, as in the last two examples. As a rule of thumb, hyphens aid understanding in such expressions when they come before the noun, but are unnecessary after:

- *they're very well known/ a well-known writer*
- *this wine is first class/ some first-class wine*
- *keep your notes up to date/ up-to-date notes.*

They can also avoid unsightly pile-ups [*sic*] between vowels, or between consonants: *de-ice, take-off, re-enter, coat-tails, part-time*. With words of this kind, as in general, US usage is less hyphen-friendly than British. For instance, Corpus shows that *takeoff* is the most common form around the world, and is used 80 per cent of the time in the US. But in the UK the proportions are reversed, and 80 per cent of the time it's hyphenated.

How often people use the hyphen is largely a matter of personal, national, or house style. But style guides universally agree that in one construction it is always an intruder: between a verb and a following adverb (in '*phrasal verbs*'). The hyphen is redundant in: '*The weekend will be kicked-off by our new correspondent . . .*' and '*Some pedigree herds have been built-up over generations.*' As Fowler said more than eighty years ago, there is one governing principle behind its use:

The hyphen is not an ornament, but an aid to being understood, and should be employed only when it is needed for that purpose. (13)

The urge to merge

In Shakespeare's day, there were dozens of ways of spelling his name—Shakespere, Shackespeare, Shaxpear, etc.—but nowadays they've been whittled down to just one. In the intervening centuries most word shapes have been narrowed down to a single spelling as well, or to two variants. Where uncertainty often reigns is about how to combine words. There seems to be a trend for words to move from two separate lives to a shared existence. Dictionaries contain dozens of examples of how this has happened historically, and the Corpus suggests which words are currently heading in this direction. *Website* is a good example. It is two words in its earliest appearance in the *OED*, and in all the citations, which run up to the year 2000. However, the Corpus shows that people now write it as one word over 80 per cent of the time.

Some very common words were once separate. Nowadays we write *anybody* without a space, but for Caxton, Shakespeare, and Jane Austen, among others, it was two words. *Somebody*, *nobody*, and *everybody* all began life as two words (*body* meaning 'person', an archaic use, from which comes *busybody*). Other common couples which to modern eyes look distinctly odd when put asunder are:

Words previously written separately

anybody	any	body
indeed	in	deed
marshmallow	marsh	mallow
nothing	no	thing
otherwise	other	wise
platform	plat	form
portcullis	port	cullis
smallpox	small	pox

When considering if two words which exist independently are best written as one, pronunciation can help. A **BLACK**bird, with one strong stress, is a bird that belongs to that particular species; a **BLACK BIRD**, with two, equal stresses, is a bird you can't identify which happens to be black. That same rule explains why *smallpox* was originally two words: it was indeed small, compared to what the *OED* politely calls '*the pox proper, or great pox*'.

Currently several words which we're used to seeing as singletons look as if they're in the process of tying the knot. For instance:

underway 54%
under way 46%

someday 75%
some day 25%

website 82%
web site 18%

anymore 62%
any more 38%

Nothing in spelling is permanent, and, as we saw in Chapter 2, and will see often again, other aspects of language are equally fluid.

4 Which is to be master?
Meaning in context

'When I use a word,' Humpty Dumpty said in rather a scornful tone, 'it means just what I choose it to mean—neither more nor less.'

'The question is,' said Alice, 'whether you can make words mean so many different things.'

'The question is,' said Humpty Dumpty, 'which is to be master— that's all.'

Lewis Carroll, *Through the Looking-Glass, 1871.*

Humpty Dumpty famously claimed to be able to make words mean exactly what he wished. So, on his lips 'There's glory for you' could mean 'There's a nice knock-down argument for you' if he so chose. His boastful claim was inspired by his rather fragile ego: only dictators—or the insane—would make the same boast. But if people individually don't decide what to make words mean, are not their 'masters', who is?

Are dictionaries masters of meaning? Clearly not. First, because language is primarily a spoken not a written medium (think of how much you speak in a day, compared with what you write), and dictionaries mostly reflect written language. People don't usually speak dictionary in hand—though they may consult one to bolster a line of argument or prove a legal point. There is a Latin tag: 'Spoken words fly, writing remains' (*verba volant, scripta manent*). And as soon as they have passed our lips, spoken words fly away, while the written word remains for hundreds, even thousands, of years. Because of our cultural tradition, it is easy to equate 'language' with the written word, forgetting that language is firstly speech and only secondly writing. And speech is uttered by speakers, a term I shall often use in this chapter to reinforce that idea.

Second, even if dictionaries are viewed as authorities on how to use words, any diktats aiming to tell people which words they may use are unenforceable—except, just possibly, in totalitarian states. As Dr Johnson wrote in the *Preface* to his dictionary (1755):

. . . academies have been instituted, to guard the avenues of their languages, to retain fugitives, and repulse intruders; but their vigilance and activity have hitherto been vain.

His realistic view is borne out by what has happened when academies have attempted to straitjacket language. Even in Johnson's day the *Académie Française* failed to regulate French. As he also noted in his *Preface*: '*The French language has visibly changed under the inspection of the academy.*' More recent attempts, such as trying to proscribe the use of words like *le tie-break* and *le software*, have met with as little success. In France, as everywhere else, no amount of huffing and puffing and tut-tutting by the language police can stop the general public using the words and phrases that everybody else does. (1)

Third, dictionaries cannot dictate what words mean, because meanings are indeterminate and fuzzy; they do not have clear borders, still less guards 'to repulse intruders'. Printed dictionaries, on the other hand, have to base their descriptions of language on the territorial and linear idea that every sense of every word is distinct from every other. Their vertical layout in columns, with different senses marked by numbers or letters, provides visual reinforcement for this idea. Here's an example, to which we'll return later in this chapter.

How does a dictionary define *classic*?

> **classic ▶ *adjective***
> **1** judged over a period of time to be of the highest quality and outstanding of its kind: *a classic novel | a classic car.*
>   **b)** (of a garment or design) of a simple, elegant style not greatly subject to changes in fashion: *this classic navy blazer.*
> **2** very typical of its kind: *I had all the classic symptoms of flu.*

Last, speakers do not use words in isolation. They use words in specific situations and specific verbal contexts, which range from phrases to texts. The fact that dictionary writers define each sense suggests that words have some kind of inherent 'meaning' which can be discussed in the abstract. This can lull people into thinking of meaning as '*something independent, inherent and unique to an item, and serving to distinguish it from all others*', and to think of individual word meanings as '*autonomous and fossilized, like flies caught in amber*'. (2) The reality of words conveying meaning in context and in use is rather different.

Speech communities

So if neither individuals nor dictionaries decide what words mean, who does? Speakers in communities of different kinds, sometimes known as '*speech communities*'. Although there is no generally agreed definition of the term, it is still a helpful tool for thinking about language. In the broadest terms, speakers belong to national—or even transnational—groups who share a common tongue: English, French, Spanish, Portuguese, are languages whose mother-tongue speakers are spread over many countries. Though English speakers from, say, the UK and South Africa can communicate well, there are many differences in the norms of language they follow. Zooming in from the larger picture, a community could be a geographical or social grouping of any size: from part of a whole country, with its own version of a language, such as north-east England where the Geordie dialect is spoken, to cities such as New York or Philadelphia, to the Gaelic-speaking areas of Ireland or Scotland. Smaller still are social networks and groups, such as urban or professional grouping, who use words and meanings in ways unique to them.

Members of these groups and communities often have expectations and norms about what words and phrases mean—though they may or may not share broader, social expectations and norms as well. It is possible to belong simultaneously to more than one speech community. Somebody might belong to the communities of: British, Geordie, football fan; or Canadian, Torontonian, foodie; or Australian, Sydneysider, blogger.

Speakers in speech communities decide what words mean; and just as they decide what they mean, so they can change their meaning. It is worth noting that speakers 'decide' what words mean in two different senses. Individually, in specific situations and verbal contexts they choose which meaning is relevant out of the several on offer. Collectively, they determine over time which meanings of words will flourish, and which will wither.

The amount and variety of data in the Corpus make it possible to analyse how different groups of people—Australians compared to the British, female bloggers compared to males, fiction writers compared to news writers, and so forth—use words in context. This chapter looks at how context makes it clear, to speakers and dictionary writers alike, which meaning of a word is intended; and at some ways in which speakers can change what words mean.

Janus words

In Chapter 2 we discussed how new words come into English, and in Chapter 3 suggested that once part of the language their graphic shape can easily be changed. And just as the shape of established words can be altered, so speakers can cause them to fluctuate wildly in meaning, or to mean multiple things. Some words can even end up signifying the opposite of what they originally did. In some speech communities *bad* and *wicked* mean 'good'. In others, *fat* rewritten as *phat* means 'excellent', as in this quote from a British blog text included in the Corpus: *'I've ordered a phat new computer, which is an absolute beast (sporting some 200 Gb of hard-disk space).'*

These double-edged words with conflicting meanings are called *'Janus words'*, or *'contronyms'*. (Janus, a Roman deity, had two faces, one looking backwards and one forwards, the better to guard doors and gateways, hence the name for these words, which seem to face in two directions at once.) Some long-established examples are:

Janus words in context

sanction = 'penalty' ← *trade sanctions; economic sanctions; legal sanctions*
sanction = 'permission' ← *official sanction; divine sanction; to receive official/governmental/etc. sanction*

oversight = 'a failure to notice things' ← *It was an oversight; They failed to do that by oversight*
oversight = 'a duty to notice things' ← *to have/exercise/etc. oversight of something; congressional/governmental/etc. oversight*

But notice how the meaning in either case is signalled by words typically found in the verbal context. These customary associations of words are known as *'collocations'*, and collocation is a fundamental concept in the analysis of meaning, and will be explored further in the next chapter. Which meaning applies in these Janus words is also signalled by grammar. *Sanctions* meaning 'penalties' are typically plural; *oversight* meaning 'failure' is preceded by *an*, or something happens *by* oversight.

A more recent example of a Janus word is *double whammy*. Derived from *whammy*, meaning a spell, or a hex, on something—which was first recorded in writing in 1940—it took off in the 1950s through the US cartoon strip *Li'l Abner*. The *double whammy* cast by the character Evil-Eye Fleegle with both his eyes was even more powerful than the single whammy cast with one eye. Though dictionaries often define it as something negative, in keeping with its origins, speakers often interpret it as something positive, as in this yachting report from a Sunday newspaper included in the Corpus: '*Oystercatcher 23 delighted in the moderate breeze, recording a double whammy of top spots on Saturday . . . with two emphatic wins in this strong class.*'

Watch the borders!—polysemy

To Humpty Dumpty's vain (= 'empty' and = 'conceited') boast about making words mean whatever took his fancy, Alice replied: '*The question is, . . . whether you **can** make words mean so many different things.*' Alice's question may be philosophically important, but in practice speakers **can** easily 'make words mean so many different things'.

Using the same word, they effortlessly convey different meanings, and their listeners effortlessly understand them. *Sanction, oversight*, and *double whammy* all have more than one meaning, as has *vain* in the previous paragraph. A word

I've been emphasizing, *speaker*, has at least four: 'someone who speaks a language'; 'someone delivering a speech or lecture'; 'loudspeaker'; 'the presiding official in the British House of Commons, and in other parliaments'. Though misunderstandings don't happen nearly as often as they theoretically might, an urban myth illustrates what could go wrong. Edgar J. Hoover, the feared head of the FBI, insisted that memos he received had wide margins so that he had room to write in them. One day he got a memo whose margins were too narrow. In big letters on the top he wrote: '*Watch the borders!*' The next day 200 agents were dispatched to Mexico and Canada. (3)

Open any general language dictionary at random and you will see that most words in general use have more than one sense and definition. These words are technically known as '*polysemous*'. This word comes from the prefix *poly-*, 'many', and *sēma*, 'sign', and is pronounced 'poli**SEE**mus' or 'puh**LI**simus'. The related noun is '*polysemy*', pronounced 'poli**SEE**mee' or 'puh**LI**simee'. Words with a single meaning are '*monosemous*'—pronounced 'monuh**SEE**mus'—for instance, *maypole, mazurka, monthly* (adjective), *midwifery*. Many scientific, technical, or specialist words are of this kind, for example some we've come across in this book: *lemma, prefix, suffix*.

Not only are many words 'polysemous'; the words speakers use most are the most polysemous of all. The more common a word is, the more meanings it has. This is an observable fact, and partly explains why people manage to communicate most of the time using only a fraction of the overall vocabulary of English. Some of the most common words have a staggering number of meanings. Take *do*, which is the third most frequent verb in the Corpus, and so the third most frequent in the language (*be* and *have* are first and second.) The *OED* divides it into over 150 meanings, yet it isn't even the longest word in that dictionary: the verb *put* holds that honour.

And if words have several meanings, then surely they are going to be very ambiguous? In theory, this is true; in practice, it turns out not to be the case. The different collocations of Janus words like *sanction* distinguish one meaning from another. Another textbook example of a potentially ambiguous word is *bank*. Out of context, does it refer to the institution you entrust your money to, or '*the land alongside or sloping down to a river or lake*'? (Not to mention the several other subsidiary meanings clustering round those primary ones.) The words look and sound the same, are both nouns, and can both be used in the singular or plural. Of course, what we know about how the world works can often remove the ambiguity. If I say, 'I have to get to the bank before it closes', your knowledge of the real world will tell you I'm talking about the financial institution, and you will discard other interpretations.

Now, imagine a computer program with the task of translating the sentence with *bank*. The program uses some sort of bilingual dictionary, but to choose the correct translation it has to understand the precise meaning of the English. How can it possibly do that? Unlike you and me, the program doesn't know that financial institutions open and shut, while river banks don't. What clues does it have to work with? Here is a concordance of twenty examples chosen at random from Fiction material in the Corpus. It's interesting to look at the first ten and decide:

Which ones refer to the financial meaning, and which to the river bank? How do you know?

scattered over the floor.* *" You 've got a	**b a n k**	account , you little turd , "Carl said
, and lying on the paved area above the	**b a n k**	was the Maudhnait. People were looking
. But instead he was stuck in front of a	**b a n k**	machine , computerized no doubt , watching
the time they had reached the Oswego local	**b a n k**	, Eric had repeatedly and furiously vented
<p>" Fine. We'll wire the money to your	**b a n k**	account . "*</p><p>*" Thanks , Gary . You
down the road and no one outside of the	**b a n k**	. Carefully , she slipped out of the trees
came to a cluster of trees that lined the	**b a n k**	. They were old , and they were tall,
aside , allowing the duo to step into the	**b a n k**	.* *Agent McGinnis flashed his badge
personal errand .* *Stacy Chapman 's	**b a n k**	card had been used at the TSB on the high
picked up a handful of pebbles from the mossy	**b a n k**	and tossed them into the lake . They landed
looked when she rode like that .* *The	**b a n k**	was made of dark wood . It was an attractive
the man you hired to take my place at the	**b a n k**	is doing a good enough job , he 's in for
knot of enemy lancers appeared on the north	**b a n k**	and opened fire .* *Now on the island
the ford from the western end to the south	**b a n k**	of the Chickahominy difficult but not impracticable
choice . Leroy 's just as focused on this	**b a n k**	as I am ! He would have been there with
looks down between his legs into the stony	**b a n k**	. " God forbid we should end up in the
albeit a barmaid with enough money in the	**b a n k**	to buy her own business in the near future
General . I had ten million in a Panamanian	**b a n k**	account , and she attacked me and stole
" Yes , my father was a partner in their	**b a n k**	. " Irene smiled . " How are you related
from the water and lay down on the grassy	**b a n k**	to dry . She was overjoyed with this place
used to getting them .* *I reached the	**b a n k**	and knelt down myself , taking my hair

In most of these examples a word in the same sentence makes it clear which meaning is operative. *Account* in example 1 signals the financial meaning; *mossy* in 10 signals the river bank meaning, and so forth. If our computer program 'knew' that *account* goes with *bank* in one meaning, and *mossy* with the other, it would be able to translate *bank* correctly. Usually ambiguity is resolved by words in the same sentence—but not always. In example 2 the phrase '*the paved area above the bank*' suggests the river bank meaning, but not conclusively. After all, a financial bank could be built into the side of a hill, or underground. However, *river* is mentioned in the previous sentence, which clears up the ambiguity.

Humans are better at understanding language than computers—so far—and don't generally need to rely on these neighbouring verbal clues: the topic under discussion or the situation will make the meaning clear. But if the meaning of a particular sentence is unclear, those clues are crucial. For dictionary writers they are also vital: they are one of the tools they use to decide how to demarcate the different senses of a word. And it is only by looking at as many examples as possible of words in context that modern dictionary writers can get objective evidence of how speakers signal meanings.

Dr Johnson divided words into senses according to how they were used in his sources. Those sources were authors he regarded as classics, and he validated his division into senses with quotations from their work. But literary sources don't tell us which meanings the majority of speakers assign to words. Modern lexicographers take a more democratic approach. They decide what a word means by looking at its use across the extraordinary range of texts provided by the Corpus and other corpora, not by poring over selected and hallowed works. They aim to describe how people in general use language, not whether such and such a use is sanctified by the great and good. As Professor John Sinclair, one of the doyens of corpus linguistics, wrote:

One of the principal uses of corpus is to identify what is central and typical in the language. . . . If we are to approach a realistic view of the way in which language is used, we must record the usage of the mass of ordinary writers, and not the stray genius or the astute journalist. (4)

In the guts of the living

> *The words of a dead man*
> *Are modified in the guts of the living*
> W.H. Auden, *In Memory of W. B. Yeats*

By conventional metaphor languages are equated to living organisms, and can be described as 'living', 'dying', 'dead', 'extinct'. Referring to Yeats, Auden inverted the metaphor, and suggested that living people—speakers—inwardly modify language. What is true of poetic language is true of all language.

You and I and all the members of our speech community inherit it, but we don't pass it on in the same state as we found it. In the course of our lives we make it our own and, in our own tiny way, assist in changing it. Every time we use a word in a particular new meaning, we strengthen that meaning; every time we don't use a word in a meaning that is declining, we hasten its demise. (5)

This happens because the union of a word with a meaning which we so often take for granted is neither unique, indissoluble, nor permanent. The idea of uniqueness is undermined because words have different meanings. The union can be dissolved, because words lose—and gain— meanings, or their meanings can be expressed by different words. And these shifts happen constantly, as will be seen from historical and contemporary examples.

Some words are Alice-like, and can get bigger and bigger, and smaller and smaller. One way in which speakers shrink the meanings of words is by confining them to a smaller sphere of activity. This process is known as '*narrowing*', and can be observed historically. In Old English the verb *steorfan*, the ancestor of *to starve*, meant 'to die'. Ousted over time by *to die*, a Viking word, it did not disappear completely: it took on the very specific meaning of 'dying of hunger'.

Similarly, in medieval times *professor* referred to anybody qualified to teach at a university, and was interchangeable with *master* and *doctor*. Over time in Britain it became confined to the holders of endowed chairs, but in the US it still applies more generally to university teaching staff. A final historical example is *affection*, which once denoted emotion opposed to reason, particularly strong emotions, as in Milton's '*A will over-ruled by enormous affections or passions*'; or Hobbes's '*Anger, Envy, Fear, Pity or other Affections*'.

In contrast, some words expand their sphere of operation, through a process known as '*extension*'. Our common-or-garden word *dog* once meant a particular breed—though nobody knows for sure which—before it became applicable to any old canine. Expansion also often happens when formerly specialist or technical words reach a wider public. *Neurosis* and *neurotic* gained wider currency through the influence of Freud and the psychoanalytic movement. *Anal*, meaning 'obsessive, over-fussy, pernickety' has similarly broadened, from a technical meaning describing a particular stage of childhood development.

Less obviously technical, but still a word which has increased its range, *issue* once referred to specific emotional and psychological problems. It now shows signs of becoming a general word for any and every kind of problem. Often the general meaning becomes more common than the technical one: *learning curve*, from psychology and education; *feedback* from electronics; *bottom line* from finances. Sometimes the meaning changes: a *quantum leap* is always large in general language, but not in science.

Mobile meanings

Apart from narrowing or expanding their range, words can be upwardly or downwardly mobile, figuratively speaking. They better themselves through a process known as '*melioration*' (from the Latin *melior*, 'better', also found in 'to ameliorate'). If you describe somebody as *sophisticated* you probably approve; and it's probably better to be working with sophisticated software than with unsophisticated. But this approving use is not recorded earlier than in Hardy's *Jude the Obscure* (1895). The meaning from which it developed had negative connotations, as the *OED* definition shows: '*deprived of primitive simplicity or naturalness.*' Ben Jonson used the

verb *to sophisticate* in its earlier meaning of 'to adulterate':
'*He lets me haue good tabacco, and he do's not Sophisticate it,
with sack-lees, or oyle.*' Enthusiasm has similarly risen above its
lowly origins and become entirely respectable. In the eighteenth
century, although the modern sense existed, it was often a
finger-wagging term used to criticize religious reformers:
'*Towards the end he [Wesley] exalted his voice and acted
very ugly enthusiasm.*' (6)

But words can go down in the world, as well as up. A classic
example is *silly*. Its ancestor in Old English, *(ġe)sǣliġ*,
meant 'happy, blissful, fortunate' (and is directly related to
the modern German *selig* and, through Yiddish, to the *Zelig*
of Woody Allen's film). From such promising beginnings
it went downhill as the *OED* shows (spellings have been
modernized):

How *silly* developed its modern meanings

Date	Meaning	Example
before 1225	blessed	*through silly martyrdom*
before 1225	pious, holy	*silly maiden*
circa 1250	happy	
circa 1290	innocent	*this silly beast*
1297	pitiable	*this silly old king*
1297	insignificant	*the silly wench*
1500s	feeble-minded	*she of love was silly*
1529	foolish, simple	*their silly souls*
1588	of words, thoughts	*thy silly thought*
		the silliest, foolishest stories
1766	lacking common sense	*silly man*

There are two names for this process: Anglo-Saxon worsening, and Latin '*pejoration*', the technical term sometimes used in linguistics. Another well-known example is *knave*, which originally just meant a young boy. From there it developed first to mean servant; then somebody in a lowly social position, as opposed to a knight, and later still, a rogue. A modern example of 'pejoration' is *gay* in the sense of 'stupid' or 'feeble', a meaning it can have mainly in US slang. This sense has even developed its own spelling, *ghey*, as in this quote from a US blog: '*no time for the ghey concept known as disclosure*'. Similarly, Disney's Mickey Mouse™ now lends his name not only to things which are small, and therefore not to be taken seriously, but also to the ineffective or the sub-standard. The next Corpus example, from a New Zealand parliamentary debate in April 2004, uses the iconic mouse in an elaborate metaphor on political 'packages', and shows how very creative the examples in the Corpus often are: '*The Government came out last December with a package, all dressed up in Christmas wrapping, and, finding it to be unacceptable to the public, it has gone about this Mickey-Mouse consultation process, tossed it back into an Easter box, and served it up as being all-new and a great answer.*'

A classic mistake: confusables

The words just discussed have had their meanings changed in a variety of ways. But there is one variety of change which is noticed and commented on more than any other: when a word starts being used in a meaning which traditionally 'belonged' to another word, or 'encroaches' on its territory. An obvious example is *disinterested* meaning 'not interested'. These changes of allegiance are often criticized by the language police, and join the long list of word pairs known as '*confusables*'. Usage books provide guidelines for when to use which word of each pair—one guide even gives an embarrassment rating for using one instead of the other. (7)

Guides and dictionaries sometimes suggest that the differences between confusables are easy to state and define, but closer inspection often shows that the distinctions are not as clear-cut as they first look. Let's take a single dictionary meaning each from the confusables *classical* and *classic*:

classical ▶ *adjective*
2 representing an exemplary standard within a traditional and long-established form or style: *classical ballet.*

classic ▶ *adjective*
1 judged over a period of time to be of the highest quality and outstanding of its kind: *a classic novel* | *a classic car.*

These definitions suggest that each meaning of each word is distinct from its other meanings, and from all meanings of the other word. But does this hold water? If you compare *classical* 2 and *classic* 1, what, in the abstract, is the difference? Both definitions refer to the notion of setting a standard over a period of time. The difference appears to lie purely in *classical* 2 relating to 'form' or 'style'. What helps to distinguish one meaning from the other, as the definitions suggest, is that we use *ballet* in the same context as *classical*, and *novel* and *car* in the same context as *classic*. In other words, these typical collocations signal the meanings concerned.

Some usage guides suggest that *classical* is (mistakenly) used for meaning 1 of *classic*, so that instead of referring to a *classic novel* people would refer to a *classical novel*. Does the Corpus confirm or disprove this? And are there are other meanings which overlap? Using a special program, it is possible to compare all contexts in the Corpus for the two words. What emerges is that many nouns can be modified by either adjective—rather more than can only be modified by one. The most frequent and most significant are shown in the table below.

Classical and *classic* in context

Noun	How many times?		How statistically significant?	
	classical	classic	classical	classic
music	4889	106	60.1	6.1
example	114	2740	12.3	54.9
ballet	614	51	54.1	18.2
liberalism	197	10	43.2	8.7
tale	16	463	5.1	39.4
mythology	132	8	37.4	7.4
dance	545	28	36.6	4.4
tradition	535	112	36.0	15.3
concert	313	8	35.2	1.3
repertoire	141	25	35.2	14.2
Greek	132	6	33.4	4.2
theory	534	91	32.8	11.0
novel	26	374	6.3	23.7

As can be seen, there is generally a very large difference between how often the same noun is used with *classical* and *classic*: '*classic example*' is nearly 25 times more common than '*classical example*'. The question is: when is either word used in a different meaning from what the dictionary suggests, that is, in the stigmatized meaning? To analyse that, we need to consider all the dictionary meanings of the two words.

How does a dictionary define *classical* and *classic*?

classical ▶ *adjective*
1 relating to ancient Greek or Latin literature, art, or culture: *classical mythology* | *classical Latin.*
  b) (of art or architecture) influenced by ancient Greek or Roman forms or principles.
2 representing an exemplary standard within a traditional and long-established form or style: *classical ballet.*
  b) relating to the first significant period of an area of study: *classical Marxism.*
3 *Physics* relating to or based upon concepts and theories which preceded the theories of relativity and quantum mechanics; Newtonian: *classical physics.*

classic ▶ *adjective*
1 judged over a period of time to be of the highest quality and outstanding of its kind: *a classic novel* | *a classic car.*
  b) (of a garment or design) of a simple, elegant style not greatly subject to changes in fashion: *this classic navy blazer.*
2 very typical of its kind: *I had all the classic symptoms of flu.*

The next table presents the overlap between the words visually. Reading down a column you will see how the collocations reflect the different meanings of each word. So *classical Greek* in column (b) reflects meaning 1 of *classical.* Reading across rows shows two things. The arrows indicate one word being used instead of the other in the same meaning. Thus, the collocation *classical novel* in row 1 occurs where *classic novel* might be expected. When the same collocation has two different meanings, the noun concerned appears in three cells. *Classic music* in row 2 refers both to meaning 1 of *classic,* as in '*classic punk-rock music*'; and to what is understood by *classical music*—Mozart, Haydn, and so forth.

Classical or *classic*?

(a) Meaning	(b) **classical:** collocations	(c) **classic:** instead of *classical*	(d) **classic:** collocations	(e) **classical** instead of *classic*
1	Greek mythology tale	← Greek ← mythology	mythology tale repertoire tradition	← tale
	novel		novel	← novel
1b	example			
2	music ballet dance concert repertoire	← music ← ballet ← dance ← concert ← repertoire	music ballet dance concert	
			example	← example
2b	liberalism theory tradition	← liberalism ← theory ← tradition	n/a	n/a
3			n/a	n/a

Classical is used with *tale, novel,* and *example,* where *classic* would be expected, according to the definitions. That bears out what the usage guides say. However, *classic* is used more often instead of *classical* than happens the other way round. Column (c) shows that *classic* is used in three out of five senses of *classical* and in ten out of these thirteen collocations. All these overlaps suggest that for certain words—at least for certain speakers—the boundaries between meanings are somewhat fuzzy. Although currently the Corpus shows there is a large difference in how often one collocation occurs compared with the other, that difference could well narrow over time.

Making a point forcibly

Like *classical* and *classic,* many confusables look and sound similar, and have conceptually interrelated meanings.

Similar sounds and meanings

ambiguous/ambivalent	emotional/emotive
connote/denote	fictional/fictitious
continual/continuous	forcefully/forcibly
derisory/derisive	luxuriant/luxurious

It's easy to see how the meanings of these words intertwine. For example, speakers sometimes use *connote* in place of *denote.* Both words refer to what words 'mean', so it's reasonable to think of them as interchangeable in that sense. But, particularly for dictionary writers, they cover different aspects of meaning. *Denote* is often used to refer to the 'literal' meaning of a word, that which can be stated objectively, whereas *connote* refers to more emotional and subjective features. So the word *magpie* denotes an identifiable bird of a particular genus and species, with particular physical characteristics; it connotes behaviours such as hoarding and scavenging. *Forcibly* and *forcefully* are another pair of confusables that it's hard or even impossible to disentangle. Historically they each have two meanings: 'with force or violence', as in '*forcibly*' or '*forcefully removed/evicted/ deported*'; and 'with great power or conviction', as in '*forcibly*' or '*forcefully expressed/reminded/argued*'. The Corpus shows that though some verbs collocate more often with one adverb than the other, there is a large amount of overlap in collocation.

Other pairs sound very similar, but originally had little or no connection in meaning, for instance: *abstruse/obtuse, averse to/adverse to, to appraise/to apprise, to flounder/to founder.* Sometimes it looks as if the sound of a word suggests a meaning it didn't previously have, or brings an aspect of its meaning to the fore. *Fortuitous* once referred to events which were accidental, without commenting on whether the event was good or bad. The current meaning of 'happening as a fortunate accident', or even just 'fortunate', is now well established. Similarly, *fulsome* seems to be losing its meaning of 'over-flattering and probably insincere', and means simply 'abundant': '*The critics have been fulsome in their praise.*'
A rare example of confusables creating a completely new word form is *behoven*, a blend of *behove* and *beholden*, which the *OED* records from as long ago as 1880, and which is used very rarely, but in both meanings, in the Corpus: '*I am not behoven to them; I think it is behoven on a civilized society to ensure that . . .*'

To enchain syllables

The original intention of the literati of Dr Johnson's day was to slow down the juggernaut of language change. When he embarked on his project, Johnson too believed this was possible; by the time he published his dictionary he saw clearly that no academy or dictionary could 'embalm' English. As a vivid reminder of how meaning changes, it is worth quoting at length his words on the subject, from the *Preface* to his dictionary. Not only are they superbly eloquent, but they also contain examples of the message they so forcefully convey. Several of his words and phrases are nowadays generally used to mean something very different; are used in different grammatical patterns; are rare, or archaic; or are not used at all. You might like to consider how he used the underlined words and what he meant, and compare it with how you would use them and what you would mean.

*Those who have been persuaded to think well of my <u>design</u>,
require that it should <u>fix</u> our language, and put a stop to those
<u>alterations</u> which time and chance have hitherto been <u>suffered</u>
to make in it without opposition. With this <u>consequence</u> I will
confess that I flattered myself for a while; but now begin to fear
that I have <u>indulged</u> expectation which neither reason nor
experience can justify. When we see men grow old and die at a
certain time one after another, from century to century, we laugh
at the elixir that promises to prolong life to a thousand years;
and with equal justice may the lexicographer be derided, who
being able to produce no example of a nation that has preserved
their words and phrases from <u>mutability</u>, shall imagine that
his dictionary can embalm his language, and secure it from
corruption and decay, that it is in his power to change <u>sublunary</u>
nature, or clear the world at once from folly, vanity, and
affectation.*

*. . . sounds are too volatile and subtile [sic] for legal restraints;
to enchain syllables, and to lash the wind, are equally the
undertakings of pride, unwilling to measure its desire by
its strength.*

5 Words of a feather
Word groupings

'You shall know a word by the company it keeps.'

J. R. Firth, British linguist, *1957*.

In the last chapter we looked at some aspects of how words convey meaning in context. But it's one thing to convey meaning through words and phrases, and another to thread those meanings together in grammatical sentences. One school of thought about how English works runs like this. Each of us has in our head a grammar ('*grammar*' here meaning 'the rules for combining words' rather than 'correct usage'). We also have a mental dictionary or 'mental *lexicon*' of words and meanings. We apply the grammar rules to the list, and thereby produce perfect, natural-sounding sentences. But can it be true that's all there is to it? Let's try a little thought experiment . . .

Intergalactic learners of English

A taskforce of extraterrestrials from the distant planet Euglossia has landed on Earth. But don't worry: they <u>come in peace</u>. They are here in a spirit of <u>mutual cooperation and understanding</u>. Their aim is to learn all Earth's languages, and to teach us theirs.

As these ETs are capable of travelling from another galaxy it is clear their brains are <u>vastly more sophisticated</u> than ours. Their phenomenal memories have absorbed nearly all the grammar and pronunciation rules of English. From a few hours watching TV and listening to radio they have also absorbed the vocabulary, which they have supplemented by memorizing dictionaries. They can carry on a conversation which is highly accurate grammatically; but because they have interacted so little with humans, their language is <u>somewhat stilted</u>. To help them speak more naturally, some earthlings have volunteered to give them conversation lessons. Let's listen in on a conversation between an ET and his tutor, Geoff.

ET: Hello, good morning, and welcome. How are we keeping today, mate?

Geoff: Fine, thanks. Yourself?

ET: I am good or well. But, listen up, please help me to be understanding of your last utterance: 'Yourself'. The verb is <u>conspicuous by its absence</u>, as your Earth journalists like saying.

Geoff: Well, I hadn't really thought about it before, but you're right. Mmm, it's a kind of ritual exchange here on Earth. You know, us humans like to use the fewest words possible.

ET: I see. I'm lovin' it, this idea of economy in language, innit. That very much <u>reflects our thinking</u> back home on Euglossia. But, <u>be that as it may</u>, might we <u>move swiftly on</u> to today's vocabulary lesson-to-be-learned-from-this-experience?

Geoff: Fire away, I mean, ask me your question.

ET: My question is about the word 'naked'. I know that your earth dictionaries say it has the meaning 'without clothes', and it applies to people and parts of the body. But, to achieve fluency and pass myself off as one of you (*'As if!' thinks Geoff*), I need to know which specific words English speakers use it with. For instance, do they say 'naked knees' and 'naked ankles'?

Geoff: No, they don't usually say either of those, I don't think. But I'm not very sure why. Ah, I've got it, maybe it's because we don't talk about those parts of the body very much at all.

ET: (*Thinks: 'If I use this "ah" word earthling Geoff will believe I too need time to think, even though I don't'*) Ah, could it be because in your society knees and ankles do not usually have erotic associations? And could it be that you use 'naked' with parts of the body which **are** erotically charged?

Geoff: Mmmmm. That's an interesting idea, but I really can't tell you. Can I get back to you on that one?

(*fade out*)

ET's grammar seems perfect, yet much of what he says sounds strange. His language is a strange mishmash of the formal and the friendly, the pompous and the direct. For instance, *listen up*, when talking to a single person rather than a group, or using *innit* and *be that as it may* in the same stretch of language. What he says breaks the subtle rules of what is suitable for his listener, and for the occasion.

His tutor—as an English teacher—will no doubt point out the social implications of using *mate* in a conversation, and explain that *I'm lovin' it* is an advertising slogan rather than part of general language. But as we can see from the conversation, a tricky area for ET is deciding which words to combine to produce natural English. That's why he asks about *naked*. (It might also have something to do with the TV programmes he watched last night.)

We can all produce natural-sounding language. From our exposure to language we know 'instinctively' which words go with which others. In fact, we must know tens of thousands of these natural associations and combinations of words, but we often can't call them to mind when we try to think about them, to 'introspect'. We might be able to say confidently that it sounds natural for *naked* to go with *woman* or *body*, because the words occur together so often, and reflect the core meaning of *naked*. But what about less common pairings such as *naked knees* and *naked ankles*? We might hazard a guess that they're **possible**, because *naked* can go with various body parts; but we can't say whether they are **probable**, and we're unsure if they sound **natural**. That's why Geoff can't answer ET's question: it needs a collection of language such as the Corpus to throw light on that.

The company a word keeps

Words do not exist in isolation. They are strongly attracted to other words, and associate with them to make regular, predictable patterns. Those patterns are part of our 'implicit' knowledge of language. In the introduction to ET's dialogue with Geoff, and in the dialogue, several word combinations are underlined: *come in peace, mutual cooperation and understanding, vastly more sophisticated*, and so forth. (Which of them ring bells with you?) They're underlined because they seem to belong together naturally.

These combinations also seem predictable: *cooperation* suggests *mutual* and *understanding*; when talking about aliens landing, '*We come in . . .*' is likely to be followed by *peace*. Sometimes the second word seems almost inevitable, given the first: *move swiftly on*. Sometimes, given a word or phrase, what comes before seems inevitable and pre-ordained: given *more sophisticated*, why does *vastly* sound more natural than *hugely*, and why is it fifteen times more common? These combinations appear over and over again in many different kinds of English texts. Their technical name is '*collocation*'. Collocation refers to the combination itself, while the individual words are known as '*collocates*'. If two or more words appear together regularly, they are said to 'collocate'.

Which single noun do you think follows *naked* more than any other?

The concept of collocation was proposed by the British linguist J. R. Firth and has had a major influence on the corpus analysis of English and other languages. As he put it: '*You shall know a word by the company it keeps.*' (1) His maxim implies that meaning is not contained within or confined to individual words, but instead emerges from their interaction with other words, just as personality emerges from a person's interaction with others. For example, part of the 'meaning' of *auspicious* is that it regularly collocates with *occasion*; furthermore, part of the meaning of *auspicious occasion* is that it often occurs in the phrase *on this auspicious occasion*. As we shall see later in this chapter, most, if not all, of the 'meaning' of *quintessentially* lies in its collocations.

Let's look at what ET's *naked* can tell us about how collocations create and shape meaning. The table below shows the top 25 nouns modified by *naked*, in descending order in the Corpus.

Top 25 nouns modified by *naked*

Rank		How many times?
1	*eye*	1398
2	*body*	1144
3	*woman*	1118
4	*man*	761
5	*girl*	323
6	*prisoner*	203
7	*lady*	183
8	*flesh*	128
9	*breast*	126

Rank		How many times?
10	*ambition*	112
11	*torso*	93
12	*aggression*	92
13	*cuticle*	87
15	*mole-rat*	78
16	*chick*	75
17	*flame*	64
18	*self-interest*	57
19	*greed*	46
20	*singularity*	42
21	*dna*	36
22	*pic*	32
23	*rambler*	19
24	*opportunism*	19
25	*sadhu*	18

What leaps out is that *eye* is the most common noun used immediately after *naked*. (Is that how you answered the question at the beginning of this section? I've tried it on dozens of people, and they never guess correctly.) The contexts make it clear that the complete phrase is *to the naked eye*, often preceded by *visible/ invisible*. This highly idiomatic phrase belongs in a meaning category all its own, and dictionaries generally agree in separating it from other meanings.

The second thing that emerges is that collocates reflecting the meaning 'not wearing any clothes' occupy eight of the top ten positions. Not until number 10 in the league table does *naked ambition* point to a different meaning, which can be defined as 'undesirable and unbridled'. In fact, two-thirds of the 25 collocates divide at first glance into these two meanings:

1 'not wearing any clothes'   *body, woman, man, girl, prisoner, lady, flesh, breast, torso, detainee, chick, pic, rambler, sadhu*

2 'undesirable and unbridled'   *ambition, aggression, self-interest, greed, opportunism*

(The '*naked rambler*' refers to a quintessentially British eccentric who decided to walk, in the nude, from one end of Britain to the other, in order to assert the rights of naturists; and '*sadhus*' are ascetic Indian holy men, who typically wear either no clothes, or a skimpy loincloth.)

Other than *naked eye*, which tops the chart, only five words cannot be assigned at first glance to one or other of the two meanings: *cuticle, flame, mole-rat, singularity, dna.*

On closer inspection, *mole-rat* goes with the first meaning: *naked mole-rats* are an African species of blind and almost totally hairless rodents which live underground. The collocations *cuticle, dna*, and *singularity* all belong to specialist language—biology and astronomy respectively. That leaves one collocate from the top 25, *flame*, unaccounted for. This is a separate meaning, which can be paraphrased as 'without its usual covering', and appears in combinations like *naked bulb* and *naked light*.

The list highlights that the commoner meanings and collocations occur much more frequently than the less common ones. The chart overleaf shows how many examples there are of each of the five different senses we have been talking about.

unbridled 5%

eye 22%

unclothed 69%

specialist 3%   flame 1%

Lists of collocations are invaluable for lexicographers and linguists, because they provide a quick personality profile for a word. Such lists also suggest which meanings are more common and which less so—their frequency. Frequency is important information for dictionary writers, because there are strong arguments for giving the different meanings of words in frequency order—and that is the order that modern dictionaries for learners of English usually follow.

Bare or *naked*?

ET nonplussed his tutor by asking whether it's possible to say '*naked knees*' and '*naked ankles*'. Introspection and intuition suggest those collocations are **possible**, but the key question is whether they are **likely**. In fact, *naked knee(s)* occurs a mere seven times in the Corpus compared to 114 for, say *naked breast(s)*. But does this simply reflect the fact that people write about *knees* less than *breasts*? It seems not, because *knee* and *knees* occur about a third **more** often in the whole Corpus. So, if *naked* collocated randomly we would expect *naked knees* to occur more often than *naked breasts*.

What about ET's hunch that *naked* refers to parts of the body viewed erotically? Does the Corpus give us information with which to evaluate it? One of the things that collocation can do is distinguish between close synonyms, and *bare* is the closest synonym to *naked* for the meanings we're discussing. (It also occurs a similar number of times in the Corpus: 25,210 times compared with *naked*'s 29,875.)

One way of looking at ET's question is to see whether, and how often, *bare* and *naked* modify the same body-part nouns. As regards how often, these body parts appear in *bare*'s top 25, but not in *naked*'s:

- *foot, midriff, chest, skin, shoulder, hand, torso, flesh, leg, arm, buttock, knuckle*

Several of these collocations suggest that the part in question is being viewed anything but erotically: *foot, midriff, hand, leg, arm. Naked*, in contrast, has only one body part in its top 25, and that is *breast* (at number 9). Why should it be the only one? The fact that the breast is the most eroticized part of women's bodies tends to support ET's claim about the eroticization of *naked*. Confirming that, as its top 25 (on p. 89) shows, *naked* has a tendency to collocate with female words such as *girl, lady, chick*.

As regards whether both adjectives can apply to the same words, *naked* can be used to refer to many of the same parts as *bare* (but not *midriff* or *knuckle*), but *bare* is a far more frequent and significant collocate for most of them, as the italicized words in the next table show. (2)

Bare versus *naked*

		How many times?		Significance rating	
		bare	**naked**	**bare**	**naked**
1.	foot	2308	46	56	6.1
2.	*chest*	824	70	49.3	16.2
3.	*skin*	669	70	42.3	13.9
4.	body	92	1144	7.8	37.8
5.	*shoulder*	554	23	37.8	4.5
6.	torso	80	93	33.2	35.4
7.	flesh	128	128	31.5	31.5
8.	breast	211	126	31	24.5
9.	*leg*	335	39	30.5	8
10.	*arm*	513	23	29.5	0.8
11.	buttock	40	22	29.4	22.1
12.	*toe*	97	7	28.6	5.1
13.	*stomach*	95	6	22	1.6
14.	backside	22	16	21.4	18.1
15.	ass	68	49	20.9	17.6

Where a collocation is equally likely with either word, as with *torso, flesh, breast*, there are no obvious clues to what motivates the choice of one over the other. Perhaps speaker attitude has a bearing, but this is often difficult to infer from context.

And what about *naked knees* and *naked ankles*? Knees are a generally undervalued part of our anatomy—when did you last give a compliment about them, or have yours complimented? —so, in line with ET's theory, they are *bare* seven times more often than they are *naked*. And *bare ankles* are 47 times more likely than naked ones. ET may well be on to something with his theory. What is truly staggering is that the brains of English speakers—which have only about a quarter of the capacity of ET's—are capable of containing all this information about which collocations are appropriate to which kind of contexts.

The quintessential New Yorker

Collocational profiles often provide a sharper picture of words whose meaning can seem hard to pin down. For instance, what exactly is the nub of the adjective *quintessential* and its adverb *quintessentially*? Does it even have a 'meaning' on its own? After all, you can't use it like other descriptive adjectives; you can't say: 'She is very quintessential.' Despite that, one dictionary defines *quintessential* as 'representing the most perfect or typical example of a quality or class'. So, would ET sound natural if he said: 'I think Cate Blanchett is the quintessential woman'? Unfortunately for him, no, because that is not how the word tends to collocate. It would probably never occur to us by introspecting, but *quintessential* is, the Corpus suggests, a bit of a closet chauvinist. It often co-occurs with nouns and adjectives in four major categories, of which the first three refer to people:

- **social, class, or national group**: *English, Englishman, Canadian, New Yorker, outsider, insider, foreigner, bourgeois, gentleman*
- **intellectual, artistic movement**: *romantic, post-modern, entrepreneur, poet*
- **outstanding example**: *hero, icon, symbol, expression*
- **work of art**: *soundtrack, movie, novel*

When it applies to people, it's curious that women are very under-represented. For example, *quintessential American* occurs 25 times, always referring to men; no *quintessential New Yorkers* are women—though one wonders what Dorothy Parker would have to say about that—; and so forth.

Quintessentially has an even stronger preference than *quintessential* for nationality words. (3) In descending order of significance, in the Corpus people and things are quintessentially *American, English, British, French, Canadian, Australian, Scottish, Irish, Indian, Parisian, Gallic,* and *European*. These, together with the remaining nationality and geographical adjectives, make up over half its collocations. *Quintessential* and *quintessentially* illustrate how some words gravitate towards whole sets of other words which share some common meaning feature.

Which adjective best completes this sentence? *The meal was ridiculously . . .*

Another adverb which clearly shows this semantic association with a group of related words is *ridiculously*. The most common adjective to complete the sentence in the box above is *expensive*. But there is a whole set of adjectives to do with the cost of something, or the level of something: *low, high, expensive, cheap, large, small, overpriced, priced*. Again, they make up a set of related words. To produce truly natural-sounding English, ET will need to absorb these semantic associations, just as we do through our exposure to English in use.

I'm unconventional; you're quirky; he's eccentric

As we have seen from *naked*, different meanings of a single word are signalled by different collocates—*eye* versus *breasts* versus *ambition* versus *flame*. Collocates also highlight differences between words which are near synonyms such as *naked* and *bare*. Many pairs of words have differences in meaning which it's rather hard to define. They include *infamous/notorious, celebrated/famous, quirky/eccentric, insolent/impudent,* and even *big* and *large*. To prove the point, why not jot down your ideas about:

How would you define the difference between *quirky* and *eccentric*?

Looking at collocates helps to tell these word twins apart. Their significant collocates suggest they differ in ways which cannot be explained by definition alone. Below are their collocational profiles, highlighting which adverbs they are modified by; which nouns they modify; and which other adjectives they appear with. The second column shows how many times the collocation appears, and the third gives a figure for its statistical significance.

Collocational profile for *eccentric*

is preceded by:			precedes:			appears with:		
somewhat	79	42.97	**millionaire**	47	32.88	*quirky*	28	36.64
slightly	95	42.26	**billionaire**	26	28.15	*reclusive*	11	29.12
rather	91	40.27	**genius**	48	27.22	*old*	84	27.23
mildly	30	39.65	**character**	152	26.53	*wellwrought*	5	26.76
wildly	31	38.83	**inventor**	22	25.87	*bizarre*	19	26.17
charmingly	12	33.35	**uncle**	40	24.19	*eclectic*	12	26.17
wonderfully	20	33.02	**loner**	14	23.82	**brilliant**	24	25.85
endearingly	9	31.8	*behaviour*	61	23.02	*irascible*	6	24.3
more	165	31.44	*singer*	46	22.74	**English**	29	24.15
decidedly	16	31.02	**aristocrat**	12	20.38	*unpredictable*	11	22.49
delightfully	11	30.13	*personality*	42	20.36	**flamboyant**	8	22.44
highly	43	29.94	**recluse**	8	20.21	*lovable*	7	22.26
wilfully	9	29.04	**aunt**	20	17.95	**British**	32	22.05
sometimes	29	26.81	**visionary**	8	17.54	*harmless*	9	21.12
increasingly	25	25.54	**spinster**	6	16.84	**charming**	9	20.75
			bachelor	11	15.85	*rich*	21	20.66
			professor	24	15.09	**colourful**	10	20.64
			Englishman	8	14.85	*elderly*	13	20.38
			lady	30	14.82	*strange*	19	20

What does this profile suggest? *Eccentric* is often preceded by words like:

- *charmingly, wonderfully, endearingly, delightfully*

and appears with adjectives such as:

- *lovable, charming, colourful.*

These show that people often react favourably to eccentrics —although *wildly* suggests they might get a bit out of hand.

Words such as *millionaire, billionaire, rich,* and *old* suggest we are likely to use it of wealthy elderly people. Collocates such as *genius, inventor, visionary,* and *professor* suggest that we associate it with cleverness. *Loner* and *recluse, spinster* and *bachelor* suggest, however, that there is a personal price to be paid for eccentricity. (That prototypical eccentric the late Howard Hughes seems to confirm all three insights.) Finally, the British, and in particular the English, seem to be more prone to eccentricity than other nationalities.

Collocational profile for *quirky*

is preceded by:			precedes:			appears with:		
little	50	39.43	**comedy**	93	31.17	*offbeat*	35	46.32
delightfully	12	33.17	**humour**	48	27.78	**funny**	66	36.22
slightly	41	32.62	*perspective*	80	26.59	*eccentric*	28	36.13
charmingly	9	30.56	**charm**	36	24.32	*absorbing*	12	29.36
engagingly	7	30.41	**character**	115	23.4	*idiosyncratic*	13	27.54
as	51	29.71	**humor**	32	23.31	*weird*	25	26.7
wonderfully	13	28.78	**lyric**	35	23.01	*romantic*	24	26.64
somewhat	23	27.67	*sense*	101	22.0	*interesting*	46	26.57
something	21	27.32	*tale*	39	20.91	**fun**	22	26.08

is preceded by:			precedes:			appears with:		
endearingly	5	24.45	*melody*	25	20.82	*comic*	20	25.85
sometimes	20	24.44	pop	25	19.53	*humorous*	13	25.15
rather	23	24.16	twist	22	18.89	unpredictable	14	24.93
more	69	23.68	sensibility	17	18.85	indie	13	24.53
willfully	5	22.18	*mannerism*	9	18.51	*clever*	18	24.44
very	44	21.22	style	60	18.29	*pop*	19	23.89
			grin	23	17.67	catchy	10	22.8
			smile	46	17.67	*colorful*	12	22.77
			instrumentation	7	14.14	bizarre	15	22.74
			individuality	7	13.95	*whimsical*	8	22.63
						cute	16	21.92

What about *quirky?* First, though it can be directly applied to people, as shown by *quirky character*, it is typically used of people's behaviour and characteristics, as shown by *humour, smile, mannerism*. It is strongly associated with being humorous or youthful: *funny, fun, humorous, whimsical, cute*. It is also associated with music and creativity in general: songs, lyrics, films, and novels may be *quirky*, but are rarely *eccentric*.

No doubt ET will be able to absorb all this information in a flash. But he'll need to be really on his toes to work out and apply the differences between larger sets of related words, such as *slender/slim/skinny/thin/ scrawny*. (Because we use English, it's easy to assume that these words distinguish aspects of reality which are somehow inherently separate in the real world. Many languages, however, do not have this many alternative words to describe body size and shape.) It's easy to distinguish *scrawny* from the others, because it has an obvious negative connotation. But—apart from their relative frequencies—what exactly is the difference between *slender* and *slim* or between *slim* and *thin*? Only a corpus can provide enough accurate data to work out these often subtle distinctions.

No man is an island

Information about collocation and semantic association is important for different groups of people using or analysing English, not just for lexicographers in their supposed ivory towers. Learners of English want what they say and write to sound natural, and knowing how words collocate is a crucial part of that. To help them, writers of EFL ('English as a Foreign Language') dictionaries provide this information, which can only be extracted reliably from corpora. Here is an entry from a well-known EFL dictionary showing how three really frequent adjectives collocate differently. Something for ET to really get his teeth into.

How synonyms collozate

big – large – great		
These adjectives are frequently used with the following nouns:		
big ~	**large ~**	**great ~**
man	numbers	success
house	part	majority
car	area	interest
boy	room	importance
dog	company	difficulty
smile	eyes	problem
surprise	volume	beauty
question	population	artist

A second group of people with a vital interest in collocation are translators. They are interested because the translation of a word into another language generally changes according to which words it's associated with in the original language. For instance, *rich* may have one translation when associated with *family*, but quite another when associated with *sauce*. If you ask any translator worth their salt how to translate a word, their first question will be: 'What's the context?'

The quotation from John Donne heading this section suggests that what applies to people applies to words. Adapting it a little:

No word (man) is an Island, entire of itself; every word (man) is a piece of the Continent, a part of the main. (4)

The tendency for words to be bound to other members of their verbal family is a pervasive feature of English. This chapter has dealt with only a few examples out of the literally thousands that could have been chosen. So pervasive are these tendencies that it has even been suggested that most of the language we produce is governed by an '*idiom principle*' (5). In other words, much of the language we use consists of ready-made chunks; we only need to create fresh language when the chunks fail to convey our messages. In the next chapter we shall be looking at some of those ready-made chunks in more detail.

6 Cats and dogs
Idiomatic phrases

In the last chapter we left ET struggling to master the finer points of combining words in collocations. However, after a few days' total immersion he was making excellent progress. But then he hit a major obstacle. Let's listen in again briefly.

Geoff: Well, ET, I think that just about **wraps up** our session for today. So, we'll start again at 9.00 tomorrow morning. Oh, and don't forget to activate your rainshield facility. It's raining cats and dogs outside.

ET: I don't understand, Geoff. I thought you 'wrapped up' presents, and how can animals 'rain'?!

Even though it sounds slightly old-fashioned to mother-tongue speakers, for ET and other learners *It's raining cats and dogs* is a startling phrase. A godsend for illustrators, who can have fun with images of cats and dogs hurtling comically from the heavens, for learners it plays to the stereotype of the weather-obsessed British. And people are intrigued about its origins, for which all sorts of ingenious theories have been put forward—for example that it has to do with the Norse Thunder God, Thor.

Which other ways of describing very heavy rain—e.g.
***It's pelting*—can you think of? Which do you use most often?**

Often quaint or poetic, and frequently very visual, hundreds and hundreds of imagistic phrases like *to rain cats and dogs* create a link between the outer world of experience and the inner worlds of thought and language. A bottomless well [*sic*] of potential cliché for the journalist, these images are a source of endless fascination and speculation for learners and speakers of English alike. The experiences they draw on and the analogies they suggest come from dozens of fields. Some typical ones are:

- **the animal kingdom:** *fat cats, the dog's bollocks, cat and mouse, no spring chicken*
- **sport:** *to move the goalposts, ballpark figure, to touch base, the ball's in your court*
- **war, combat:** *to put your head above the parapet, to shoot somebody down in flames, a battle of wits*
- **human bodies and faculties:** *to put your foot in it, behind someone's back, to fall on deaf ears, to turn a blind eye*

A corpus-based dictionary of idiomatic phrases groups them under 32 different themes, which suggests how pervasive they are. (1) Themes include:

- **decision-making:** *to bite the bullet, the jury is still out*
- **love:** *to bill and coo, there are plenty of other fish in the sea, to be smitten*
- **mental faculties:** *the lights are on but nobody's at home, mad as a box of frogs, a kangaroo loose in his top paddock*

In the last chapter we suggested that much of the language we use consists of pre-ordained collocations. In this chapter, we look at other chunks of language which are similarly ready-made, but which are also non-literal, or special in some way, such as:

- **idioms:** *it fell off the back of a lorry;*
- **conversational formulae:** *if you catch my drift; don't mind if I do;*
- **quotations and allusions:** *green and pleasant land;* and
- **similes:** *as daft as a brush.*

What links them all is that their meanings cannot be derived from the individual words making them up. I shall refer to them in general as '*idiomatic phrases*'.

Cats and dogs is a high profile idiomatic phrase because of its striking image and much-discussed origins. Not all idiomatic phrases are so visible, but such phrases are certainly plentiful, and run into the thousands. In an earlier chapter we saw that the most common words have the most meanings; they also have the most idiomatic phrases associated with them. One dictionary lists thirteen of them just for *easy*. The selection below shows the different kinds of phrase that will be discussed in this chapter, apart from idioms proper.

- **easy on the eye/ear** (*informal*) pleasant to look at/listen to.
  METAPHOR
- **I'm easy** (*informal*) said by someone when offered a choice to indicate that they have no particular preference.
  SPOKEN FORMULA
- **to be easier said than done** to be more easily talked about than put into practice: *going on an economy drive is easier said than done.*   **CATCHPHRASE**
- **as easy as pie** very easy: *using the camera was as easy as pie.*
  SIMILE

Language often conveys attitudes and evaluations of situations and events, rather than pure information, and that's exactly what all these phrases do.

A universal tendency? Metaphor

It is easy to think of metaphor as a literary affectation, the preserve of poets, writers, and the literati. In fact, it pervades all the language we use, and is a vital tool for conceptualizing ideas and experiences. Researchers have argued persuasively that we all have a natural tendency to understand and express abstract ideas and processes in <u>concrete</u> terms. It is clear that <u>behind</u> many words and phrases we use lie <u>images</u>, but they are so deeply <u>embedded</u> in our consciousness and our language that we no longer perceive them as such.

The last paragraph contains four underlined images. *Concrete* refers to physical substances, and is applied to language precisely because we conceive of ideas and words as physical substance ('*I **take back** what I said*'). *Behind* firstly refers to space, so '*behind . . . words and phrases*' above suggests that language is located somewhere in physical space. We see *images* and we often use analogies based on the sense of sight to describe understanding ('*do you **see** what I mean?*'). Finally, *to embed* means 'to fix something firmly in its surroundings', reinforcing the conceptualization of language as substance.

These images are metaphors. So, what is the definition of metaphor?

A word or phrase used to describe somebody or something in a way that is different from its normal use, in order to show that the two things have the same qualities and to make the description more powerful . . . (2, 3)

There is a lot of debate among scholars about how exactly metaphor works, but that definition highlights some widely accepted key points.

Metaphor projects onto thing, animal or person *A* qualities associated with thing, animal or person *B*, in order to highlight certain features of *A*. The resulting metaphorical statement can be seen as literally untrue, or impossible. For example, to describe an experienced politician as '*a wily old fox*' cannot be literally true, but the image makes the characterization more powerful and evocative than just saying he is 'wily'.

Some authors suggest that our pre-verbal experience moulds the way we think and the verbal images we use. For example, our experience as babies is initially of our own bodies, which is why so many idioms refer to body parts. (4) We perceive the external world through our senses, and that is why images based on our sense organs and perception are common: e.g. *There's more to this than meets the eye.* Before we can even stand up, our activity consists of purposeful movement (picture an unstoppable pre-toddler zooming across the carpet to see just how purposeful it can be). That explains why activity is often seen as movement: *We're making progress; We're getting there.*

There are scores of such parallels. Their relevance to everyday life is suggested in the very title of one of the key works on the subject: *Metaphors we live by.* (5) This book suggests that there are deep-rooted conceptual metaphors which govern the way we think and act. The most famous is: ARGUMENT IS WAR, or STRUGGLE. This is manifested both in the way we conduct arguments, and in the language we use: *a war of words, hatchet job, handbags at dawn, 'You win!', to go in/come out all guns blazing.* Another famous conceptual metaphor is LINGUISTIC ITEMS ARE CONTAINERS. That would explain why Geoff spoke about 'wrapping up' the lesson at the beginning of this chapter.

Scholars have detailed the complex networks of images used by English to express these parallels. (6) One major tendency is for abstract entities to be viewed as concrete:

- **society** = a **building**: *to undermine the very foundation of our democracy*
- an **organization** = a **ship**: *The company runs a tight ship.*
- **organizations** = **living things** ('personification'): *Companies live and die by cash.*

Personifying organizations and groups, and even events, comes naturally to us. Most of the time we are not aware of how bizarre it might seem to draw a parallel between an abstraction and something which is living—or how someone from another planet, like ET, might not think the same way as us. The next examples from the Corpus show how powerful and pervasive the parallels are.

> **alive and kicking:** *the old school tie <u>network</u> is alive and kicking*
> **shot in the arm:** a *much needed shot in the arm for <u>rugby</u> north of the border*
> **kiss of death:** *this is the kiss of death for large <u>corporations</u>*
> **to be on its last legs:** *a decadent <u>aristocracy</u> on its last legs*
> **bring something to its knees:** *losses that have brought the <u>company</u> to its knees*
> **to be a death blow:** *it would be a death blow to Newtonian <u>physics</u>*
> **death knell:** *the death knell came in the 70th minute*
> **a dead duck:** *for me <u>marriage</u> is a dead duck, a relic of a bygone age*
> **dead in the water:** *that <u>theory</u> is dead in the water*
> **to bite the dust:** *traditional <u>theatre</u> has largely bitten the dust*

All these exemplify a special kind of metaphorical language: idioms. Idioms are multi-word phrases whose overall meaning cannot be deduced from the meanings of the individual words. To take the last example, '*traditional theatre has largely bitten the dust*': how can theatre, an abstraction, 'do' anything? And even if it could, what is this dust, and why is it biting it?

Idioms are conventional metaphors which have become part of the language everyone uses. You or I could invent a colourful phrase tomorrow, but if other people don't follow suit, it isn't part of the language: it isn't 'institutionalized'. An acquaintance's wife says, *'It's enough to make you bust your gusset!'*, but the rest of the world hasn't adopted it yet. A second crucial feature of idioms is that they are phrases of some kind. Although language is full, as we have seen, of single words embodying a metaphor—*concrete, behind, image*—an idiom is usually understood to consist of several words.

Hark! hark! The lark . . .

The animal kingdom has been mentioned as a fertile source of metaphorical and idiomatic phrases. To illustrate just how rich a source it is, here is a selection from the Corpus involving bird imagery. The ones marked with asterisks have abstractions as their topics, rather than people.

> **People are like birds**
> - people **look** like birds
>   *as bald as a coot; no spring chicken; ugly duckling*
> - people **behave** like birds
>   <u>eating</u>: *gannet; to eat like a bird*
>   <u>observing</u>: *to watch like a hawk*
>   <u>reacting</u>: *to bury one's head in the sand; to run round like headless chickens; like water off a duck's back; a game old bird; like a duck to water; to smooth ruffled feathers; the vultures are circling*
>   <u>time-keeping</u>: *an early bird; up with the lark; up at sparrow fart*
>   <u>singing</u>: *sing like a nightingale; sing like a lark*
>   <u>wellbeing</u>: *as happy as a lark; sick as a parrot*
>   <u>movement</u>: *the bird has flown; as the crow flies; a bird of passage*

- homes are **nests**
  *to fly the nest; to fly the coop; *to come home to roost; like an
  old mother hen; like a homing pigeon; empty-nest syndrome;
  to build a nest*
- people/animals can be **free**, or **confined**
  free as a bird; cooped up; like battery hens
- events and actions are **evaluated** in bird terms
  *an albatross round someone's neck; *to be strictly for the
  birds; *to be a lame duck; *a wild-goose chase; *neither fish
  nor fowl; to give sb the bird [= a) to boo sb; b) to make a rude
  gesture]; *to lay an egg [= not be successful]; *to be a turkey*
- common/uncommon
  a rare bird; rara avis; as rare as hen's teeth
- proverbs
  *one swallow doesn't make a summer; what's sauce for
  the goose is sauce for the gander; birds of a feather flock
  together; don't count your chickens before they're hatched;
  the early bird catches the worm*

I can hear the rain . . .

The Eskimos are commonly supposed to have dozens of
words for snow (they haven't, but it's one of the most enduring
language myths around). But even supposing it were true,
English speakers could play them at their own game when it
comes to rain. The standard expressions listed below describe
torrential rain, and every single one is idiomatic. As has been
seen in earlier chapters, the Corpus can show the relative
frequency of items, and these rain phrases are listed in
ascending order. (The numbers refer to how I've classified them.)

It's raining pitchforks (3)
It's lashing down (2)
It's bucketing down (1)
It's raining stair rods (3)

It's raining cats and dogs (4)
It's pelting down (2)
It's pissing down (peeing down, piddling down) (1)
It's pouring (1)

The images are of four kinds: water metaphors (1); metaphors of hitting or striking (2); analogies based on shape (3); animals (4).

People have come up with several explanations for the cats and dogs image, which comes only fourth in the ranking above. One suggestion is that it's a corruption of the obsolete French word *catad(o)upe*, meaning 'waterfall' (7); another, popularized by the internet, peddles the idea that cats and dogs sheltering in the thatch of houses were washed out by heavy storms; another that because of poor drains dead cats and dogs could be seen floating down the streets during rainstorms, making it look as if they'd fallen from the sky. There seems to be no reason to entertain these homespun etymologies for a phrase which can be explained by the power of metaphor alone.

If it can rain *stair rods* and *pitchforks*, why not *cats and dogs*? There are clear analogies at work, and a strong dose of exaggeration. Torrential rain can sometimes seem as if it's falling in long, narrow shapes rather than drops. Stair rods and pitchforks are long, cylindrical objects which are like torrential rain, and clatter like driving rain when hitting the ground. The stair rods and pitchforks metaphors link the realm of natural events with the realm of man-made things, and similar images are used in several other languages. *Cats and dogs* connects the realm of natural events with the realm of living things, specifically animals, and many other languages draw similar parallels, as can be seen opposite. Welsh even goes one step further, by bringing in humans rather than animals, and combining them with man-made objects: 'It's raining old women and sticks.'

How it pours in other languages

	Cylindrical objects	Animals
Spanish	*Caen chuzos* de punta* It's raining sticks tip downwards (literally, 'sticks are falling tip downwards')	
French	*Il pleut des cordes* It's raining ropes *Il pleut des hallebardes* It's raining halberds* *Il pleut des clous* It's raining nails	*Il pleut des crapauds et des chats* It's raining toads and cats *Il pleut des vaches* It's raining cows
Brazilian Portuguese		*Chove pra cachorro* It's raining 'for the dog'
German	*Es regnet Bindfäden* It's raining pieces of string	
Welsh	*Bwrw cyllyll a ffyrc* It's raining knives and forks	
		Bwrw hen wragedd a ffyn It's raining old women and sticks

(*The *chuzos* in the Spanish idiom are not just any old sticks, but long poles with metal tips formerly used by nightwatchmen; halberds were military weapons, a fearsome combination of spear and battle-axe.)

However, it would be wrong to think that these images are universal. For example, the most common Japanese idiom is apparently:

土砂降りの雨です

doshaburi no ame desu

It means literally 'It's raining falling earth and sand' and supposedly originates in the regular landslides that happen in Japan when there is heavy rain.

Other languages may conceptualize an idea similarly to English, but the exact wording differs.

Spanish v English idioms

Spanish	English
la noche está en pañales 'the night is in nappies/diapers'	the night is young
a paso de tortuga 'at a tortoise's pace'	at a snail's pace

However, sometimes the metaphor can be very different indeed:

aburrirse como una ostra 'to be as bored as an oyster'	to be bored stiff
estar más loco que una cabra 'to be madder than a goat'	to be as mad as a hatter

Or the metaphor can reflect an altogether different cultural experience:

llamar al pan pan, y al vino vino 'to call bread bread, and wine wine'	to call a spade a spade
cortarse la coleta 'to cut off one's pigtail'	to hang up one's boots

(At their last bullfight before retiring, bullfighters ceremonially cut off their pigtail.)

How's tricks? – formulae

Often the language we use is highly regulated, allowing for little—or minimal—variation. There are standard written 'formulae' for dozens and dozens of situations, from lonely hearts ads to wedding invitations, and from job applications to letters of condolence. What is perhaps less obvious is that similar rules often apply in speaking.

The situation, with its social and cultural expectations, dictates strictly and precisely the words we can use—unless, of course, we are determined to be rude or eccentric. As Professor David Crystal suggested, nobody meeting the Queen is likely to say: *'How's tricks, your Majesty?'* (8) Similarly, when greeting someone we know well, our first word will be *hi* or *hello*, but that would be highly inappropriate in most job interviews.

In conversation we draw on a huge repertoire of formulae. Take a very common word, *there*. A comparison of three corpus-based dictionaries shows it appears in at least twenty highly idiomatic formulae. The following selection gives some idea of just how expressive, subtle, and versatile they can be.

Formula	Function/meaning
There, there!	comforting, especially a child
Been there, done that!	commenting on an experience, and suggesting
(and bought the t-shirt)	you don't want to repeat it
We've all been there	expressing or asking for support or understanding
You've got me there!	a) = 'I don't know' (and I'm not quite sure what I feel about not knowing)
	b) = 'You win'
There goes . . .	regretfully accepting something bad that's just happened e.g. *There goes my theory/chance/inheritance*
Hello there!	friendly greeting
You there!	hostile greeting
But there again . . .	modifying something said earlier

One of the features of idiomatic phrases is that it is difficult or unusual to change them, and formulae illustrate this. For example, you can't change the tense and say: *Was there, did that!* While you **can** change *There goes my career* to *There went my career*, it doesn't occur very often in that tense in the Corpus. *Goodbye there* instead of *Hello there* would be meaningless—or sarcastic—, and *We've all gone there* entirely changes the meaning.

Jolly hockey sticks! – catchphrases

When spoken formulae are associated with a particular person—real or fictional—they are defined as 'catchphrases'. Many come from films and TV. Perhaps even more than other idomatic phrases, they depend on speaker and listener sharing the same cultural experience: if you haven't seen the film or watched the TV show, you won't get the meaning. For that reason, catchphrases tend to date very quickly, and have a high turnover. Here is a very small selection.

- *bovvered* – for British people this spelling of 'bothered' immediately sums up the cheeky but naïve, couldn't-care-less attitude of the monstrous teenager Lauren, a cult character in the British TV series *The Catherine Tate Show*. '*Some people hate being mentioned in the blog. Am I bovvered? No, not really.*'
- *jolly hockey sticks* – suggests that a woman is rather gushing and sporty, and probably frightfully posh. It was first used by the British comic actress Beryl Reid, who claimed to have invented it, in a 1950s radio show. It can be used as an adjective too: '*Joanna Trollope seems—and sounds—terribly English in a jolly hockey sticks sort of way.*'
- *I'll just get my coat* – is a way of admitting that you've just said something completely daft, or put your foot in it in a

big way. It comes from the comedy series *The Fast Show*,
and is still alive and kicking. Several examples are from
blogs.

- *You are the weakest link. Goodbye!* – Anne Robinson's
  gleefully sadistic phrase is a new favourite.
- *Time to musk up* – meaning 'time to put on the after-shave
  or cologne' is a catchphrase for lads wanting to smell
  good for the girls. It comes from the Will Ferrell film,
  Anchorman.
- *That'll dink dank do for me* – an alliterative way of saying
  'that's great, that's fine', was coined by British comedian
  Peter Kay.

Read on Macduff! – quotations

Which one of these did Shakespeare **not** coin?
cruel to be kind; to the manner born; faint heart never won fair maid.

Similar to catchphrases, but usually much more ancient, are
quotations. As Shakespeare gave us so many words, it is no
surprise he also coined many idioms. Shakespeare scholars
or not, we have undoubtedly all quoted him in our time—but
usually without knowing it. Apart from the obvious ones—
'*to be or not to be*', '*Alas poor Yorick*', and so forth—there
are dozens of less noticeable idioms that English has merrily
plagiarized from the 'Swan of Avon' (another allusion turned
cliché, as so often happens). Here are ten common
Shakespearean idioms, with their sources and how
often they appear in the Corpus.

Ten Shakespearean allusions	
at one fell swoop (*Macbeth*, IV, iii)	747
cold comfort (*King John*, V, vii)	318
wild goose chase (*Romeo & Juliet*, II, iv)	315
tower of strength (*Richard III*, V, iii)	221
sorry sight (*Macbeth*, II, ii)	111
to eat out of house and home (*Henry IV*, II, i)	94
primrose path (*Hamlet*, I, iii)	56
cruel to be kind (*I must be cruel only to be kind*) (*Hamlet*, III, iv)	55
to the manner born (*Hamlet*, III, iv)	45
to beggar all description (*Antony and Cleopatra*, II, ii)	31

These ten idioms, chosen at random, coincidentally illustrate a couple of things that regularly happen to quotations and allusions. People love wordplay, and love to pun on the originals. For instance, a tenth of the examples based on *to the manner born* modify the original wording. Sometimes they just take the structure and change the noun: '*who wears the sarong as though to the costume born.*' Sometimes they pun. A worried mum—mom, actually, as she was American—gets this advice from an agony aunt about her daughter's horsy obsession: '*Your daughter is one of those who's obviously to the manure born.*' Someone criticizing a restaurant writes: '*The lunch menu is laminated, which is difficult to bear if you are to the menu born like me.*'

A damp squid in one fowl swoop

Quotations, like stories, can also change in the telling. In a sort of historical Chinese whispers the original *to the manner born* has become *to the manor born* in nearly half of all examples. This change has happened for two reasons. The words sound identical (technically they're '*homophones*', words which sound the same but mean different things); and people make sense of the phrase by associating it with the hereditary wealth and privilege of the manor.

In fact, people can be very determined in squeezing a meaning which makes sense to them out of language which doesn't, so to speak, volunteer it. Their determination is one of the ways in which they change language, in a process known as '*folk etymology*'. Folk etymology is what happens when people alter a word shape that seems strange, and make it fit their personal understanding of English. A classic example is *bridegroom*. The *-groom* element started life as the Old English *-guma*, a poetic word meaning 'man'. It was reinterpreted as *groom*, in the sixteenth century, when *groom* still meant 'man' in general rather than a stable lad.

People use folk etymology to tease sense from idioms containing rare words—which is where the title of this book comes in. It is very common to hear *damp squid* instead of *damp squib*, to mean a disappointment, and there are many examples on the Web. The reason for the change seems clear and perfectly logical in its own terms. The word *squib* means a firework, so the original idiom was transparent: a damp squib would not light, and would be a great disappointment. As the word *squib* now rarely appears outside the idiom— though still used in some areas, for instance parts of Scotland— it no longer makes sense to some people. Replacing it with the word *squid* does two things: it links it to a word that people know, and it breathes new life into an otherwise dead metaphor. *Squid* intensifies the idea of dampness; and there is, arguably, a strong metaphorical link between dampness and disappointment: *a wet blanket, to rain on someone's parade, not set the Thames on fire, to go belly-up, to pour cold water on something,* and so forth.

Another phrase which is being folk-etymologized is the Shakespearean *at one fell swoop*. The obsolete adjective *fell* (= 'cruel, ruthless') puzzles people, so they reinterpret it. Bird imagery, as we saw earlier, is very common in English, so it is not surprising to find *in one fowl swoop*. (For other variations on *fell*, see the section on 'eggcorns' in Chapter 3.)

Happy as the grass was green—similes

> Now as I was young and easy under the apple boughs
> About the lilting house and happy as the grass was green
> Dylan Thomas, *Fern Hill*

Dylan Thomas famously likened his happiness to the green of grass, and simile in the right hands is a powerful, sit-up-and-take-notice-of-me poetic device. We non-poets, however, usually have no option but to make do with the hand-me-down similes that English passes on to us: *as happy as a clam, as Larry, as a sandboy, as a lark*.

Structurally, English similes are simple. They make use of two recurrent patterns: *as* + adjective + noun group; and verb + *like* + noun group:

- *as happy as a pig in mud*
- *as drunk as a skunk*
- *as cheap as chips*
- *as safe as houses*
- *to eat like a horse*
- *like water off a duck's back*

Research suggests that there are only between 100 and 150 such common similes, and another 100 to 150 peripheral ones. (9) However, a select handful that appear in the Corpus lend themselves to virtuoso variation. As with puns on Shakespearean quotations, people seem to leap at the chance to indulge in linguistic creativity within the confines of a very set structure.

For instance, if people want to pooh-pooh the usefulness of something, they can take the basic frame and elaborate on it to their heart's content. While there appear to be two or three repeating forms, like *as useful as a chocolate teapot*, *as useful as a condom in a nunnery*, and *as useful as an ashtray on a motorbike*, variations on the theme can be extremely inventive, not to say baroque, and often hilariously tasteless. To my mind, they are a tribute to English speakers' everyday, rather than poetic, creativity.

Ironic degrees of usefulness

as useful as:

a bikini in the snows of Antarctica
a bus pass in the Mojave
a fan heater in a desert
a game of musical chairs on the deck of the Titanic
a one-legged man in an arse-kicking competition
getting shaving tips from Brian Blessed
strippers in a nudist colony
a hand brake on skis
a powerboat in the Sahara

7 Grammar that can govern even kings (1)
What do we mean by grammar?

MISS PRISM: (*calling*) Cecily, Cecily! Surely such a utilitarian occupation as the watering of flowers is rather Moulton's duty than yours. Especially at a time when intellectual pleasures await you. Your German **grammar** is on the table.

. . .

CECILY: (*coming over very slowly*) But I don't like German. It isn't at all a becoming language. I know perfectly well that I look quite plain after my German lesson.

Oscar Wilde, *The Importance of Being Earnest, 1895*.

Is English grammar easy?

Grammar and *glamour* are related, but for most people studying grammar seems about as glamorous as it is for Cecily. (2) No doubt she finds German unbecoming because it has a lot of 'grammar'. And grammar in this sense means how individual words change according to their role in a sentence. To see what Cecily had to grapple with, let's look at the German *mein* ('my'):

He's my brother – Er ist **mein** Bruder
I love my brother – Ich liebe **meinen** Bruder
My brother's book – Das Buch **meines** Bruders
I played with my brother – Ich spielte mit **meinem** Bruder

Mein changes its endings according to whether it refers to the subject or the object, whether it's possessive, and according to the preposition used.

In contrast, English words have few different forms, so English grammar is often thought of as easy, almost non-existent. It is true that its fewer than a dozen different standard endings seem somewhat puny beside the 70 or more basic forms of Spanish verbs, and the staggering 20,000 or so theoretically possible verb forms of Finnish. (3) But the study of how words change shape is only half the story of grammar. (Its technical name is '*morphology*' with the *morph* part coming from the Greek for 'shape', so it is literally 'the study of shapes'.) (4) English morphology is very simple compared with that of German, but grammar consists of much more than morphology.

Morphology's sister is '*syntax*' (5). This deals with how you put words together to make sentences—which, hopefully, other people can understand. And English syntax, unlike English morphology, is far from simple. One of the classic grammars of English lists no fewer than 3,500 items in its index, as David Crystal has pointed out. (6) Learners of English whose mother tongue has a more complicated morphology than English—and just about all the European languages do—often claim to find English grammar—that is its word shapes—easy, but admit to struggling with its syntax.

If all this seems a bit abstract, you might be surprised how much syntax you know—without realizing that you know it. Try rearranging the jumbled sentence below.

jumped moon the over cow the

You will have used several rules of English syntax to unjumble it. Among them:

- The rule that *the* (the '*definite article*') comes before the noun (*cow* and *moon*) it refers to.

It may appear self-evident that you put the article before the noun, but that's because you probably learned English word order as a child. Had you learnt Romanian or Danish as a toddler, you would find it just as natural to tag the article on to the end of the noun. If you were Russian you would feel utterly at home using no article at all.

- Second, putting *over* (the '*preposition*') before *the moon*.

As its name suggests, a **pre**position comes before the thing it refers to. But many languages, such as Chinese, have '*postpositions*', and put the word with this function **after** the noun.

- You also know that the normal English order is to put *over the moon* (the '*prepositional phrase*') after the verb, and *cow* before *jumped*. Only in poetry and flowery prose could you change that order: *over the moon jumped the cow*.

All those rather abstract rules—which you didn't know you knew —are syntax rules. They suggest that English grammar, in this wider sense, is not quite as simple as it is often perceived to be.

Grammar Nazis

But if grammar is such an abstract notion, how can it be the emotive topic that the Corpus suggests it often is? Let's look at some examples from the Corpus which show how strongly people feel about it.

*This week, for example, we've had two obnoxious teenagers banned from the centre of Weston-super-Mare for terrorizing the town. Their evident delight in their achievement suggests people who have never been taught to judge themselves, merely to appreciate themselves whatever they do. Related to this idea of undiminished self-esteem at all times is the fashionable rejection of the importance of the boring basics of a subject such as English **grammar**.*
(British English)

The link suggested between delinquency and grammatical ignorance is hardly a one-off. It's a recurrent theme when educational and social standards are discussed, and is a topic on which the great and the good, including Prince Charles, can have very firm views: *'We've got to produce people who can write proper English. It's a fundamental problem.'* (7)

Bad grammar not only rots your soul. In journalistic rhetoric, it may rot your teeth too:

*Benjamin's ragtag warriors show off their earthiness and love of liberty by baring their bad teeth and their bad **grammar** while the British, led by General Cornwallis, are sleek snoots who can't wait to get back to their gold chandeliers and Chippendale.*
(American English)

On the other side of the ideological battle-lines, grammar itself is viewed as excess baggage, and getting rid of it as liberating:

*And Bama . . . has found a voice, . . . which . . . flouts the standard dictates of **grammar** and spelling, and unabashedly uses the Dalit dialect even for narration.*
(Indian English)

Sometimes grammar is a conspiracy:

*Prescriptive **grammar** has very little to do with maintaining the clarity and precision of the language. What it really has to do with is maintaining the dominance of the upper classes and enforcing social norms.*
*. . . Prescriptive **grammar** is a tool of the kleptocracy.*
(American English)

Those who understand or care about its finer points are slated as fascists:

> *. . . I have felt completely burned out (burnt out? help me,*
> ***grammar*** *nazis) . . .*
> (Australian English)

And it can even be rapped—albeit rather intellectually:

> Step into that cypher if you're fittin' to battle.
> You're like a baby, and post-modernism's your rattle.
> You don't have any candy,
> I'd be better off robbing that pansy
> Ben Johnson [*sic*] for style.
> You're just a little child,
> Oral spittle and cute smile .
> In this big-boy world your English is in denial.
> The sun is coming up on English **grammar**
> and your ivory tower is in the dark—Stammer, bitch
> (American English)

Surely these emotionally loaded quotes can't be talking about the same dry subject that made poor, bored Cecily look so plain?

It all depends what you mean by . . . (8)

And they aren't. The following entry adapted from the corpus-based *Oxford Dictionary of English* assigns *grammar* no fewer than seven meanings.

How does a dictionary define *grammar*?

grammar ▶ noun

1. [mass noun] the whole system and structure of a language or of languages in general, usually taken as consisting of syntax and morphology (including inflections) and sometimes also phonology and semantics. • 2. [usu. with modifier] a particular analysis of the system and structure of language or of a specific language: *Chomskyan grammar.* • 3. [count noun] a book on grammar: *my old Latin grammar.* • 4. **a set of actual or presumed prescriptive**

notions about correct use of a language: *it was not bad grammar, just dialect*. 5. • the basic elements of an area of knowledge or skill: *the grammar of wine*. 6. • (Computing) a set of rules governing what strings are valid or allowable in a language or text. 7. • (Brit. informal) a grammar school.

– ORIGIN late Middle English: from Old French *gramaire*, via Latin from Greek *grammatiké (tekhné)* '(art) of letters', from *gramma, grammat-* 'letter of the alphabet, thing written'.

The Oxford Dictionary of English (revised edition). Ed. Catherine Soanes and Angus Stevenson. Oxford University Press, 2005.

The German grammar Cecily struggled with is *grammar* in meaning 1. But the meaning over which people cross swords is number 4: '*a set of actual or presumed prescriptive notions about correct use of a language.*' Some key words in that definition raise questions that lie at the heart of debates on grammar in education and politics. Is there one 'correct' use of language? Many non-linguists say there is; linguists tend to say there isn't. Are there rules—'prescriptive notions'—to follow, such as: '*If I were* is always correct, *if I was* is always wrong'? And, if such rules exist, what is their status, and where do they come from?

These underlying controversies exposed by the definition help explain why 'grammar' is the explosive topic the Corpus quotations suggest it is. But they are only a selection, and may well be skewing the picture. Only looking at major amounts of data can give a more accurate and balanced view of how people really use the word.

Grammar anxiety?

So, is grammar anxiety a neurosis of pedants, conservatives, and literati? Or is grammar a concern for the world at large?

The word certainly appears in the Corpus remarkably often. With nearly 10,000 examples, it ranks among the 7,000 most common English lemmas—the 7,000 which make up 90 per cent of everything we write. In the ranking it sits just below *aspire*, and above *deception*.

***Grammar* in the frequency league table**

Rank	Word
6771	cosmetic
6773	skepticism, scepticism
6774	coral
6775	emit
6776	Medicare, medicare
6777	aspire
6778	perpetrator
6779	**grammar**
6780	puff
6781	trek
6782	uranium
6783	deception
6784	blessed
6785	reconcile
6786	redundancy
6787	flap

Do people in some countries worry more about grammar than in others? The Corpus suggests so. The quotations used come from all round the world, but the British, the Australians, and New Zealanders seem more obsessed by the word than other English speakers, since it occurs with higher than expected frequency in their examples. What do people mean by *grammar* when they write about it? Detailed analysis of a representative sample confirms very strongly that people are mainly concerned with correct usage. The 'correct grammar' meaning is the one intended in over half of all examples.

What do people mean by *grammar*?

Rank	Meaning	Percentage of examples	Definition
1	'Correct grammar'	52.2%	4
2	'Language system'	27.4%	1
3	'Book'	8%	3
4	'Particular analysis'	6.1%	2
5	Computing meaning	2.9%	6
6	'Elements of knowledge'	0.8%	5
	Ambiguous/other meanings	2.6%	

And how exactly do people express their anxieties about 'correct' grammar? The adjectives they use give a good indication of their strength of feeling. In the structure *grammar is* + ADJECTIVE, two-thirds of examples criticize their own or other people's grammar. Grammar is:

- *improper, atrocious, wrong, bad, terrible, poor, horrendous, sloppy, crappy*

Similarly, when *grammar* comes before another noun, the context is often negative: *grammar mistakes, grammar errors,* and *grammar corrections* are the commonest collocations, while those who try to apply it are described as *grammar Nazis* or *grammar freaks*. And when most people discuss grammar, they write about very limited aspects of it: the aspect of 'getting it right'. (The next chapter has examples of *grammar* used to mean precisely that: 'correct usage'.) Among the very few positive notes are: '*You are a grammar god!*', and a lone voice proclaiming: '*I am a grammarian. Grammar is fun. Grammar is exciting.*'

Pease pudding hot: words changing shape

> Pease pudding hot, pease pudding cold,
> Pease pudding in the pot, nine days old
> Some like it hot, some like it cold
> Some like it in the pot, nine days old.

The traditional rhyme 'Pease Pudding Hot' illustrates in miniature a key fact about grammar: like every other aspect of language, it does not stand still. *Pease* is our modern *pea* in medieval apparel, and is an example of a word that has changed shape (its 'morphology') over time. The grammar we use today has developed from earlier versions of grammar, and will inevitably change into something different. To see how it has evolved in the past, and how it may be changing in front of our eyes, let's look at two grammatical changes—or, strictly speaking, 'morphological' changes—through historical and modern examples.

First, nouns can switch from singular to plural, and vice versa. For instance, *pease* was once singular, with a plural *peasen*. In Chapter 2 there were several examples of words being 'back-formed', such as *edit* from *editor*. Our modern *pea* is a 'back-formation' from *pease*. What happened is that people interpreted the final 'eez' sound of the singular as a plural, and so created the singular form *pea*. Are similar processes at work today? Let's see what the Corpus can tell us.

A useful criteria

> Which of these would you say?
> *This is the only criteria we should use.*
> *This is the only criterion we should use.*

Several nouns which English inherited from Latin and Greek and which end in *-um* and *-on*, such as *stratum*, *criterion*, and *phenomenon*, appear to be undergoing the opposite process to *pease*. People are treating their plurals in *-a* as singulars. It is quite common to hear '*a criteria*' as in: '*This is the only criteria we should use.*' What light does the Corpus shed on this? How often does *criteria* show up in writing as a singular? And what other forms of the word occur?

Criterion and *criteria* occur over 60,000 times, which makes this 'lemma' one of the 3,000 most common in the corpus. *Criteria* is more than four times as frequent as *criterion.* (9) A random sample suggests that, though the singular use of *criteria* is not a rare bird, it still belongs to a relatively small flock, as shown by the figures below.

singular 7%

plural 70%

not clear from context 23%

And how does it behave in context? In seven out of every 100 examples the immediate context shows unambiguously that it is singular, as signalled by words like *a, this, only*, and *is*: '*There is another criteria for evaluating a great editor.*' In just over 70 per cent of cases context in the same sentence shows that the word is plural, for instance '*different criteria*' and '*criteria such as race, class, and gender*'. However, that leaves nearly a quarter of cases (23 out of every 100) where the context does not make it clear whether *criteria* is to be understood as singular or plural: '*But by what criteria?*' Is that singular or plural? Which raises the question: do these ambiguous uses reinforce the trend to use *criteria* as singular?

It is notable that in a random sample of **spoken** material *criteria* is a singular nearly three times as often as in all material. This suggests that in spoken language *criteria* is taking wing as a fully-fledged singular. As time goes by it seems likely that more and more people will forget that *criteria* started life as a plural. If we were to carry out a similar analysis ten years hence, I have a hunch we would find that *criterion* has been ousted still further in writing by what some people regard as a cuckoo in the nest.

Phenomena as a singular appears to be even more frequent, making up nearly 10 per cent of occurrences of the form. The trend towards singular for plural is less evident in the case of other words examined: *stratum*, *consortium*, and *stadium*. For instance, a random sample of *stadia* suggests that it is used as a singular in fewer than 2 per cent of cases.

Dove as if he were a beaver

It is not only nouns that morph into different shapes; English verbs too have gone through many incarnations. For instance, the past tense and past participle of *to dig* are nowadays always *dug* in 'standard' English, but up to the eighteenth century *digged* was an acceptable variant. The *King James Bible* tells us: '*And all the Egyptians digged round about the river for water to drink*' (Exodus, 7:24), when the Nile was turned to blood. Conversely, if we came across the verb form *oke*, we might scratch our heads in puzzlement until we saw it in context, as in Langland's '*though all my fingers oken* (=ached)' from the fourteenth-century English allegorical poem *Piers Plowman*. (10)

These variations are due to the existence of two different families of verbs. Verbs like *to intend*, and *to save*, which form the past tense by adding -*ed* or -*d*, are called '*weak*' verbs; '*strong*' verbs, such as *sing* and *come*, change more radically.

These are ancient verb patterns, inherited from Old English and shared with modern German and Scandinavian languages. English strong verbs, however, have been on the wane for centuries, and new verbs entering the language have tended to be weak. Some verbs have migrated from one type to another.

The examples with *dig* and *ache* show changes over time. But there are also variations within and between English-speaking countries, some of them very well known. The alternation between *dived* and *dove* is a highly visible example. In *The Song of Hiawatha*, published in 1855, Longfellow tells us that Hiawatha:

> . . . called aloud to Kwasind,
> To his friend, the strong man, Kwasind,
> Saying, 'Help me clear this river
> Of its sunken logs and sand-bars.'
> Straight into the river Kwasind
> Plunged as if he were an otter,
> **Dove** as if he were a beaver,
> Stood up to his waist in water,
> To his arm-pits in the river,
> Swam and shouted in the river, . . .
> *Hiawatha vii*

A quote from two years later suggests, perhaps ruefully, that in Canada *dove* as the past tense was already the norm by then.

In England when a swimmer makes his first leap, head foremost, into the water he is said to dive, *and is spoken of as having* dived *. . . Not so however, is it with the modern refinements of our Canadian English. In referring to such a feat here, it would be said, not that he* dived, *but that he* dove. (11)

To older British ears *dove* can still sound markedly transatlantic, and *The Oxford A–Z of Usage* recommends: '*In Britain it should still be avoided in careful writing.*' (12) However, the *Merriam–*

Webster Online Dictionary gives *dived* as the first option, with *dove* as an alternative. It also has a usage note on the topic which confidently states:

Dove . . . *has become the standard past tense especially in speech in some parts of Canada. In the United States* dived *and* dove *are both widespread in speech . . . In writing, the past tense* dived *is usual in British English and somewhat more common in American English.* Dove *seems relatively rare as a past participle in writing.*

How far does the Corpus bear out this statement? The chart below shows the relative percentages for the two uses in four English-speaking countries.

UK   dived 92%
      dove 8%

AUS   dived 68%
      dove 32%

US   dove 65%
      dived 25%

Can   dove 75%
      dived 20%

The chart shows that both forms are used in each of the four countries, but in very different proportions. It is noteworthy that in American English *dove* can be used in all eight meanings identified by the *Oxford Dictionary of English*. These include the sense of 'to drop suddenly' as applied to prices, profits, and so on. This meaning is always expressed by *dive* in British English, possibly suggesting that to British ears phrases such as '*the Nasdaq dove*' and '*crime rates dove*' still sound unusual, and more markedly novel than when the verb is used in its core senses.

> Which of these would you say?
> *I texted him yesterday*, or *I text him yesterday*.
> Which would you write?

As has been mentioned, new verbs coming into English are generally weak, adding *-ed* in the past. But there is an up-to-the-minute verb whose status does not yet appear settled. If you listen out for people talking about *texting*, you may notice that the past tense is sometimes *text*, and sometimes *texted*. Can the Corpus shed any light on this?

Cases where the verb 'lemma' TEXT comes immediately after a pronoun or noun showed that in writing *texted* is about ten times more common than *text*. (13) Is *text* used as the past tense in all kinds of writing? It seems not. It occurs only in the **Weblogs** and **Fiction** domains. Now, weblog writing often comes closer to speech, and *text* for the past struck me as a feature of speech. So I wondered if the proportion of *text* to *texted* in Weblogs would be different from what it is in all domains. However, as so often happens, the evidence confounds expectations, and there is no difference.

He speaks to Me as if I was a public meeting

(Attributed to Queen Victoria, talking about her prime minister, Gladstone)

So far we have looked at changes and variation in individual word forms—'morphology'. But morphology is only one part of the story. What about areas of syntax which are changing? As an example of how the Corpus can throw light on that, we're going to look at some structures containing *if* where the following verb can be *were* or *was*:

> *If I were* or *was you . . .*
> *If only he/she/it/I were* or *was . . .*
> *If it were* or *was up to . . .*

By using *were* instead of *was* in these phrases you are using the *'subjunctive'*. (Don't be put off by the terminology. If you have unpleasant memories of the subjunctive from school French, the English subjunctive is child's play in comparison.) A relic from an earlier stage of English grammar, in modern English it takes three forms. The first is very widely used, especially in formal American English.

- Sentences such as: *He suggests that she* **speak** *to her husband* (rather than *speaks*) use the *'base'* form of the verb, rather than the form with -*s*, after words like *suggest, recommend, insist.*

The second type cannot be applied in new situations, and occurs only in formulae.

- *So* **be** *it! Far* **be** *it from me to . . . , God* **save** *the Queen! Hell* **mend** *him! God* **rest** *her soul!* **Suffice** *it to say . . .*

The third kind of subjunctive is used in clauses which begin with *if,* as in our three examples, or otherwise express a hypothetical situation.

Some people insist that *were* is the only correct form, particularly in the phrase *if I were you*—though the quote from Queen Victoria suggests that even she may not have lived up to the standards set by some purists. Is the purists' view reflected in how people actually write?

The structure *if I* **were** *you* is roughly ten times more common than *if I* **was** *you*. Perhaps surprisingly, *if I was you* does not turn up in spoken material at all. The picture for the other two structures, however, is rather different. In *if it were/was up to* . . . , there is still a preference for *were*, but it is nowhere near as strong, making up about 60 per cent of cases. With *if only*, the proportion drops further, to 55 per cent.

One possible explanation for *were* clinging on in *if I were you* is that we perceive and process it as a formulaic phrase which allows no variation. Another factor could be that when people use this phrase they are very aware that their choice will tell people a lot about them, and they are therefore particularly chary. Also, over three-quarters of examples in the Corpus of *if I were you* come from the Fiction domain, so the authors may be exercising particular care, and not representing language as it is really used.

Personally I'd bet that within a few years *if only it was* and *if it was up to* . . . will oust the versions with *were*, but *if I were you* will cling on.

Mesdames et Messieurs, faites vos jeux.

8   Style wars
Usages people hate

'When I split an infinitive, God damn it, I split it so that it will stay split.'

Raymond Chandler, *1947.*

In typical tough-guy style, Raymond Chandler slugged the received wisdom that split infinitives are incorrect. But even now, some people still believe that it is inherently wrong to put an adverb between *to* and the verb, as in *Star Trek*'s famous '*to boldly go where no man has gone before*'.

This rule—or, rather, superstition—is one of a handful of what can be described as the folk commandments of English usage. Like the originals, they are mainly negatives:

- thou shalt not end a sentence with a preposition (1)
- thou shalt use *shall* rather than *will* with 'I'
- thou shalt not say *disinterested* when thou meanest 'not interested'
- thou mayest not start a sentence with *and* or *but*

and so forth.

The fact that many people have these usage rules imprinted on their psyches raises questions which we'll look at in this chapter. Questions such as: what do people mean by 'usage'? What kinds of usage do they object to? And, where do ideas of correct usage come from?

Some favourite usage bugbears

Which of these—if any—set **your** nerves on edge?

to interface with someone
hopefully
at the end of the day
synergy
I personally think
at this moment in time
with all due respect
*pron**ou**nciation*
nucular for *nuclear*
less people
absolutely (= 'yes')
Add your own bugbear here:

Usage is a slippery eel of a word. It can mean two things: the way people actually use language; or the way one group of people feels other people ought to use it. In the second meaning it's equivalent to 'good' or 'proper' usage, with the 'good' or 'proper' understood. Which meaning is intended in any context is sometimes far from clear. The definition in the *Oxford Dictionary of English* neatly sidesteps the ambiguity with the use of the word 'and': '*the way in which a word or phrase is normally and correctly used*'. But as we shall see, many people consider that for certain words and phrases there is an absolute abyss between how they are normally used and how they are 'correctly' used.

The first person we know of who made *usage* refer to language was Daniel Defoe, at the end of the seventeenth century. He did so while arguing for the creation of a society to police how English should be used: '*The Voice of this Society should be sufficient Authority for the Usage of Words.*' In other words, the 36 members he proposed would be able to dictate to the six million or so English speakers of the time which words they should use, and how they should use them. (2) In a notable phrase, which no doubt some linguistic conservatives would endorse even today, he suggested that this clique of the great and good would be '*the allowed judges of style and language, and no author would have the impudence to coin without their authority*'.

For contemporary British English speakers the most famous authority on correct usage is H. W. Fowler's *Dictionary of Modern English Usage*, and Fowler defines usage as '*points of grammar, syntax, style, and the choice of words*'. These are useful headings under which to group many contentious language issues. As we shall see later, they are all topics that people still get very exercised about.

Remarkably, according to the Corpus, *usage* is one of the top 7,000 lemmas of the English language, the ones which make up 90 per cent of everything we ever say and write. In the ranking it sits just below *locally*, and just above *Friday night* and *casino*. Can this really mean that in binge-drinking, gambling-addicted Britain more people are interested in the niceties of language than in having fun?

How frequent is *usage* in the Corpus?

Rank	Word
4625	conscience
4626	stiff
4627	slaughter
4628	inherent
4629	assuming
4630	locally

4631	*usage*
4632	pioneer
4633	suite
4634	Friday night
4635	vague
4636	casino
4637	magistrates
4638	conception

Unfortunately not, since, as we have seen before, it is necessary to look at how often people use meanings of words, rather than just the words themselves. There are more than 21,000 examples of *usage* in the Corpus, but most of them have to do with the other meaning of the word: '*the action of using something or the fact of being used*', as in *energy usage* and *phone usage*. (In this meaning the word could often be replaced by *use*, and using the longer word is something Fowler criticized.)

The meaning of 'correct usage' emerges in the company of some evocative key words. For instance, *usage* often collocates with *correct* as a noun or adjective: '*I don't think that this is a completely correct usage of the term.*' In other words, anybody mentioning usage is likely to be querying it, and will probably want to correct it. *Acceptable* is the most significant adjective in the structure *usage is . . .* : '*In a 1969 survey the usage was acceptable to only 38 per cent . . .*' Again, this collocation is indicative: deciding whether a particular feature of English is acceptable, and to whom, is the crux of debates on usage.

Pundits and princes

When it's a question of safeguarding language, there are plenty of people ready to take up the cudgels. Journalists such as John Humphrys in the United Kingdom or William Safire in the

United States; educationists (or should that be educationalists?); literary critics; publishers and writers. Most major publishers produce usage books, and there are dozens of websites offering similar content. A few usage gurus, like Safire or Fowler, have become part of the cultural landscape. They and other writers on usage have a professional stake in the matter, but there are also groups of enthusiastic amateurs raring to tilt at the windmills of incorrect usage.

Not least among them is Prince Charles, who was quoted in 1989 as saying: '*We've got to produce people who can write proper English. It's a fundamental problem.*' (3) That same year he also criticized some of the media, and the education system, for reducing English to being '*so impoverished, so sloppy and so limited*'. (4)

How far do you agree with this statement?
The BBC has a responsibility to maintain proper English.
Not at all   Up to a point   Very much   Completely

As the most visible and audible of the media in Britain, the BBC might be expected to come under attack. And in October 2007, 310 years after Defoe presented his proposal for a society, the Chair of the BBC Trust received an open letter from a group of British worthies advocating a similar idea.

Signatories included the highly vocal Conservative MP Ann Widdecombe (for whom the word *strident* could have been invented); the former Chief Inspector of Schools; the former chief of the Defence Staff; and Ian Bruton-Simmonds, a member of the Queen's English Society. (5) At a time when the BBC had just announced major staff cuts, the letter suggested, apparently without irony, that somebody should be appointed to scrutinize correspondents' use of English '*syntax, vocabulary and style*' (echoing three out of four of Fowler's list). Promoting the *proper use of language* was important, it claimed, because of mass communication. To help with this task, a group of 100 voluntary monitors would listen out for grammar and vocabulary slips and report back to the language czar, who would tell broadcasters what they ought to have said.

In the three centuries between Defoe's proposal and this letter the world, and our knowledge of it, has changed out of all recognition. The English language too has changed—though not beyond all recognition. What has remained constant is that certain groups of people believe they are entitled to tell others how to speak and write, and to dictate what 'proper' English is. Though people no longer believe that the sun revolves around the earth, many are prepared to abide by usage rules which are just as devoid of any scientific or rational basis. Though nobody believes the Philosopher's Stone will turn base metal into gold, many hope 'poor' English can somehow be magicked into 'good' English by rules.

It would be a mistake, however, to imagine that only those who write for a living, or reactionaries, snobs, and philologists, are interested in 'good' English. Some recent examples from the British media can help illustrate how emotive a topic it is for people who are none of those things.

Sloppy, slipshod, and lazy

What kinds of usage questions do people worry about? The answer seems to be: just about everything. For instance, the *Daily Mail* featured an article about the letter to the BBC from the Queen's English Society and there was lively online discussion. (6) The points people raised cover the whole gamut of usage—syntax, grammar, style, and choice of words—as well as pronunciation.

The key words and phrases used online to describe the state of current English are the ones that always crop up when these issues are discussed: '*poor grammar*', a '*decline in standards*', '*misuse of the Queen's English*'. What people should be aiming for, it was argued, was '*proper use of the English language*', and '*decent, standard English*', which needed to be taught in our schools. As often happens, the way other people use grammar came in for a lot of criticism, although complainants rarely gave specific examples of grammatical mistakes. So it looks as if *grammar* is often a generic way of referring to any aspect of English that people object to.

People can get very heated about transgressions of what they view as linguistically acceptable. Nobody would like to be called '*sloppy and slipshod and lazy in one's expression*'. But those were the words applied online to speakers on the BBC. The 'sloppy' echoes Prince Charles's comments about modern English but takes the moral condemnation several steps further. There is a wealth of disapproval on display here.

Critics of language usage commonly stray beyond language itself into the realms of morality; they see people who misuse language as fundamentally morally flawed. At the same time, in their view defending 'proper' English has become a moral (and often patriotic) duty. This tradition lives on in phrases such as: '*The BBC—and all of us—have a duty to maintain standards.*' (7)

Failed fatwas

Another insight into public concerns about language comes from the BBC itself. The journalist and writer Vanessa Feltz, whose show on BBC London 94.9 features phone-ins, took violent exception to what she saw as the overuse of the phrase *at the end of the day*. Her objection was that it was creeping into dialogue everywhere, and making it impossible to hold a conversation without it.

She tried to impose a 'fatwa' on callers to her programme using it. Her crusade failed, as she later had to admit, because callers clearly couldn't communicate without the phrase slinking sooner or later into their conversation. To stop them using it would have been to censor them. (Sadly for their instigators, this appears to be the fate of most linguistic crusades which have purely stylistic or linguistic motives, rather than social or political ones.) Vanessa Feltz also asked listeners to phone in with words and phrases which they wanted consigned to the linguistic scrapheap, and they did so with great gusto. (8)

Both the online *Daily Mail* group and radio callers took pot-shots at these particular *bêtes noires*:

- shifts in the meaning of words
- words and phrases being overused
- saying the same thing twice in different words ('*tautology*')
- words and phrases seen as imports

Let's look at some things the Corpus can tell us about each of these.

Meaning shifts

Do you think this sentence is correct usage?
Outwardly she appeared disinterested in what Doug was saying.

There is possibly no redder rag to the usage police than using *disinterested* to mean 'not interested', instead of *uninterested*. The second edition of *Fowler's Usage* (1965) noted: '*A valuable differentiation is thus in need of rescue, if it is not too late,*' and

Bill Bryson suggests that '*the distinction is a useful one and well worth fighting for*'. (9, 10)

Can the Corpus tell us who has won this particular skirmish in the style war? The news from the front is mixed.

It might dismay usage watchdogs that the Corpus shows *disinterested*—by about 25 per cent (2,732 against 2,204). But the key question is how often it means 'impartial' instead of 'uninterested'. The 'uninterested' meaning applies about 50 per cent of the time, the 'impartial' meaning about 40 per cent (10 per cent of examples are ambiguous). So, that 50 per cent of *disinterested* is still less common than the word *uninterested*. Traditionalists could take some comfort from the fact that when people wish to express the meaning 'not interested' it seems they still prefer to use *uninterested*—at least in writing.

A second example of a disputed meaning shift is *epicentre*, but here it's a case of a single word changing, rather than one word driving another out. Though not on the tip of everyone's tongue, *epicentre* and *epicenter* are often used instead of *centre* and *center* by journalists in search of lively copy. It seems to be an article of faith with some writers of usage guides and others policing language change that you should only use it in its technical meaning of: '*the point on the earth's surface vertically above the focus of an earthquake.*' For instance, one writer on the topic cautions: '*Do not use it as a fancy word for "centre", which too many pretentious writers do.*' (11) Arguably, it is sometimes pretentious, but the Corpus shows that in practice writers are deaf to the strictures of stylists.

In addition, while people sometimes use it as an inflated alternative to *centre*, in many cases it seems to carry an extra connotation. First of all, it's used to refer to the centre of undesirable, natural events, such as outbreaks of disease, epidemics, and famines.

The epicentre of . . .

Word	How often?	How significant?
earthquake	47	47.52
quake	28	45.85
epidemic	10	24.01
outbreak	9	22.01
explosion	7	17.56
instability	5	16.51
terrorism	7	15.27
revolution	6	15.25
universe	6	15.25
storm	6	15.11
crisis	7	13.81
Monday	6	12.54
activity	7	10.36
world	10	9.96

Its use then extends further to describe undesirable human activities, such as crime waves, child prostitution, and hooliganism. Finally, it comes to be used to heighten descriptions of physical locations as the centre of creative, cultural, or political movements: '*It* [Amsterdam] *was the European epicentre of the youth revolution in the 1960s.*' So, it seems that the word has taken on a lively metaphorical existence of its own, away from its scientific roots, a point which any blanket condemnation tends to overlook.

For our last example under this heading, a member of the public objected to *with regards to* used to mean 'with reference to', instead of the standard *with regard to*. Here again the processes of analogy that we have seen at work elsewhere come into play. Because the noun *regard*, being somewhat formal in register, does not cross most people's lips very often, they replace it in speech with the more familiar *with regards to*. The Corpus suggests that at the moment *with regard to* is holding its own in writing: it occurs nearly eight times as often as the other form. The British usage police often view the United States as a major source of linguistic infection, and shun transatlantic borrowings as the illegal immigrants of language. In the case of *with regards to*, however, Corpus shows that the biggest culprits of this supposed language crime are the British themselves.

At the end of the day

We grow tired of anything that is repeated too often—an anecdote, a joke, a mannerism—and the same seems to happen with some language. Overusing phrases is certainly something the general public notice and grow tired of. As I mentioned earlier, the British broadcaster Vanessa Feltz waged an unsuccessful campaign against *at the end of the day* in the meaning of 'ultimately, in the final analysis'. (Having read this, listen out for it and see how often it crops up in conversation.) What can the Corpus tell us about how it is really used?

One question is: how often do people use it instead of possible alternatives? Alternatives used to summarize and conclude presenting a point of view are: *ultimately; in the end; when/after all is said and done; when push comes to shove;* and *in the final analysis*. The sections of the Corpus I looked at were British news material and British informal. Even discounting contexts where *at the end of the day* had a literal meaning ('*police patrolling the school gates at the end of the day*'), it was by far the most common phrase.

Another style crime for language watchdogs—and for many other people—is expressing the same idea twice in different

words. This is known technically as '*tautology*', and is something
John Humphrys describes as '*the linguistic equivalent of having
chips with rice*'. (12) An example often quoted is *general
consensus*. Critics of the phrase argue that because dictionaries
define *consensus* as 'a general agreement', *general* is redundant.
(As most of us don't have the dictionary definition in mind when
we use words, this seems a particularly pedantic language
prescription.) Other examples where the tautology is more
obvious are *return again, future prospects*, and *repeat again*.

Other usages to which people object vehemently are *Personally,
I feel* and *at this moment in time*. (13) Objections are partly
based on an appeal to logic: you don't need *personally* with *I*
because the *I* makes it personal enough already (after all, who
else would you be talking about?); and you don't need *in time*
because moments are a period of time in any case. However,
logic is usually an unreliable guide to analysing natural
languages. If it were more reliable, our watchdogs should also
take issue with arguably tautological phrases such as '*there
wasn't a cloud in the sky*' (in the sea? on the ground?) or '*there
wasn't a soul to be seen*' (to be smelled? to be touched?).

A 'descriptive' approach to these usages is to try to find out
whether they convey a difference in meaning or connotation.
Watchdogs view them as arbitrary and unnecessary variants;
linguists tend to take it for granted that it is unusual for a
language variant to be arbitrary.

Usage crimes the public loathe

Tired idioms

- *between a rock and a hard place*
- *at the end of the day*
- *to sing from the same hymn sheet*
- *it's a nightmare*
- *it's not rocket science*

Tautology

- *and also*
- *at this moment in time*
- *personally I think*
- *me as a person*
- *the problem is, is that . . .*
- *so therefore*

Pronunciation

- *reguly, particuly, itinery*
- regional accents; 'ficko' and 'fug' voices
- letter *h* pronounced as 'haitch'
- making a statement with the voice going up at the end, so it sounds like a question

Grammar & syntax

- singular noun with a plural verb
- *shouldn't of*
- *has ran, we was,* and similar verb mistakes
- *fairly unique*
- *less* instead of *fewer*

Exaggeration

- *yeah, totally*
- *absolutely* (= 'yes')

Americanisms

- *fruitloop*
- *heads-up*
- *to touch base*
- *24/7*
- *Can I get . . . ?* instead of *I'd like . . .*

Personally, I feel . . .

People accept *personally* when it is used to mean either 'with the person specified being present', as in '*I met him personally*'; or 'relating to the individual concerned' as in '*I took it personally*'. What they find objectionable is the meaning that can be paraphrased as 'in my view': '*I personally feel that it's vital to . . .*'

Three basic questions which the Corpus can help us answer are: how often do people use *Personally, I* . . . as opposed to just *I*? Is there a pattern to how people use it? And what does the larger context suggest about why they do so?

In answer to the first question, the Corpus shows that *personally* is used with other verbs than *think*, although it is by far the most common verb. The next commonest ones are *feel, believe*, and *find*. Nearly all the verbs *personally* is used with can be grouped under the headings of 'views', 'understanding', 'liking', and 'wishing'. Apart from the ones already mentioned, they include *know, see, hope*, and *want*. You can say or write both *Personally I think/feel/etc.* and *I personally think/feel/etc.*, but the first pattern is more prevalent. That pattern makes it clearer than the second one that *personally* is a comment on the whole sentence, a little like *frankly* in the infamous: '*Frankly, my dear, I don't give a damn.*'

The kinds of verbs people use *personally* with suggest that its use isn't capricious or tautological. Rather, it is a method that speakers use to soften a statement about their views and likes, in an attempt to forestall disagreement, since views and likes can be controversial. The contexts in which *personally* is used suggest that some of the topics and situations are highly controversial: religion, politics, court proceedings, public enquiries, and the like. People who condemn its use as illogical, however, need not worry that it is invasive, like a sort of linguistic knotweed. The most common verb it goes with is *think*, and the structure *I think that* is vastly more common than *Personally, I think that* or *I personally think that*.

Another phrase which came in for criticism was *safe haven*. The argument runs like this: the idea of 'safe' is inherent in the word. Therefore there can't be an unsafe haven; or, if it is unsafe, it isn't a haven. While the definitional logic is impeccable, it overlooks the differences in real use between *haven* and *safe haven*, as well as being a disguised version of the 'etymological fallacy' (see pp. 152–3). A *haven for tourists* is a resort to which tourists flock, and which welcomes them; but a *safe haven for tourists* implies a contrast with other tourist destinations which are clearly dangerous.

Some usage myths

Defoe, Swift, and their contemporaries argued in favour of taking steps to fix English usage and stop it from changing. They were worried that if it went on evolving the writing of their day would be impossible for future generations to understand. A standardized and agreed form of the language was also thought to be the only way to achieve a worthy vehicle for people to express all the concepts which new discoveries and inventions were making possible in an age of great social upheaval.

During the eighteenth and nineteenth centuries a flood of books aiming to fix the words, spelling, grammar, and pronunciation of English were produced: dictionaries, grammars, books on rhetoric, style, and elocution. Though some writers argued that the 'common usage' of everybody should be the final arbiter, the argument was won by those who viewed the usage of 'authorities' as the final guide. This enabled self-appointed

authorities to impose rules exactly as they saw fit on a public
who were keen to have simple rules they could adhere to.

That whole tradition has helped shape people's views today
about what 'proper' usage is. It has also helped create what
Randolph Quirk described as people's '*linguistic morality*'. (14)
The following ideas are some that have recurred in discussion
of language issues over the centuries, and still seem to maintain
their vitality. It is worth examining them.

- *There is only one version of correct English, and it is
  appropriate regardless of circumstances.*

This assumption is the essence of the debate on 'good', 'proper',
or 'standard' English. Oceans of ink have been spilled elsewhere.
Here I would just point out what seems like a very obvious flaw
in the logic of this presumption. If there were only one version,
speakers would have to use language in exactly the same way at
all times. That this is not the case is shown by people (people's?)
adjusting what they say to suit who they're speaking to, and to
the formality of the occasion. For instance, the same person
could, on different occasions, call a drink any of these:

- *alcoholic beverage* (official)
- *refreshment* (formal, official)
- *drink* (general)
- *swift pint, swift half* (informal)
- *bevvy* (Scots, Northern English, informal)
- *wee dram* (Scots, friendly)

Which of those is the 'best' English usage?

Tongues, like governments

'*Tongues, like governments, have a natural tendency to
degeneration,*' Dr Johnson wrote in the *Preface* to his dictionary,

a view which appears to have many followers even today. There seems to be a widespread belief that left to its own devices the English language will degenerate. Every age, it seems, bewails how decadent and enfeebled its own language has become, compared with its vigorous, pure beauty in earlier times.

The idea that words have a fixed meaning with which you tamper at your peril seems to be very deep-rooted. An early defender of English usage, Jonathan Swift, put it this way: '*I see no absolute Necessity why any Language should be perpetually changing.*' (15)

> How far do you agree with this view?
> Not at all   A little   Very much   Entirely

- *Any change to language is inevitably for the worse.*

If you speak of 'worse' you are clearly making a judgement that what went before was better. It also implies that you accept in principle that change happens. So, to say that an earlier version of language is 'better' would logically entail accepting as meaningful statements such as: 'The English language was better on 25 May 1997 than it was on 17 August 2003.'

The absurdity of maintaining this position was wittily captured by Victor Hugo. A fellow member of the *Académie Française* claimed that the rot set in for the French language in 1789. To which Victor Hugo replied: '*À quelle heure, s'il vous plaît?*' ('At what time, please?'). (16)

- *A corollary of the previous assumption is that earlier uses and meanings of words and phrases are better.*

This assumption is the '*etymological fallacy*'. It maintains that the older or first meaning and use of a word is more valid than and preferable to newer, later ones. It can be seen as an attempt to bolster with rational arguments the irrational idea that language shouldn't change. Furthermore, because the vast majority of people nowadays have no knowledge of Latin and Greek, when watchdogs appeal to what an English word meant in those languages, they can easily come under suspicion of being elitist. (17)

Not the least of the many problems with the etymological line of argument is that one of the ways language evolves is through metaphor—*line* in this sentence being an example. Speakers often strive to make what they say more pictorial, vivid, and dramatic (the widespread use of *awesome* to mean 'very good' is another case in point). With that in mind, it is legitimate to view *epicentre*, discussed earlier, as just one of the thousands of words which have taken on non-literal meanings. To prune language of such metaphorical growth would be to neuter it.

Another major problem with this argument is that what traditionalists believe to be the older meaning is not necessarily the original one, or not the earliest one recorded in writing. It is true that the geological sense of *epicentre* comes, inevitably, before its figurative use. But, according to the *Oxford English Dictionary*, the first recorded use of *disinterested* was by John Donne (before 1612) precisely in the meaning 'not interested'.

English for the English

- *The purity of the English language is corrupted by words from abroad.*

Linguistic nationalism and morality are sometimes cosy bedfellows. The slogan 'English for the English', though it could well be contemporary, comes from a copy of the *Leeds Mercury*, quoted approvingly in Henry Alford's *A Plea for the Queen's English*, of 1864. The link between foreign words and immorality is made quite explicit:

*But it is not only on literary grounds that we think the
bespanglement of our language with French and other foreign
phrases is to be deprecated. Morality has something to say in the
matter. It is a fact that things are said under the flimsy veil of
foreign diction which could not be very well said in plain
English.* (18)

In English culture, the French have often got the blame for
undesirable states of affairs, especially in sexual matters, and
there is a touch of lip-smacking prurience in this paragraph too;
perhaps even a suggestion of the virginal English language being
tartily adorned with foreign fripperies.

There is a hoary tradition of British antipathy to 'furrin' words.
Sir John Cheke, who in the sixteenth century was firmly opposed
to the mass import of classical terms, warned of the dire
consequences with a balance of payments simile:

*I am of this opinion that our tung should be written cleane
and pure, vnmixt and vnmangeled with borrowing of other
tunges, wherin if we take not heed by tijm, ever borrowing
and never paying, she shall be fain to keep her house as
bankrupt.* (19)

The author of the first English dictionary, Robert Cawdrey, had
this to say in 1604, using another financial image:

*Some men seek so far outlandish English, that they forget
altogether their mothers language, so that if some of their
mothers were aliue, they were not able to tell, or vnderstand
what they say . . . one might well charge them for counterfeyting
the Kings English.* (20)

Dr Johnson had a long list of words which he wanted to
banish from the language. Among them was *ruse*, which he
denounced as '*a French word, neither elegant nor necessary*'.

Most intransigent of all was the member of the House of Lords who, in 1981, blamed William the Conqueror and suggested an extremely drastic remedy:

The result of the Battle of Hastings dealt a blow to brevity from which our language has never recovered. It is time we went back to 1065. (21)

Nowadays, the French are off the hook, and British language watchdogs tend to be most suspicious of American imports. Cynics would say it is a case of the older sibling being jealous of the younger sibling's success. British BBC radio discussions which pose the question, '*Who has the better grasp of English: the British or the Americans?*' (22) certainly seem to spring from linguistic sibling rivalry. The nationalist, British bulldog sentiment behind the next comment is more obvious: '*Any self-respecting media organisation or official in this country should at least try to use "English" terminology.*' (23)

A possibly apocryphal story illustrates perfectly the mixture of jingoism, snobbery, and one-upmanship that can underlie prejudices against American usage. An American student let his tutor know he was in Oxford and would like to contact him, to which came the Olympian rejoinder: '*I am delighted that you have arrived in Oxford. The verb "to contact" has not.*' Meanwhile, a quotation from Mark Twain sums up the supremacy of US English over British English, much to the chagrin of many British speakers:

There is no such thing as the Queen's English. The property has gone into the hands of a joint stock company and we [i.e. the Americans] own the bulk of the shares!

Now that watchdogs and pundits of different kinds have had their say, let's conclude this chapter with some common sense about language change from a primary-school child. A primary teacher in Ellon, Aberdeenshire, had been telling her class about the Battle of Bannockburn, and finished by saying they could visit the site of the battle. One of her class asked: 'Is that www.bannockburn.com, Miss?' (24)

'*Out of the mouths of babes*', to use the famous, if slightly misquoted, quotation. (25)

Epilogue
Dictionaries then and now

Lingua franca (1)

While you are reading this, more people are learning English around the world than speak it as their mother tongue. There are possibly 350 million people learning it in China alone: six times the population of Great Britain. English has an unprecedented reach as the *lingua franca* of global communication, and is used to some extent by probably around a quarter of the world's population. Among them are the roughly 375 million people who speak English as their first language, from Alaska to Australia, and from Guyana to Guam. Tens of millions of learners and mother-tongue speakers alike at some stage consult a dictionary. 'The dictionary' in the form we think of it today, as a guide to, or an authority on, our own language, has existed for a little over four centuries. Its forerunners generally had quite a different purpose: to translate from one language into another.

Given its current pre-eminence, it is easy to forget that the worldwide spread of English is decades rather than centuries old. In Europe, for well over fifteen hundred years Latin dominated international communication, religion, administration, and practically all intellectual exchange. If you wanted advancement in any sort of career, you had to know Latin. English dictionaries as we know them today are seen by many scholars as ultimately springing from this practical need to get to grips with the grammar and meanings of Latin.

An example of this need to understand Latin is contained in one of Britain's greatest cultural treasures. Voted, like the *Oxford English Dictionary*, an English icon, the seventh-century Lindisfarne Gospels contain the Latin text of the four Gospels. (2) Celebrated for their fantastically elaborate decoration, which mixes pre-Christian with Christian symbols, they also provide a sort of crib of the Latin biblical text. Around AD 970 Old English translations of the Latin words were added between the original lines and in the margins. This was done by the Northumbrian Aldred—'unworthy and most miserable priest' as he described himself—provost of the Minster at Chester-le-Street, in County Durham, which housed the Gospels at the time. In turbulent and often violent tenth-century northern England he wanted to make sure that the Word of God would be understood by the faithful. (3)

Such translations added to a text are called '*interlinear glosses*', and during the Middle Ages in Europe thousands of Latin manuscripts were annotated—glossed—in this way. Often glosses from individual texts were gathered together and put into a single collection, a '*glossary*', organized sometimes alphabetically, and sometimes by topic. They were essential tools for people dealing with Latin every day, particularly clerics.

Evidence for how words were used was usually completely lacking in these collections, *glossae collectae*, as neither the Latin nor the English words were shown in context. They did, however, have great authority: for not only was Latin the language of the universal Church; it was also sanctified as the language of Classical rhetoric and wisdom, and the foundation of any kind of education at all.

A garden of words

It was a collection of, and commentary on, biblical words that was first referred to as a *dictionary* in English (*dictionary* comes from the medieval Latin noun *dictionarium*, meaning a collection of *dictiones*, or words). The first quotation of the word in the *OED* is from 1526, from a book published by Caxton's successor, Wynkyn de Worde: '*And so Peter Bercharius in his dictionary describeth it.*'

The dictionary in question was a '*Moral Dictionary*' (*Dictionarium Morale*). This was part of a larger work compiled in the fourteenth century by the French cleric and influential scholar Pierre Bersuire (Petrus Berchorius in Latin). It explained—in Latin—the meaning of 3,000 Latin words from the Old and New Testaments.

The first two books to be called 'dictionaries' were both bilingual dictionaries, one Latin—English and the other Welsh—English. The first was:

• *The Dictionary of syr Thomas Eliot knyght* (1538)

It was dedicated to King Henry VIII by its humanist author, Sir Thomas Elyot, who wrote in the preface: '*About a yere passed I beganne a Dictionarie, declaryng latine by englishe.*' He promised to improve people's Latin within six months.

The second work was by the clergyman and translator of the New Testament, William Salesbury, and was published in 1547.

• *A Dictionarie in Englyshe and Welshe, moche necessary to all such Welshemen as will spedly lerne the Englyshe tongue.*

There was something of an explosion of dictionary publishing in the sixteenth century, for Latin and modern European languages. At that stage, there was no consensus over what to call such books, and *dictionary* was far from being the standard term. Alternatives ranged from the does-what-it-says-on-the-tin '*Vocabula*' (literally '*Words*', 1496), through the poetic '*Garden of Words*' (*Hortus Vocabulorum*, 1500), to the marketing-friendly

A Worlde of Wordes (1598). Similarly, the book generally regarded as the first dictionary of English for English speakers does not feature the word *dictionary* in its title. Furthermore, it contains hardly any of the features we have learned to expect in a modern dictionary.

A Table Alphabeticall by Robert Cawdrey, published in 1604 (the same year in which it was decided to undertake the translation that has given us *The King James Bible*), was rather different from our modern idea of a dictionary. Compiled— actually, largely plagiarized—by a schoolmaster and his son, and containing a modest 2,500 or so lemmas, it could be seen as an early example of niche publishing, directed at '*Ladies, Gentlewomen, or any other unskilfull persons*'. (*Unskilfull* here means 'lacking in education'.)

For, in a period of massive importation of words from Latin and modern European languages, amounting to a linguistic balance of payments crisis, hundreds of flowery, 'inkhorn' terms were in use which were, almost literally, all Greek to many people. Such words were called '*hard words*' and *A Table Alphabeticall* set out to make them comprehensible:

A Table Alphabeticall, conteyning and teaching the true writing, and understanding of hard, usuall English wordes, borrowed from the Hebrew, Greeke, Latine, or French, &c, With the interpretation thereof by plaine English words, gathered for the benefit & helpe of Ladies, Gentlewomen, or any other unskilfull persons.

Whereby they may the more easilie and better understand many hard English wordes, which they shall heare or read in Scriptures, Sermons, or elsewhere, and also be made to use the same aptly themselves.

Cawdrey's dictionary explained these 'hard words' mainly by using synonyms, sometimes short definitions. It marked words

which came from French or Greek (otherwise they were
assumed to come from Latin), and that was about the limit
of the information it gave:

§ aberration, a going a stray or wandering

§ abut, to lie unto or border upon, as one lands end meets
with another

There were no examples of the words in context, and thus
no evidence of how they were really used, nor were any
sources cited. The authority of the text as an interpreter was
taken for granted; in any case the intended audience were
hardly in a position to question it. It is also interesting to note
how that aspirational message of the last sentence on the title
page, '*and also be made to use the same aptly themselves*', isn't
a million miles from modern advertisements offering to help
us boost our word power. (4)

The proportion of an Englishman to a Frenchman

Beginning with *A Table Alphabeticall*, the seventeenth century
witnessed a profusion of English dictionaries. Their authors
plagiarized each other with a carefree incestuousness that
could make Oedipus blush, and keep modern copyright lawyers
permanently in business. Nevertheless, their books proved
popular and many went into several editions and revisions.
The first dictionary of English to call itself such was Henry
Cockeram's *The English Dictionarie* of 1623. The first person to
start using the published works of British authors as authority
for his definitions was Thomas Blount, in his *Glossographia* of
1656. But though he cited the names of authors, he did not
include quotations from their works.

In the decades after the publication of Blount's dictionary, the
English literary elite was becoming alarmed that the English

'tongue' was in a state of terminal decline and needed to be protected from further decay. Luminaries such as Dryden, Defoe, Swift, and Pope made suggestions about how to achieve this. One idea often mooted was that an Academy or Society should be established to 'fix' the language—to stop it from changing. Its members would have the authority to decide which words were acceptable: '*and no author would have the impudence to coin without their authority*', in Defoe's words. But how could an impartial decision be made about which words would get past these language czars? The answer lay in referring to hallowed British authors, or 'authorities'. If they used a word in a particular meaning it was acceptable; if not, it was beyond the linguistic pale.

The first person to include quotations from English literature in an English dictionary was Samuel Johnson. For quotations for his 1755 *Dictionary of the English Language* Dr Johnson turned to writers who were part of the literary canon, as well as to writers on more technical matters. His book contains almost three times as many quotations as it does headwords—a ratio which is, incidentally, on a par with many modern dictionaries which boast about the number of examples they provide. Johnson's description of words' histories—their etymologies— was often patchy, as in:

RAGAMÚFFIN n.s. [from rag and I know not what else.] A paltry mean fellow.

Yet even for such a simple word he produced citations from Shakespeare, Butler, and Swift. And he exemplified slang too, as in *what the dickens* (a phrase which goes back as far as Shakespeare). Johnson's frankness about not knowing the origin of the word is disarming, though clearly not something any dictionary user would accept nowadays.

DÍCKENS a kind of adverbial exclamation, importing,* as it seems, much the same with the devil; but I know not whence derived.

Where had you this pretty weathercock?
—I cannot tell what the dickens his name is my husband had him of. Shakesp. Merry Wives of Windsor

What a dickens does he mean by a trivial sum?
But han't you found it, sir? Congreve's Old Batchelor

* importing = 'meaning'

Scouring English literature from the Elizabethans up to his contemporaries, he tracked down—editing, if it suited him—apt illustrations of meaning. Once he spotted them, he marked the relevant passage for his assistants to copy out. It was a laborious, time-consuming process, with Johnson single-handedly choosing both the words to include and the examples to validate their meanings. Nevertheless, his dictionary was published within nine years of being commissioned, whereas the 40 members of the *Académie Française* took 45 years to produce theirs.

After the event, the comparatively short time it took him was a source of patriotic pride in the unending history of Anglo-French rivalry. But even before undertaking his Herculean task Johnson was nothing if not chauvinistic. This is his reply to a Dr Adam, who doubted he could complete it in the three years agreed with the booksellers who commissioned it:

Adam: *But the French Academy, which consists of forty members, took forty years to compile their dictionary.*

Johnson: *Sir, thus it is. This is the proportion. Let me see; forty times forty is sixteen hundred. As three to sixteen hundred, so is the proportion of an Englishman to a Frenchman.*

Knowledge is power

So scribbled James Murray, the self-taught Scottish polymath, on the flyleaf of one of the books from which he relentlessly harvested information. Few lives can have been more inspired by an all-consuming thirst for knowledge than his. Having left school at the age of 14, he educated himself comprehensively, above all in languages and philology, and was ultimately appointed editor of what was to become the *OED*. In that role, the task that fell to him, his assistants, and fellow editors, working away in their dank, cold scriptorium—whose very name harked back to their monastic predecessors but which was actually a corrugated iron shed—was to track down and collate evidence for the historical development of every meaning of every English word in use from 1150 onwards.

With a democratic disregard for academic hierarchies and niceties, the decision was taken to involve volunteers from the great British and American public in this mammoth task. They can be seen as the pre-electronic equivalents of the wordhunters of today's TV series *Balderdash and Piffle*. A notice inviting people to join in the great enterprise was printed in newspapers and magazines, and distributed in libraries, in bookshops, and from news-stands. The appeal struck a patriotic chord, and during the half century it took to create the dictionary, over five million quotations were submitted, each noting the word referred to—the 'catchword', as Murray termed it—the name of the author whose quotation was being used, bibliographical details, and then the quotation in full.

Using this mountain of evidence it was ultimately possible to build up the most comprehensive picture ever of the development of English. Its current version describes more than 615,000 word forms and contains nearly 2,500,000 quotations.

The *OED* is recognized around the world as a unique linguistic achievement, and a cultural monument. It seems entirely fitting that such a unique resource should be supported, for modern English, by the *cornucopia* (853 examples, and most frequent in the Life and Leisure domain) of evidence that is the Corpus.

Notes

A sea change

(1) This does not mean that English contains two billion **different** words, such as *life, death, love, war,* etc. It means that a rather smaller number of words appear from once to several million times, and thereby make up the total. For instance, the word *the*, the commonest word in English, occurs nearly 100 million times, while even a rare word, such as *otiose*, appears 198 times.

(2) *Time-honoured* is another Shakespearean gift to English, from the first line of *Richard II*, when King Richard greets John of Gaunt: '*Old John of Gaunt, time-honour'd Lancaster.*'

(3) Whitman strikingly omits *and* from his long list of six nouns, a rhetorical device known as *asyndeton*. Its related adjective, *asyndetic*, crops up just seven times in the Corpus, that is, roughly once every 300 million words. As an average-sized book contains 100,000 words, you might need to read 3,000 books, if chosen randomly, to find *asyndetic*.

Chapter 1

(1) The *Brown University Standard Corpus of Present-Day American English,* or the *Brown Corpus* for short, consisting of 500 extracts of 2,000 words each from fifteen categories of texts.

(2) Clive Upton & J. D. A. Widdowson, *An Atlas of English Dialects* (Oxford: Oxford University Press, 1996); Bill Bryson, *Mother Tongue* (London: Penguin, 1990), p. 97.

(3) See www.acronymfinder.com.

(4) See the *OED* entries for those words.

(5) In the *Preface* to his Dictionary (1755).

(6) David Crystal, *The Cambridge Encyclopedia of the English Language,* 2nd edn (Cambridge: CUP, 1997).

(7) David Crystal, *The English Language,* 2nd edn (London: Penguin, 2002), p. 49.

Chapter 2

(1) Defoe, Daniel, *The True-Born Englishman*, 1701.

(2) Albert C. Baugh & Thomas Cable, *A History of the English Language*, 4th edn (London: Routledge, 2002), pp. 57–61.

(3) Mark Twain, *The Awful German Language*, 1880.

(4)   **Words from the Old English Lord's Prayer in Modern English**

Word	Rank	How often (per million words)
to	3	23,638
and	4	23,135
of	5	23,071
that	8	10,841
be	13	7,540
on	15	6,333
as	18	5,671
from	26	3,722
we	27	3,520
will	32	2,861
who	46	2,125
come	76	1,259
us	86	1,116
our	90	1,059
day	102	886
lead	231	360
father	444	193
earth	1042	82
daily	1381	59
evil	1409	57
heaven	2734	24
forgive	2863	22
guilt	3661	15
thou	7123	5

The second column shows their rank, and the third how often we use them per million words. For example, the table shows that 'to' is used 23,368 times per 1,000,000 words. If you divide the larger figure by the smaller, you get roughly 40. This means that 1 in every 40 words we **ever** use is *to*. Similarly, 1 in every 92 words we use is *that*. At the bottom of the scale, however, on average we can only expect to come across *guilt* every 66,666 words.

(5) Baugh & Cable, op. cit., p. 55.

(6) Baugh & Cable, op. cit., p. 105.

(7) David Crystal, *Words, Words, Words* (Oxford: Oxford University Press, 2006), p. 59.

(8) W. H. Auden, 'But I Can't', in *Selected Poems*, ed. Edward Mendelson (London: Faber & Faber, 1978).

(9) Martyn Back, of Le Robert, personal communication.

(10) Dates refer to the relevant meaning only, not to the first appearance of the word.

(11) The British regional word *mimsy*, meaning 'prim; careful; affected; feeble', is first recorded after Carroll's word. It is not clear which examples in the Corpus refer to it and which to his meaning.

(12) Ruth Wajnryb, *New-Word Lists* in *Sydney Morning Herald, Spectrum*, 16 February 2008.

(13) Loanwords are discussed in Baugh & Cable, op. cit., *passim*.

(14) *Taboo* is another loanword, from Tongan, a Polynesian language, first recorded as being used in English by Captain Cook, in 1777.

(15) Geoffrey Hughes, *A History of English Words* (Oxford: Blackwell, 2000), p. 45.

Chapter 3

(1) Thorstein Veblen, *The Theory of the Leisure Class*, 1899.

(2) The form ending in -*able* appears in the *OED*, albeit labelled archaic. The definition is from Robert Burchfield's *The English Language* (Oxford: Oxford University Press, 1985), p. 91, as noted in Bill Bryson's *Mother Tongue* (London: Penguin Books, 1990), p. 111.

(3) *The Times*, 20 August 2007.

(4) From press release of the American Literary Council and the Simplified Spelling Society, 29 May 2004.

(5) The sounds are not exactly the same phonetically, but the differences are not meaningful.

(6) So phonetic is Spanish that many bilingual dictionaries do not give the pronunciation of the Spanish words at all; the phonetic symbols would merely repeat the headword letter for letter.

(7) The two pronunciations not covered by the verse are th*ough*t and thor*ough*.

(8) David Crystal, *How Language Works*, 2nd edn (London: Penguin Books, 2002), p. 129.

(9) Paul Christophersen, *An English Phonetics Course* (London: Longman, 1956), p. 63.

(10) This version is widespread in the US, and is given as a variant in the online *Merriam–Webster* dictionary, with its origins noted as folk etymology.

(11) This statement is not true in parts of the north of England such as Cumbria and Yorkshire. There, *beck*, from Norse and meaning a stream, still exists, particularly in place names. But there is no relation between the two words.

(12) Lynne Truss, *Eats, Shoots & Leaves* (London: Profile Books, 2003), p. 169.

(13) Sir Ernest Gower, ed., *Fowler's Modern English Usage*, 2nd edn (Oxford: Clarendon Press, 1965), p. 255.

Chapter 4

(1) Governments and organizations can of course prohibit or recommend the use of any words they wish in official and organizational texts. For instance, in Quebec, the *Office de la Langue Française* creates for official use hundreds of French words to replace English ones. The Chinese government systematically removes references to Tibet from any dictionaries made available in China.

(2) Rosamund Moon, 'The Analysis of Meaning' in J. M. Sinclair, ed., *Looking Up* (London: Collins, 1987), pp. 86–103.

(3) Julia Vitullo-Martin and J. Robert Moskin, *Executive's Book of Quotations* (New York: Oxford University Press, 1994).

(4) J. M. Sinclair, *Corpus, Concordance, Collocation* (Oxford: Oxford University Press, 1991), p. 17.

(5) According to one analogy, speakers could be thought of as shaping the 'weather' of language, which in time will affect its 'climate'. See Michael Stubbs, *Text and Corpus Analysis* (Oxford: Blackwell, 1996), p. 44–5.

(6) From Horace Walpole's letters, as quoted under *enthusiasm* in the *OED*. All unreferenced quotes in this chapter are from the *OED*.

(7) Philip Gooden, *Who's Whose?: A No-Nonsense Guide to Easily Confused Words* (London: Bloomsbury, 2004).

Chapter 5

(1) J. R. Firth, 'A Synopsis of Linguistic Theory, 1930–1955' in *Studies in Linguistic Analysis*, Special Volume, Philological Society, 1–32, 1957.

(2) The figure for significance answers the question: 'Of all the times that the two words could have occurred together, in what proportion did they

actually occur together?' So if word *a* occurs 50 times and word *b* occurs 50 times in the Corpus, they *could* have occurred together 50 times. The higher the figure, the more strongly associated the two words are.

(3) This example was suggested by an example in Michael Stubbs, *Text and Corpus Analysis* (Oxford: Blackwell, 1996), p. 175.

(4) John Donne, *Meditations*, XVII.

(5) J. M. Sinclair, op. cit., 1991, pp. 110–15.

Chapter 6

(1) *The Collins Cobuild Dictionary of English Idioms*, 2nd edn (Glasgow: HarperCollins, 2002), in the *Thematic Index*.

(2) The definition is from *The Oxford Advanced Learner's Dictionary*, 7th edn (Oxford: Oxford University Press, 2005), p. 963.

(3) The word *metaphor* is itself a dead metaphor, but one we don't recognize because it comes from a dead language. It is from the classical Greek *metapherein*, which means 'to carry across', 'to transfer', i.e. to transfer a concept from one domain to another.

(4) Data from a very wide-ranging corpus study of idioms tends to confirm this. The twenty most frequent words in idiomatic phrases include *hand*, *head*, *heart*, and *eye*, which are not in the top twenty for the corpus data as a whole. See Rosamund Moon, *Fixed Expressions and Idioms in English* (Oxford: Clarendon Press, 1998), pp. 75–8.

(5) G. Lakoff and M. Johnson, *Metaphors We Live By* (Chicago: Chicago University Press, 1980). See also M. Johnson's *The Body in the Mind* (London: University of Chicago Press, 1987), and G. Lakoff's *Women, Fire and Dangerous Things* (Chicago: Chicago University Press, 1987).

(6) See Chapter 2, 'Root Analogies' in Andrew Goatly, *The Language of Metaphors* (London: Routledge, 1997).

(7) The French word, which refers specifically to the Nile cataracts, seems to have died out by the nineteenth century. It comes from the Ancient Greek.

(8) David Crystal, *How Language Works* (London: Penguin Books, 2006), p. 276.

(9) See Rosamund Moon, 'Conventional *as*-similes in English: a problem case', *International Journal of Corpus Linguistics*, 13/1, 2008. I am also grateful to Dr Moon for suggesting a typology which I have adapted for this chapter.

Chapter 7

(1) '*Grammar that can govern even kings*' is from Molière's *Les Femmes Savantes*. The wannabe bluestocking mistress of the household has decided to sack her maid for having broken a rule of grammar. See note 7 for references to the Prince of Wales's view that, in fact, princes can govern grammar.

(2) *Glamour* is a corruption of *grammar*, and was used in Scotland to mean a magic spell. The connection between the two was created because grammar was perceived as the preserve of those who had Latin, and their skills were assumed to include the occult. The modern meaning of 'attractiveness' is a mid-twentieth century shift.

(3) The only regular patterns are: four different forms for the verb: *like, likes, liking, liked*; -*s* for plurals; -'*s* and -*s*' to show possession; the -*er* and -*est* endings in e.g. *bigger* and *biggest*; and the -*ly* ending used to create adjectives, a total of ten.

(4) *Morphology* is the most frequent word in the Corpus containing the element *morph-*. Though Greek in form, it is a loanword borrowed from German. It is also a 'celebrity' word, as Goethe reputedly coined it, though with a biological rather than linguistic meaning. The linguistic meaning is first recorded as being used in English in 1870.

(5) The earliest known citation of *syntax* in this meaning is in the third edition (1613) of *A Table Alphabeticall*, whose first, 1604, edition is recognized as the ancestor of modern English dictionaries. See the Epilogue.

(6) David Crystal, *The English Language* (London: Penguin, 1998), p. 22.

(7) See Michael Stubbs, op. cit., pp. 160–4 for remarks by Norman Tebbit and Prince Charles about 'bad English'.

(8) '*It all depends what you mean by . . .*' was a well-known catchphrase in Britain in the 1940s and 1950s. It was used by C. E. M. Joad, a radio celebrity on *The Brains Trust* discussion programme, and a popularizer of philosophy.

(9) The plurals *criterias* and *criterions* also exist, but are very uncommon, occurring in less than 0.01 per cent of cases. The singular *criterium*, which has occasionally been used historically as a Latinized version of the Greek, also crops up, but only in tiny numbers. *Criterium* with a capital *C* is generally used in the very specific sense of a 'bicycle race over public roads', mostly in American and Australian sources. This form comes to English via French, rather than directly from the Greek, as in the case of *criterion*.

(10) In the original, '*þauh alle my fyngres oken*'.

(11) In the *OED* entry for *dive*, verb, meaning I, 1 a.

(12) Jeremy Butterfield, *The Oxford A–Z of English Usage* (Oxford: Oxford University Press, 2007).

(13) There were 225 examples of *texted* as a past; and 27 cases of *text* as past. *Text* occurred 75 times as a simple present, and 22 as a historic present. (There were also six examples of *text messaged*, and two of *text'd*.)

Chapter 8

(1) This belief in particular is still very much alive. For instance, the style checker in Microsoft Word flags up sentences ending with a preposition. The first grammarian known to have stated it as a rule was Lindley Murray in his well-known *English Grammar* of 1795, and the issue is discussed in detail in David Crystal's *The Fight for English* (Oxford: Oxford University Press, 2006).

(2) Daniel Defoe, *An Essay upon Projects*, 1697.

(3) Reported, not verbatim, in newspapers on 29 June 1989; quoted in Michael Stubbs, op. cit., p. 161.

(4) *Daily Telegraph*, 29 December 1989, quoted in Tony Crowley, *Proper English: Readings in Language, History and Cultural Identity* (London and New York: Routledge, 1991), p. 9.

(5) The Queen's English Society is devoted to '*preserving and improving the beauty and precision of the English Language*'. 'To preserve' and 'to improve' seem contradictory; if you wish to preserve something, you presumably don't want to change it: if you wish to improve it you admit that it needs to be changed. Curious.

(6) Article by Laura Roberts, published in the *Daily Mail*, 28 October 2007.

(7) From online discussion of the *Daily Mail* article.

(8) Telephone calls to Vanessa Feltz, BBC London 94.9, 4 November 2005.

(9) H. W. Fowler, revised Sir Ernest Gowers, *Fowler's Modern English Usage* (Oxford: Clarendon Press, 2005), p. 134.

(10) Bill Bryson, *Troublesome Words* (London: Penguin, 2002), p. 57.

(11) Ted Nield, 'Chief Sub', *The Journalist*, November 2007.

(12) The *Oxford English Dictionary* defines *tautology* as:

The repetition (esp. in the immediate context) of the same word or phrase, or of the same idea or statement in other words: usually as a fault of style.

The article 'Tautology' in *Fowler's Modern English Usage* explains the concept in detail. The John Humphrys quote is from *Lost for Words* (London: Hodder & Stoughton, 2004), p. 112.

(13) In 2004 the Plain English Campaign took a poll of the clichés its supporters detested most. Top of the list were *at the end of day*, followed by *at this moment in time*.

(14) Randolph Quirk, 'Towards a description of English usage', *Transactions of the Philological Society 1960* (Oxford: 1961), pp. 40–61. He has some wise words on why people are so interested in usage.

> *One must fully recognise how widespread and deeply entrenched among the educated—including language students and scholars—are concepts of right and wrong, good and bad, at all strata of linguistic usage . . . There must be some investigation of what beliefs and precepts obtain; they cannot be sneered or shrugged away as the inheritance of prescriptivism as though this was to demonstrate that they lack significance or influence. They are features of our linguistic morality as deeply and as complicatedly entrenched as our licensing laws.*

(15) Jonathan Swift, *A Proposal for correcting, improving and ascertaining the English Tongue*, 1712.

(16) Quoted in Guy Deutscher, *The Unfolding of Language* (London: Arrow, 2004), p. 15.

(17) For example, Ian Bruton-Simmonds, in his 2003 Christmas Lecture to the Churchill Society, said of *meticulous* that:

> *Until its particularity was ruined its meaning was overcareful from fear . . . Meticulous is irreplaceable. There is no single English word that carries its core meaning.*

This is an appeal to its original Latin meaning, and to an earlier meaning in English which has long since disappeared.

(18) Tony Crowley, op. cit., pp. 173–80.

(19) Baugh and Cable, op. cit., p. 217.

(20) Thomas Cawdrey, 'To the Reader', *A Table Alphabeticall*, 1604.

(21) Quoted in Sidney Greenbaum, *Good English & the Grammarian* (London: Longman, 1988), p. 8.

(22) This was a question I was invited to discuss on BBC London 94.9's *The Late Show* on 2 August 2007.

(23) From online discussion of the *Daily Mail* article referred to in note 6.

(24) Ken Smith, *Diary* column, *The Glasgow Herald*, 3 December 2007.

(25) '*Out of the **mouth** of babes and sucklings*', Psalms 8:2.

Epilogue

(1) *Lingua franca*, from Italian, means literally 'Frankish tongue', i.e. 'Europeans' language'. It was a pidgin of simplified Italian and various

middle-Eastern languages used by medieval merchants trading in the Middle East.

(2) As voted on the website: www.icons.org.uk

(3) For more information on the Lindisfarne Gospels, see: www.bl.uk/onlinegallery/themes/euromanuscripts/lindisfarne.html

(4) An edition of *A Table Alphabeticall*, with a foreword by John Simpson, Chief Editor of the *OED*, is published by the Bodleian Library, Oxford; see www.bodleianbookshop.co.uk

Index

Words in italics (other than titles of books, etc.) such as *acronyms* are technical terms, and are explained in the text.

The Gifted Boss

The
Gifted Boss

How to Find, Create and Keep

Great Employees

★ ★ ★ ★ ★

Dale Dauten

wm

WILLIAM MORROW
An Imprint of HarperCollinsPublishers

To three friends

who have raised my standards and my spirits . . .

Jim Fickess,

Richard Gooding and

Roger Axford

FIRST EDITION

Designed by Cathryn S. Aison

The Library of Congress has cataloged the previous edition as follows:

Dauten, Dale A.
    The gifted boss : how to find, create and keep great employees / by Dale Dauten.
    p. cm.
    ISBN 0-688-16877-9
    1. Executive ability.   2. Executives.   3. Employees—Attitudes.   I. Title.

HD38.2.D38 1999
658.4'09—dc21   98-54390
                                                                                    CIP

ISBN 978-0-06-205953-6 (revised edition)

11   12   13   14   15   WBC/BVG   10   9   8   7   6   5   4   3   2   1

Success follows doing what you want to do.
There is no other way to be successful.
—MALCOLM FORBES

There are two kinds of talent,
man-made talent and God-given talent.
With man-made talent, you have to work very hard.
With God-given talent, you just touch it up once in a while.
—PEARL BAILEY

The Six Realities
of
Gifted Bosses and Great Employees

1. The "talent-squared" workplace is possible because gifted bosses and great employees want the same things from a workplace:
    - Freedom from...
        management,
        mediocrity and
        morons.
    - A change.
    - A chance.

2. Gifted bosses don't just hire employees, they acquire allies.

3. Great employees don't have jobs, they have talents. They enter the job market once (if at all), and thereafter their talents are spotted, courted and won over.

4. Great bosses and employees often reverse the typical job search: instead of the employee doing the "hunting," it's the boss. The process more resembles a "talent search" than a "job market."

5. While many gifted bosses have created such special work environments that they have virtually no turnover, many others embrace substantial turnover and become masters of "the secret skill" of firing.

6. An alliance between a gifted boss and a great employee is a kinship of talent, often creating a bond that can last a lifetime.

An Introduction to the New Edition

When I presented one of the first copies of this book to an old friend, he weighed it in his hands, turned it sideways, then asked, "Where's the rest of it?" (Some friend.) Anticipating future wisecracks, I decided that I would respond, "It's good enough to read twice."

Well, it turned out that no one complained about the length; just the opposite, I received frequent compliments on the book's compactness. Better yet, I've heard many times from those who actually had read the book twice, sometimes more. Imagine my delight when I phoned one executive to congratulate him on a big promotion and he replied, "I went home the night I got promoted and read *The Gifted Boss* for the eighth time."

That comment haunted me when I began to prepare this new edition. I had a list of all the new examples and research studies I might add. . . . *But,* I asked myself, would someone read a bulked-up version eight times? I ultimately decided in favor of simplicity; it is, after all, a story of one wise old man and one young manager, and in their conversation is the timeless story of leadership.

What makes this book different, and the reason that people still read it, is that it's not a collection of "tips" about managing people but rather, it shows how wise leaders create alliances of talent, where the best employees and best bosses energize each other's careers. Here's the premise: Study one group of ordinary bosses and another group of great bosses and figure out how the two types differ. As we shall see, a day in the life of the gifted boss is not like a day in the life of the ordinary boss.

Rather than clutter up the gifted boss conversation with more examples, I chose to add two brief new sections to the end: one is a discussion guide for management teams; the other is a quick-start list.

These new sections arose from the many speeches and seminars I've given on the Gifted Boss principles, and perhaps I'll meet you at some future meeting. Till then, I invite you to explore the leadership materials at www.dauten.com.

What a Fool I'd Been

We keep hearing the cliché "I never met a man who looked back upon his life and wished he had spent more time at the office." Okay. Terrific. But what are we supposed to do with that insight? When people look back on their lives, what *do* they wish they'd spent more time doing?

Those two little questions ended up changing my life. I decided I would seek out the oldest, wisest people I could find and ask them to reflect upon their lives. I soon learned an important lesson: It's impossible to get wise old people to talk about regrets. With wisdom comes acceptance. The wise blame no one but themselves, and then they forgive themselves. The examined life is a process of peeling away the layers of stupidity. It may be that the greatest wisdom of all is to say, "What a fool I was!" and then to laugh.

And that discovery is where my story begins, for I have gained the freedom to see what a fool I'd been for most of my career.

"Only Connect"

My "wisest/oldest" project eventually led me to telephone Max Elmore. I'd saved him for last. He's an eccentric old sage I'd first met at O'Hare Airport, the two of us stranded together by a freak May snowstorm. At the time, I was a disheartened young bureaucrat, feeling stifled and stymied—feelings intensified that night by being one of thousands of frustrated travelers trying to nap while slumped against the walls, using our carry-on bags as pillows. Unable to relax, I watched glumly as an old guy in plaid pants appointed himself social director for all the restless children in the terminal. Once he exhausted them, he sat beside me, and I responded grouchily to his questions about my life, pouring out my frustrations. Instead of leaving me there to sulk, he cajoled me, then educated me, and ended up changing my life—literally overnight.

During our hours of conversation Max taught me that you can't get to *better* without first getting to *different*. And he showed me how to delight in flukes and coincidences and other offerings of the angels of creativity. I learned a new motto that night: Experiments Never Fail. Within a few weeks I had established a reputation within my company as an innovator, and I'd gotten pulled into a stream of new projects and eventually into a series of promotions.

In fact, the success that followed my night with Max had led directly to the conundrum I now faced: I had more career than I wanted.

So it was fitting that I put off calling Max till the end, counting on him to help me pull together what I'd heard. And when I had him on the phone, I told Max that the more I searched, the more lost I had become.

He responded by asking, "So now that you've talked to all these wise old people, what do you think you should do more of?"

"Truly live. Experience life."

"Good. But what's the main ingredient of those experiences?"

"Other people."

"Yes. The goal isn't just to experience life, but to experience it together. Remember E. M. Forster? 'Only connect.' That's a two-word philosophy of life."

Those two words did indeed strike me as an important truth. But I was knee-deep in important truths. I said to Max, "I've been going in circles, reflecting on life. And since my life is mostly spent working, I've spent a lot of time reflecting on my career." I paused here, knowing I was about to say something that chilled me to contemplate, and I had to make sure my voice would not betray the powerful emotions I was feeling: "I've found myself wondering if I should quit my job, maybe become a consultant. Spend more time with my family."

There was a pause, and I couldn't decide if I would be pleased or disappointed if he agreed. Mine was an enviable job. Solid people, my coworkers. Good salary and benefits. Then again, I found myself not wanting to go to work some mornings, so much so that when the company started a little TGIM campaign, like we should all be thrilled to see Monday morning come around, I had to bite my tongue like it was a piece of Juicy Fruit.

Max finally responded by saying, "I remember hearing John

Madden, the football coach, talking about his decision to become a television announcer. It happened not too long after he left coaching. He said something like, 'I quit coaching to spend more time with my family. But after a while, I realized that my family didn't want to spend more time with me. So I went back to work.'"

Max laughed, adding, "I'm picturing you quitting your job, and after a year or so, you discover that your wife and children are sneaking around, hiding from you." He feigned a child's high voice, "Shhh . . . get down. Here comes Dad again, trying to spend time with us."

We laughed together. Max knew me well enough to know that I already had a close family. Looking back, I suspect he understood that I was simply worn down and looking for an exit. I remarked, "So now I'm more confused than ever."

He said kindly, "I don't think the answer is 'not working.' The answer is carrying 'only connect' into your work. Business at its best is all about human involvement. The problem is that we've stripped work of its natural zest. I thought the old command structures were breaking down, but mostly it's been a sham. We talk about teams and coaches, but usually they turn out to be committees and managers working under aliases."

He was right about the company where I worked. I had left corporate life and built a small business of my own, then sold out to a larger company. Now I was a "team leader," which meant I was head of a small division. I had a couple of dozen people who worked for my group.

"So," Max said, "do you truly 'connect' with your bosses?"

"Sort of," I replied, knowing I sounded wishy-washy. They were bright, committed people, but it seemed I spent half my time trying to figure out how to get around their bureaucracy.

"Do you love them?"

"I wouldn't have chosen that word."

"Do you want to be more like them?"

"No."

"And how about the people who report to you? Do you 'only connect'?"

"I care about them."

"Not good enough. You undoubtedly 'care' about saving the whales. That's not the same as connecting."

I got a bit defensive here, because I am a good boss who has devoted himself to his division. So I threw out some objections while Max let me talk myself into a corner. Then, when I'd been "set up," Max took me into a brief conversation that changed forever the way I view work relationships.

"Have you ever had a *great* boss?" Max asked. "Someone you looked forward to seeing, who lifted you up to a higher plane?" I hesitated, debating one possibility in my mind. That's when he added, "Peter Schutz, the former CEO of Porsche, once described for me the type of relationship I'm talking about. He described it as 'I like *me* best when I'm around *you*.'"

With that I knew my answer—I'd never had a boss like that. And then he asked about my own management. I unburdened myself, explaining that my relationship with my employees was mostly as a problem solver. I spent my days with them lined up waiting to see me, and they invariably brought in their obstacles and screwups. I came through for them, and in doing so, I had stopped doing what I thought of as "actual work"—which I was good at, and enjoyed—and started being a corporate plumber, my life concerned with leaking projects and clogged pipelines.

Max started laughing as I finished my griping. "What?" I demanded. He responded, still amusing himself, "I just thought of a remark by Emperor Hirohito, commenting on how his life had changed after the war. He said, 'You can't imagine the extra work I had when I was a god.'"

He waited for me to laugh, but I merely forced a chuckle because I didn't find much humor or any applicability. He said, "Don't you see, you're trying to be the god of your department. It's a lousy job, being a god."

And then he asked me about the people who worked for me, and he wondered if I had any "great employees," whom he defined as people who not only needed no management but who also made me do better work, and who raised the entire department to a higher standard. So I had to say no, although I felt myself a bit of a traitor to say it. And then we got to the real goods. . . .

The Best Place for the Best People

"So tell me your philosophy of hiring," Max said.

I didn't have one, of course, other than believing that I was a good manager and could get good performances from the competent people that Human Resources sent over. After some conversation, he summed up my hiring in a startling way:

"Let me get this straight. You hire from the candidates that HR sends over. And HR runs ads or gets unsolicited résumés in the mail and puts them in some sort of database. If you were a college basketball coach, these are what would be known as 'walk-ons'— people who just showed up and tried out. Which means that you and a team made up of 'walk-ons' are playing against teams that have searched the world for special talent."

This didn't sound like a terribly good strategy on my part. So I added something about networking (meaning the one employee I had hired after meeting her at a professional group).

"Okay," Max said. "But what do you do to make yourself attractive to great employees?"

I explained that our company offered "competitive wages and benefits" and that we had a "professional environment."

At this he snorted "No, no, NO!" so loudly that I had to hold the phone out, away from my ear. "Listen to yourself. Think about those words. Those are dangerous phrases. When you say 'competitive wages' what you are saying is 'ordinary, average, about like everyone else's.' And when you say a 'professional environment' you are saying the same thing. 'Professional' means that it's typical of the profession, which is another way of saying that it's what's common, standard. So you have, in effect, told me that your policy is to offer average rewards in an average environment. In other words, you are trumpeting your mediocrity."

This didn't sound right, but I knew it was true all the same. That's when he said, "What you want are the Wild Brains, the original thinkers, the self-reliants. They are the ones who lift up their coworkers and even their bosses. They set new standards. And they are *not* walk-ons. They rarely look for work. Only a moron of a boss lets one get away, although thank goodness there are such morons. But mostly you have to go to where the Wild Brains roam and coax them into following you home. And you can't coax extraordinary people with ordinary claims.

"Here's a little sentence that I use. Consider it a nine-word employment policy:

"The best place for the best people to work."

There was no mistaking the power of that statement, and I could immediately see how it would change almost everything about our work environment. Then again, it would never apply where I worked, not with the ax man continually cutting our budgets. I said simply, "I wish I could afford the best, much less the great employees with their Wild Brains."

He responded, "Once you understand what it is that great employees want, you'll see that it doesn't have to be expensive to hire the best people. In fact, all of my experience suggests that the best employees are a bargain."

Max paused, but I said nothing, not certain I believed in such magic employees, bargain or not.

I was glad to hear him say, "I can hear your eloquent silence, and it tells me that we have much to discuss, my friend." And then he made an offer that I jumped at: "If you want to learn how to be a great boss, worthy of great employees, and also learn how to be a great employee, worthy of a great boss, we need to get together and talk. We need a day—twenty-four hours. How about"—I heard him flipping a calendar—"oh, this could be perfect . . . there's something I want you to witness. A week from today in Phoenix?"

And that's how it was that I came to fly to Arizona to rendezvous with the eccentric business genius Max Elmore.

Sky Harbor

Max's instructions were for me to meet him at Sky Harbor Airport, in the oldest terminal, under a statue of a phoenix bird rising.

Finding Max is never difficult. As I hustled down the corridor, my plane late, I spotted his plaid pants at a hundred yards. As I came closer, I could see his gray hair combed straight back and his bolo tie—black strings below some sort of turquoise-in-silver piece. Being Max, he was entertaining strangers with some story. He was trying to remember a book title, and as I approached I could hear his self-deprecation: "I have a photographic memory— unfortunately it stopped offering same-day service." He laughed loudest of all. That was pure Max: He lived full volume, despite being in his seventies and having known the success that would have judged his silence as profundity.

When he spotted me, he roared a greeting and grabbed me up in a hug, slapping my back and barking profanities.

Then, pointing above his head, he asked how I liked the statue they'd done in honor of me and my career. It was a giant, gaudy phoenix, and naturally it was rising from the flames/ashes.

After retrieving my bag, we went to where he had parked a

rented Chevrolet Malibu in a yellow-striped zone designated for Truck Loading and Unloading. He'd left the trunk open, which, he explained, was enough to convince Security he qualified.

He said he was staying in the house of a friend, and I would be too. The friend and his wife were away in New York, so we'd have it to ourselves. It turned out to be south of South Mountain, on a street of Santa Fe–style houses that backed up to the rocky hills. He pulled into the drive of a long low house of pink stucco. Inside were Spanish tile floors and wildly colorful paintings.

It was a jewel of an October day—warm sun, cool breeze—and Max suggested that I settle down in one of the chocolate brown wrought-iron chairs on a back patio. There was no fence, just a low wall, and beyond that was an expanse of desert sloping to the rock cliffs. There were hundreds of those tall cactuses with arms, the saguaros, and a startling stillness that suggested that time had come here to rest. It was easy to picture Geronimo and his warriors riding their horses over this land.

My reflections were interrupted by the sound of a pop-top can being popped. Max handed me a Pepsi and said, "We have an appointment this afternoon." He sat across from me and began. "But before we go, here is our objective: I want your employers to be *crazy* about you. I want them to lie awake at night and thank the Lord that you work for them, and then lie there worrying that you might leave. I want them tossing around, trying to think of ways they can make you happier. Okay so far?"

Naturally I thought this was a solid objective, although I wanted to tell Max that it wasn't going to happen, not where I worked.

He said, "But because you are in the middle of the organization, not only do you want to be a great employee, you need to be a great boss. I'm going to show you how to turn your division into what I call a 'magnetic workplace.' I want all the best employees—the

Wild Brains—to hear of your work and dream of being a part of it. Okay?"

I could only laugh and say, "Check. My bosses lying awake thanking God for me. The best potential employees dreaming of working for me. Everybody in bed, accounted for."

He leaned across from his chair to cuff me on the shoulder: "I'd forgotten what a smart-ass you are. Now I remember why I liked you."

Then Max announced that we would begin with a discussion of just what it is to be a "great boss" or "great employee." He began with a vocabulary switch. He said, "I'm going to refer to these great bosses as 'gifted bosses.' It will make sense as we go along." And then he offered the first revelation of the day.

The Gifted Boss
and the Great Employee

"It turns out," Max began, "that both gifted bosses and great employees want the same thing from a workplace." He opened a leather portfolio that I hadn't noticed and pulled out a page of paper. "I prepared worksheets," he said, as though it were a natural thing for an eccentric old genius to do on behalf of a confused corporate bureaucrat.

The first page contained this:

1. The "talent-squared" workplace is possible because gifted bosses and great employees want the same things from a workplace:
    - Freedom from ...
        management,
        mediocrity and
        morons.
    - A change.
    - A chance.

This list befuddled me, starting with the "talent-squared" business, but before I could start in with questions, Max explained:

"When I began asking about great bosses, I soon learned that a major proportion of talented people—perhaps one out of three—have never had what they believed was a 'great' boss. Very few people have had more than one. But when I found those who'd had the experience, I asked how the boss had differed from the ordinary. The first and most passionate response was nearly always something to do with freedom—

"'He trusted me.'
"'He insulated us from the bureaucracy.'
"'She never got in the way and didn't let anybody else get in the way, either.'

"Then, in the next phase, when I asked the best bosses to describe the best employees, their first response category was *identical to that of the employees:* freedom. In the case of bosses, it was freedom from having to watch over an employee, from having to supervise and admonish.

"'She knew more about what needed to be done than I did—she'd tell me what to look for.'
"'I never have to worry about his work—he has higher standards than I do.'

"In other words, the gifted boss and great employee save each other from the agonies of management. And that's what I meant when I quoted on the phone that line from the late Emperor Hirohito, 'You can't imagine the extra work I had when I was a god.' The best bosses know how he felt: They have given up the role of knowing all, controlling all. When great bosses and great employees join together, many of the traditional functions of managing—giving assignments, supervising the work, checking up—become irrelevant. Supervision is replaced by trust, and trust requires no paperwork."

Max paused after that speech and let his eyebrows dance about, questioning.

"I'm with you," I said, "although I can't imagine employees who don't need any management. My biggest problem at work is that I can't do any real work, since I spend all my time helping the employees."

Max shook his head, saying, "That's the fundamental problem with management. Let's do a bit more figuring."

He took a legal pad, one with pink paper instead of the usual yellow, and wrote a large "10." He said, "This is the number of hours some guy in a corporation works—ten a day. And naturally, this person wants to get some help. So he convinces management to let him hire an assistant. Now the guy is a manager, and he cuts back to eight hours a day, the same as his new assistant."

Max wrote:

> Manager: $10 - 2 = 8$
> Assistant: 8

"Now, say the manager spends two hours a day training, helping and supervising the assistant. Of course, the assistant also spends those same two hours being managed."

He changed the numbers on the legal pad.

> Manager: $10 - 2 = 8$ Then, $8 - 2 = 6$
> Assistant: $8 - 2 = 6$

"So you add up the two new totals and what do you get? Twelve. And then you look where we started, and it was ten. So the corporation went from ten hours of work a day to twelve hours a day. But it costs the company nearly double. No wonder organizations are reluctant to add headquarters staff. And no wonder that individual managers think hiring is a great idea. That creates a natural tension in an organization."

He reached over and poked my knee for emphasis as he added, "And what if the boss spends another hour a day in managing, plus half an hour in conversation? Adding a new employee would actually reduce the number of hours worked per day." The poke turned into a squeeze. "That's why the gifted boss is engaged in a lifelong war with bureaucracy."

He sat back and said, "And the 'spoils of victory' in that war are the chances to put gifted bosses and great employees together and get what I call the 'talent-squared' effect. Both sides are freed from the drudgery of managing. Instead, each side inspires the other. True synergy. When you hire a great employee, suddenly you have lots of ideas about becoming more efficient, and soon you are each turning out more than either one of you could alone."

I nodded, trying to match his enthusiasm, although I had plenty of doubts. He read my mind and said, "Picture a five-person department, and you take the weakest employee away and add instead someone who is incredibly productive and creative, someone who not only turns out lots of work, but who also lifts the standards of the other employees, and who comes up with better ways to do the work. That one great employee can double the output of the entire department."

Then Max gave a finger-pointing, air-jabbing conclusion, "But . . . but . . . that will only happen if you're a gifted boss, secure enough to accept and to inspire greatness."

The Ordinary Boss

Versus

the Gifted One

Max leaned back to enjoy the breeze and watch the lizards chase one another along the wall. When he began anew he asserted, "The fundamental task of the best manager is not to manage." He looked hard at me. "Did you catch that one?" And then he repeated the business about the manager not managing. He continued: "The job of the gifted boss is to create a magnetic environment, one capable of attracting great employees—the kind who don't need management, who lift up their coworkers and even their boss. Agreed?"

I was still skeptical that such miracle employees existed, but I consented that it would be an ideal state.

"I can see you're not sold," he said, leaning back to give me a William F. Buckley Jr. dubious look, making me feel found out. "But you think that way," he said, "because Wild Brains don't come around very often. They don't go out looking for jobs. You have to believe in them in order to see them. Like fairies." This amused him so much that he brayed that whole-body laugh of his, which started him coughing.

He recovered soon enough and explained that he'd made a list of a few of the differences between typical bosses and extraordinary ones. He handed me the list and let me read it over.

Looking at the list of traits of exceptional bosses, I said I could understand why Max had chosen the word *gifted* to describe the best bosses. Max responded, "When we turn to employees, you'll see that it would be easy to justify the same label for them. Both require skills that usually come with the IQ/EQ/AQ package that we drag along when we enter the workplace." He then said, mostly to himself, "Or does it drag us along?"

He shook his head, as if to shake away the distracting thought, then continued: "Back to the point. I've written down the qualities that seem to me to define the great bosses, who, in order to undertake even half of the items on the list, must have an exceptional energy level, plus a 'feel' for people that approaches the clairvoyant and/or charismatic. So 'gifted bosses' it is. And if you care to add that label to the best employees, you won't get an argument from me."

And with that he started in on the list of traits, beginning with one that seemed designed to tweak me.

The ordinary boss: offers good jobs, at competitive wages/benefits.
The gifted boss: offers an exceptional environment, including the opportunity
to be exceptional. Knows that his/her employees are in constant
demand and so sets out to create a workplace that is magnetic.

"Most companies are imitations," Max said, returning to a theme I'd heard at O'Hare Airport the evening we'd met. "They start small and imitate the ways of the giants in their field. This means that workplaces resemble one another. And when a company has an employment strategy like yours"—he paused long enough to put on a face and tone of great condescension—"of 'competitive' wages and benefits, it has put up the flag of mediocrity."

He leaned in to press the point: "I suppose that every manager looks in the mirror and believes that a leader is looking back, but in that reflection is usually just a bureaucrat with embossed business cards."

I realized at that minute that I did take pride in my business cards. After all, once you reached the "senior" level at our corporation, you got the more expensive cards—not just embossed, but color.

He continued: "First, the gifted boss envisions and creates an environment that people want to be part of. You find major programs like"—he repeatedly snapped his fingers into a bunch, as if to literally pull recollections out of the air—"3M's '15% Rule'—where employees are encouraged to devote 15 percent of their work time to pet projects of their own choosing. That's the sort of program that announces to the world, THIS IS NO ORDINARY WORKPLACE." He said the last phrase in a booming orator's voice.

"But," he said, poking the air, "the same announcement is often made in smaller, less serious ways as well. For instance, the CEO at China Mist Tea, Dan Schweiker, replaced the table in the conference room with a pool table. That may sound like a trifle, but it's important as a cultural statement. Just like when Dan got rid of the reserved parking spaces for executives. And beyond such symbolic changes, there is a different feeling—the air seems different, the people bounce. One of Dan's employees said to me, "After many years in a stuffy, driven environment, this new job is almost like being on vacation."

Max stopped to scrutinize my reaction. Not satisfied, he added: "Or take Insight—it's a thriving computer retailer that we're going to visit tomorrow morning. It was founded by two brothers who even now are only in their thirties. When one of them, Eric Crown, was helping design the new headquarters building, he had it built in the shape of a giant X. He wanted the different departments to pass in the halls, to figuratively, if not literally, bump into one another. And instead of 'dress-down Fridays,' they created what they called 'dress-up Mondays,' having one day a week when employees can choose to take off the casual wear and put on traditional business attire. And they've subcontracted with two firms that work with the handicapped to staff one of their departments. You should see these folks in action. They are delighted to be working. And they lift the whole organization with their everyday courage. It's hard to be depressed over the cold sore on your lower lip when the person working down the hall struggles to walk."

He pressed on: "Or there's the example of a company called Tires Plus, a chain of tire shops. At their headquarters, they have not only a fitness room but also a massage room and a *meditation room.* They are in the tire business, but they have a meditation room . . . can you imagine?"

Max was clearly enthralled with these stories, but I was still doubtful. He tested my reserve with a touching story about a worldwide project undertaken by Lenscrafters. They set a goal to donate a million eye exams to impoverished people around the world. Employees compete for the privilege of taking part, earning a trip to a Third World country to do eye tests and pass out eyeglasses. With that as background, Max told me of the time he met the company's CEO, Dave Browne, who told him of his own experience with the program:

"Browne joined a group of employees spending a week in rural Mexico. Because he had no experience at the actual measuring and adjusting, he was assigned to setting up and cleaning up. Then, after days of observing and helping, he got his chance to actually fit glasses. It was going well, villager after villager, when up came a young woman who was legally blind. At twenty years of age, she had literally seen almost nothing of the world. Her vision reached a few blurry inches, and she made her living doing needlepoint, spending her days with the material and thread virtually touching her nose as she squinted to do her patterns.

"Browne found the strongest pair of glasses they had, and as he slipped them onto her face, she grabbed at them, falling to the ground, shrieking. He could only think that he had stuck her in the eye, and knelt beside her wondering, Oh Lord, what have I done to this poor girl? As he tried to comfort her, an interpreter heard her screams and rushed over, only to smile down at Dave Browne and the weeping young woman. 'She's saying that it's a miracle, that she can see, that she has been touched by the hand of God.' Touched by the hand of God. That is a kind of miracle, isn't it? Wouldn't that change the way you think of work?"

I was moved by the story and said so. But I had to add that all these efforts struck me as "nice," but not "decision criteria" for choosing where to work. When I voiced my doubts, Max flopped back in his seat, acting offended. He said, "That's the rut you're in and you don't even know you're in it. It's a glass rut. It's funneling you along and you don't even see it."

I smiled at the image.

"Yes, A ... GLASS ... RUT!" He said the words loudly, leaning forward to slap the table for emphasis, causing the cans to shudder. Max didn't notice because he had realized the time and was standing up. He said, "Enough talk. It's time to go visit a magnetic workplace."

And so we were back in the car, headed for downtown Phoenix. "I have to tell you about John Genzale," Max said as we headed

up Central Avenue. Just that name sent Max chuckling. "His employees call him the Lion and bring him all sorts of lion crap—
stuffed animals and posters, that sort of thing. I love to tease him
about it. That's who we're going to meet."

We eventually stopped at a low building among the high-rises,
the offices of the *Phoenix Business Journal*. We came into the reception area but got no reception—it was deserted. Although just
four-thirty, it appeared that work for the day had ended earlier. Max
continued on toward a room in the back, waving for me to follow.
We slipped in quietly and there found twenty or so employees,
some in chairs, others on the floor, all intent on a man who was
reading poetry. "That's him," Max whispered. "Our lion."

Well, he paced in a leonine way—loose jointed and self-
assured—but more closely resembled a television news anchor—he
wore an expensive suit coat, a quiet but assertive tie in a perfect
knot, and the shirt had French cuffs with gold cuff links.

That first poem was by Tennyson, I learned later. One passage
ended with a line that seemed particularly appropriate:

> "Some work of noble note, may yet be done.
> Not unbecoming men that strove with gods.
> The lights begin to twinkle from the rocks:
> The long day wanes: the slow moon climbs: the deep
> Moans round with many voices. Come, my friends,
> 'Tis not too late to seek a newer world."

The Tennyson reading went on for a while, followed by a discussion of the images and the wordings. But it wasn't all serious,
there was joking fun too, like a scene from the movie *Dead Poets
Society*. And then Genzale took up a book of love poems, saying
that it had been brought in by one of the employees named Steve.

This was deemed to be funny by the audience. I guess you had to know Steve.

The reading and chatting went on for half an hour, with no one showing anything less than complete attention. After the employees had headed home, Max and Genzale embraced and reminisced and then got around to discussing what I'd just seen. Genzale explained: "We're a weekly business paper. It's not what most of us went to journalism school to do. And we don't have the resources of a big daily paper. But that doesn't mean we can't grow and develop as writers, that we can't set a standard for passionate writing. So I started weekly poetry readings in the newsroom. And what happened was that we got everyone reading poetry, which got everyone thinking about fine writing."

Max put his arm around Genzale and added, "Forget about what that says to the world, think about what current employees can say to potential employees: Hey, where we work, we're evolving as writers . . . we even have poetry readings."

Max beamed at me, and I said truthfully that I was impressed—not just that the group had found something to be passionate about, but that they all had committed the time to be passionate together. That's when Max told me that I needed to "find my poetry." He added, "What we're really talking about is 'niche marketing.' You have to think of yourself as marketing your department to the company, and also as marketing your department to prospective employees. You identify that one trait that you want associated with your department, and then you find a way to evolve that strength. That second part is important: Too often a manager or a company president will declare a 'vision' or a 'mission' and then do nothing to support it. It's one thing to declare that you're going to be innovative; it's another to find ways to evolve creativity, to get everyone thinking creatively.

Genzale offered an example to support Max's point: "There's an ad agency with offices here in Phoenix and in Atlanta called After Dark. As a reward for meeting their annual goals, they all went to Paris. They did the trip right too. For small money you could bring your spouse or a friend. And it wasn't 'mandatory fun' where they had a lot of planned events. They split up, explored on their own. But what they did during the trip, and after, was to talk about all the design elements they had seen. They immersed themselves in beauty. Now they're planning their next trip—Italy."

We talked a while longer before leaving the newspaper. After we got back in the car, I told Max that the poetry reading idea suggested some things I could do with my department . . . or part of it at least. I told Max, "I could apply that to the professional group. But more than half the people who work for me are clerical or technical. I feel sorry for those people. I have to tell you, those are dull jobs."

Max didn't hesitate. He responded with this story:

"Take the case of Maggie Lifland, who built three insurance agencies in resort towns in Colorado. She started out with the typical assembly line approach, where you break jobs down till they are simple enough for anyone to do. Even the smallest mind grows bored. So the structure ensures turnover and discontent, and thus you enter a downward spiral where the jobs get ever simpler as you have to constantly replace the people doing them. But, as Lifland put it, *'If you're a manager and you create jobs that are so boring that you wouldn't want to do them, why should your employees?'*

"She observed that the employees were isolated and sedentary, and that the employees highly valued the activities outside the office—after all, they were in resort towns in Colorado.

"The existing setup for the insurance offices was for each person to have a set of accounts and to handle everything to do with them. Lifland decided to centralize the files so the employees shared clients and could cover for one another. And once everyone shared work, the company was able to institute a four-day work week, three weeks of vacation per year, and an environment where 'day-swapping' is encouraged. And the company also started quarterly growth bonuses that are split equally.

"The agencies saw an immediate drop in turnover and, over time, the ability to attract highly talented employees, the sort who can be choosy about a workplace. All it took to begin was one question: If I wouldn't want to do the job, why should they? A leader doesn't just share the profits, but the wealths—the joy and satisfaction and flexibility and freedom of *ownership*. And these new jobs give an employer a story to use to romance great employees."

"But," I said, enjoying the chance to ask what seemed to me a tough question, "it's *still* pretty dull work."

He gave a hard grimace. "Okay, you're right. Some jobs are just jobs. Of course, there are plenty of people who just want to leave work at work and don't seem to mind 'dull' so much. In fact, there's a guy named Ron Healey—nothing dull about him—who's a consultant with a program called 30/40, where manufacturing firms replace a forty-hour week with thirty hours while pay stays the same. The employees come in for a six-hour shift and work straight through. Output goes up, as does the number and quality of job applicants. Turnover, absences and mistakes go down."

"Six hours straight?" I moaned in sympathy for those employees. "I'm not sure that's an improvement."

"The logic is that employees are only really productive about six hours a day, no matter how many hours they are there, so why not let them put in those hours and leave. As Healey puts it, 'We give people their lives back.' And he also is willing to admit that a lot of the jobs are just monotonous chores, being assistants to machines. He's stopped trying to pretend that they can be made deeply rewarding. Instead, they let people have time to do other things. He had one employee say, *'I don't have a great job, but I have a great life.'*"

Max concluded by saying, "Notice that the NO ORDINARY WORK-PLACE sign is lit. There's a waiting list to get on at those companies, despite the type of work and the labor shortages at competitors."

Max smiled as he continued driving along Central Avenue, through downtown. "Now, you're ready for a story that you won't believe. Dave Thomas—you know, Wendy's hamburgers—told me that he didn't have a business plan when he started the company and still doesn't have one. Instead, he had a simple dream: to own his own restaurant, and maybe if things went well, to own three or four around town."

He saw me looking underwhelmed. "No, that's not the 'hard to believe' part. What's hard to believe is that when he started the first Wendy's, it was after he'd spent years as a gifted boss while working at Kentucky Fried Chicken. Thomas knew so many great employees that he didn't have room for all of them. And he began to expand for the sake of the employees, trying to fit them all in. He explained it to me: 'I had people who I'd worked with before who wanted to work for me. I'd tell them, "I can't pay you very much." They'd say, "That doesn't make any difference." So I had to open up more stores. When you have people who are with you, and believe in you, you have a responsibility to them.'"

Max again saw my skepticism and said, "I know it sounds implausible but sitting with him, I believed it. And I've felt it in my own business life. When you know a great employee, it starts you dreaming: What could we do together?

"The fellow I mentioned to you before, the one with the tea company, Dan Schweiker, told me that for years he had done all the selling for the company. He and his partner had been considering hiring some salespeople but decided to wait another year. Then right after they had made that decision, two competitors' salespeople called him and said they wanted to work there. Two. From different companies. On the same day. And he took that as a sign that maybe he should let go of some of the selling. So he hired them both and told them, 'I'm not going to try to tell you what to do. We're hiring you to learn from you.' That was one of the great leaps forward in the history of the company."

Max stopped and inhaled. "I get so excited talking about all this that I almost forget to breathe," he said. "See what I mean about 'magnetic'? Your competitors' best people coming to you. And you can even turn your customers into headhunters. Suzanne Mollerud, who runs a chain of hair salons in Minnesota called Kids' Hair, told me how one of her best stylists came to work there. The stylist called and said, 'One of my customers has been telling me about what a great atmosphere you have at your salons.'"

And he inclined his head to me as he said, "That's ..." and waited for me to finish. I wasn't sure if he was looking for No Ordinary Workplace or the Magnetic Workplace, so I mentioned both.

Then he circled right back to finish up a point. "And don't forget that part about Thomas saying, 'I can't pay you very much.' There's the magic of a gifted boss. Some companies pay exceptional wages in order to attract top performers—in the words of one executive, 'I don't know how to motivate employees, but I know how to bribe them.' But once employees have experienced a gifted boss, they know that they'll get something more important than a starting salary—a chance and a change. Knowing the gifted boss, they know they'll get opportunities, and trust that income will follow."

Max's Magnetic Workplace was interesting, in an academic way. After all, I was in the midst of a large corporation, tightly controlled by the management structure and by the Human Resources department. "It's a beautiful dream," I told him. "And maybe I should get out of corporate life and start up my own company again. But till I do, I don't see it happening."

Loving nothing more than a challenge, Max made a face and then told me to get out the list of traits. At the next stoplight he leaned over to point at the sheet I held, saying, "Let's jump ahead to this one. Yes, this is it. The example I have for this one comes from a man who was in the military. You think you don't have much latitude . . . HA!" And then he sat back to let me read the following.

> *The ordinary boss: has clear rules and ethics.*
> *The gifted boss: has few rules but high standards. (The best one-sentence*
> *summary of good management I've ever heard: "Be big about*
> *the petty stuff and be petty about the big stuff.")*

"Listen to the story of John Welker," Max said, wagging his head in a show of cockiness. "He's now a stockbroker with Merrill Lynch, but he had this realization during his days in the army. He was given the assignment of heading an artillery battalion stationed in Germany. Soon after arriving, he decided to test his troops by simulating an attack. In other words, a situation where the guns needed to be set up as quickly as possible.

"He issued the order to prepare to fire, then stood and watched.

Then stood and watched some more. His troops put on a bumbling display of incompetence. After half an hour, he walked away, his troops still struggling. It was *The Three Stooges Go to War*. A joke."

Although I'd never been in the military, I'd had enough employees to relate.

"So," Max continued, "what to do? Yell? Study procedure manuals? The next morning Welker called a veteran artillery officer and asked, 'How long should it take to set up guns?' The answer: 'About nine minutes.' And that morning Welker went to his troops and announced that they should figure out how to get the guns ready to fire in eight minutes. He didn't tell them how to do it—he established a standard and let them work it out. And a few days later, one of them came to him, trying not to smile, and said, 'Sir, we're ready for you to time us.' And of course they beat the time easily. That experience inspired Welker to replace a two-hundred-page procedure manual with a one-page list of standards. And within a year, his battalion was named the best of its type in the world."

Knowing he had gotten to me with that story, Max grinned and added, "Did you catch that? The best in the world. That incident changed Welker's life. He gave up on policy manuals in favor of standards—not rules, but definitions of excellence."

I liked the story and knew I could learn from it. But I told Max that I wasn't clear on the difference between a rule and a standard. And I also remembered how Max liked to belittle the whole planning and goal-setting process. So, just to provoke him, I told him it sounded like "goal setting" to me.

He did a long lip-farting exhalation. "Okay, it may seem like mere semantics—rules, goals, standards . . . same difference. No. *Rule* comes from the Latin *regula* for *rod*, as in a ruler. Rules are part of formal procedure, the currency of bureaucracy, and are, of course, 'made to be broken.' As for *goals*, the origin is unknown, presumed to be derived from some forgotten sport. It suggests a 'line' to cross, a possibility.

"Now, my young and I must say *cynical* friend, compare those two words to *standard*, which is not just a 'benchmark' but an 'upright support,' as in construction and as in a flagpole. *Standard* has two possible origins—the Frankish word, *standard*—that is, 'stand hard,' or Old French *estandard*—that is, 'rallying place.'

"A standard can shape a company and its employees. When I did some work for Procter & Gamble, the staff told me proudly of the company's standard for entering a new household product category: P & G's product would be introduced only if it could beat the existing category leader in a consumer test using unlabeled products. That simple statement shaped the entire company. It told the folks in R & D not to waste their time on 'me-too' products. It told the sales force that their time wouldn't be wasted hawking mediocrity. It eliminated countless debates and meetings. And it imbued the organization with a world-beater attitude.

"And that is the beauty of a standard. It *stands up* and proclaims: Here's what we *stand for*, the ground we *stand upon*; here's how we *stand apart* and *stand out*; and this is where we *stand together*."

Here he paused to give my knee another of his iron grips. He said with some emotion, "One standard is worth a thousand committee meetings."

He pointed to the sheet of traits that I still held and instructed me to write in a new one:

The ordinary boss: understands how to function within the bureaucracy.
The gifted boss: knows how to work outside the bureaucracy.

And after writing, he added, "Now, does your employer have more restrictions than the U.S. Army?"

"I think not."

"And could you not adopt standards for your division?"

"I already have some in mind."

At that he slapped me on the shoulder. "Now, that's my boy!"

Trying to join in with his mood, I said, "Just because I work in a bureaucracy doesn't mean I have to think like a bureaucrat."

"What you have to do is to think like an antibureaucrat. It's that glass rut I was talking about earlier. Your mind is being conditioned to think just like everyone else's around you. Nothing sinister about it, that's just the way it works. And so if you want to distinguish yourself, you have to make a conscious effort to do so. Just like you have to make a conscious effort to create a unique workplace."

Here we were, venturing into the lessons Max had taught me years before. I repeated back to him one of his favorite lines: "You can't get to 'better' without going through 'different.'"

He nodded. "By being a gifted boss you are going to create a workplace that sells great employees on the idea of working for you. And if you're going to sell, the best way to sell is via word of mouth. You need to give them something to talk about." And he sang, badly, some lines from the song "Something to Talk About." He got to the part where it goes, "How about love?" And then he said, "That is our goal here. We are talking about love. Not about benefits or 401(k)s—we're talking about love."

He pulled into a parking garage for a large complex called the Arizona Center, saying, "I thought we'd eat here, but these old bones are getting tired of sitting. Let's go for a stroll first." He instructed me to take along the list.

It was late afternoon as we left the parking garage, the sun sharp between shadows. We walked along the downtown streets, past the Herberger Theater with its line of statues of frolicking nudes, past Symphony Hall.

As we walked, I read aloud from Max's list.

The ordinary boss: has answers.
The gifted boss: has questions. (Understands that letting employees figure
out the answers is more important than the answer itself.)

This one seemed aimed at me. I said, "If you could show me how to stop being the department Answer Man, it would change my life overnight."

He laughed and said, "You're too easy. That one is . . ." And he snapped his fingers. "I learned that lesson from Peter Schutz, the former CEO of Porsche who I've told you about. I once complained to him that I was working too hard. He asked me how I spent my time, and I said 'Solving problems.' And he practically yelled at me, 'STOP DOING THAT!' I was falling into the same trap that you are now in. If people can come to you to get their problems solved, they'll just keep coming back. Why should they take the risk of solving problems? If you solve them, then you get the blame. And that's what most companies are about—avoiding blame."

This reminded me, I told Max, of an article I'd read that said the number one reason people say no to salespeople is the fear of making a mistake. And this had changed the way I sold my ideas to the company. I realized that while I was going on about the wonderful things we might accomplish with some new project, the executives were sitting there thinking only one thing: *What could go wrong?* So I'd learned to "inoculate" against fears by explaining how we could minimize any risk, especially the risk of management looking bad.

One of the things I'd learned from my previous conversations with Max was a motto that I used when presenting ideas: "People hate to change, but love to experiment." A change is a risk. An experiment is something you can undo, can walk away from wiser. So I'd learned to make new projects into experiments, usually with small pilot programs.

Max enjoyed hearing me feed back his insights, and put his arm around me. I felt like a character in a movie, walking through the twilight with this sage beside me.

"Now," he said, squeezing my shoulder before turning loose, "you have explained your own solution. When employees bring you their questions, what are your experiments?"

"Turn the tables and ask them the questions."

"Exactly. You could run a department by asking two questions all day long: 'Is there a better way?' and 'Is this the best you can do?' The best employees will tell you how their work could be better. And they will love you for insisting they do it. Which takes us to the next of the traits."

The ordinary boss: buys employees' time and effort.
The gifted boss: buys help.

When I looked up, Max had started in on what seemed to me to be an irrelevant digression, but he soon proved me wrong.

"You know those little news items where they go out to a church and show some everyday item where the face of Jesus or the Virgin Mary has appeared?" I nodded, chuckling at the abrupt shift in subject.

"Well, a few months back I was watching one such report and found myself admiring the warmth and earnestness of those who had come to visit, especially as compared to the know-it-all newscasters who had come to scoff. And that's when this thought occurred to me: You will only spot the face of Jesus in a tortilla if you spend a lot of time thinking about Jesus. Your tortilla is a mirror of your mind."

This was such a silly image that I had to smile, but Max was in a dreamy state, adding, "I knew, of course, that I had merely reinvented the Rorschach test. But doing so, I rediscovered the importance of prevailing perceptions, and how we must take care as to what we allow ourselves to dwell upon. All of which leads to an interesting workplace question: What's in your organization's mind?"

My answer was going to be "How to get out of work." But Max had meant it to be rhetorical, and he provided his own answer: "Our corporations train their employees to think about the corporation, about rules, and, as you were saying a minute ago, about what can go wrong. In other words, we bathe ourselves in bureaucracy and then expect people not to act like bureaucrats.

"So," he continued, "the job of a great boss becomes to manage the corporate version of the 'collective unconscious.' I once fell into a conversation with a doctor who told me that he'd gone through fourteen assistants in one year. None seemed to live up to his standards of patient care. Finally, he went to a friend, a surgeon whose office he had visited, and said, 'You have the most wonderful staff here. How do you do it?' The surgeon said that the candidates go through three interviews, not just with him but with the other staff members. But all three interviews only screened out candidates, setting the stage for a single question that determined who got hired. That question is, 'What compassion do you have to offer my patients?'

"Using that question, the doctor solved his turnover problem. Why? Because he was able to hire people who understood pain, who understood illness, and who wanted to do something about it. It seems so simple, doesn't it? Imagine a medical office full of people who radiate compassion. And now compare that mental picture to the typical behind-the-glass, fill-out-the-forms medicrats."

Max continued: "Not every business wants to put compassion first, of course. But every organization could go in search of a related trait—the willingness to help. Shame that most newspapers have stopped calling the job ads the Help Wanted section. I know when I hire someone it's *help* that I want. It's much easier to get employees than to get help. There's an entire philosophy of business in that single word *help*. Here's a two-word employee handbook: *just help*. And how's this for a two-word mission statement: *we help*."

He turned to me and I nodded in agreement.

He continued: "It's easy to spot an organization bathed in bureaucracy versus one bathed in helping. For instance, there's a health club near where I live, one of those giant ones, with an acre of chrome torture equipment in back and a sales operation in the front. On the wall near the sales desks is a sign: PLEASE DON'T ASK TO USE THE PHONES. If you care about helping your customers, and they repeatedly asked to use the phone, you'd install a phone for customers to use, right? That's just what they've done at Blockbuster Video, at least the one near my home. There's a phone that encourages you to call home and discuss movie choices. That's helping your customers.

"All of which reminds me," Max said, "of Jay Goltz, a man who turned a frame shop in Chicago into a ten-million-dollar business. Goltz argues that 'there is always a better answer than just yes.' He gives the example of the guy who moves to a new city and is trying to find an auto repair shop to service his Lotus. He calls several and asks each of them if they work on Lotuses. A few say yes, but then one says, 'Absolutely, we specialize in imports, and the shop's owner drives a Lotus.' Ah, a better answer. Any good employee will answer a question, but only a few actually understand the customer and truly seek to help.

"That is a trait of a great employee, of course. But it's the job of a gifted boss to find such people and to create an environment in which everyone is thinking about helping."

He stopped then and turned to me: "So, what compassion do you bring along to work? What preoccupies the mind of your division? That's what will be waiting for you in your tortilla." And then he laughed that great laugh of his and started walking again.

We walked on for another block, neither of us needing to talk. The air at dusk was somehow richer than usual and seemed worthy of taking in slowly and savoring. This serene mood was interrupted by Max saying, "Are we lost?"

"I don't think so. Isn't that next cross street the one that runs past the place where we're eating?"

He seemed a bit disappointed by this answer. I guessed that Max is the sort who enjoys being lost. He said, "Let's ask, just to be certain." And with that he wandered up to a sidewalk café and started talking to a tableful of businessmen. Max asked directions, but that merely started a conversation, and we ended up sitting in with them, sharing their pitcher of margaritas.

Refreshed by our break, we resumed our walk. The night air was cooler, but it still felt thick and welcoming. Passing under a streetlamp, I read the next trait out loud for Max.

The ordinary boss: allows you to keep growing.
The gifted boss: kicks you up to the next rung in your personal ladder of evolution.

Max started by quoting a comedian named Brian Kiley: *"I went to a bookstore the other day. I asked the woman behind the counter where the self-help section was. She said, 'If I told you, that would defeat the whole purpose.'"*

"I love that line," Max continued, "because one of the distinguishing traits of the gifted boss—a trait that would justify by itself the use of the word *gifted*—is the 'feel' for bringing along an employee. Often an employee is hired not for current skills but for potential. The gifted boss is like a chess master, operating several moves in the future, sensing just when an employee can succeed at something new, often before the employee knows it." He had me stop at the next streetlamp to show me that he'd put several subheadings under this trait. Max gave an example to go with each one. Here's my best recollection of what he said:

MAKING PEOPLE UNCOMFORTABLE

"I talked with Angelo Petrilli," Max said, "when he was a vice president of one of the divisions of Bell Sports. He said of his employees, 'I find people with heart—you better hire it, because you sure can't put it in there.' And working for Petrilli is not for the faint of heart because he says, 'I believe in putting people in situations a little above their heads. Put them where they are uncomfortable. I'm not looking for maintenance people.' In fact, he takes comfort as his signal to introduce change. He said, 'For instance, I had an employee who gave a presentation to me. Marvelous. I told her, "Come with me and *you* present it to the CEO." She said, "I can't do that." And I told her, "It's not that you can't do it, you just don't know you *can* do it." Or, if I have staff people who get comfortable, I'll have them work directly with a client. They get comfortable with that, and I have them go along on sales calls. Later I might have them make some sales calls, ones where their expertise is a good match.'"

Max added, "What Petrilli wants is for his staff to be on a personal adventure as well as a corporate one. You've heard that expression 'wheels-within-wheels'; well, the gifted boss offers 'adventures-within-adventures.' The company or the department is experimenting, and within it, the boss is pushing the employees into their personal adventures. Earlier I said that you could manage with the question, 'Is that the best you can do?' Well, I guess we should modify that to include the possibility of not accepting the first yes. The great boss knows how to expect more than the employees expect of themselves."

PASSING THE BATON

"One trait of gifted bosses is letting go of authority. Indeed, they don't just let go of it, they shove it over to someone else. Nancy Loftin is the chief legal counsel for APS, a major utility company here in Arizona. Her predecessor was promoted to CFO, so he was still around and seemingly still available for legal opinions. Loftin told me, 'Not only had the other executives relied upon his advice for years, but it was quite a change for the company to have a woman in my position. Besides, he was a genius, and had a photographic memory. So it's not surprising that people still went to him with questions. But he wouldn't answer them. He'd just say, "I don't know—check with Nancy." He knew the answer—oh, he *knew*. Saying he didn't was his way of passing the baton.'"

As we waited for a streetlight, Max turned to me to say, "It sounds like an easy matter, to refer questions to the new person, but imagine the self-confidence it takes to say, 'I don't know,' and thus end any second-guessing. And speaking of self-confidence, the old boss built up Loftin's confidence with other quiet refusals. She would go to him to try to get him to intervene in tricky corporate matters, and he would say, 'You can handle it.' She said of those occasions, 'It sounds dismissive, but it wasn't. It was his vote of confidence. And I admired him so much that if he had confidence in me, I had to have confidence in me too.'"

WIN BY LOSING

As we continued walking, Max asked me if I was ready to have a real challenge to my own self-confidence. I said I didn't think so, which made him punch my shoulder. "In that case," he said, "put this one away for later. But you should know that the most daring way of challenging employees is simply by being wrong, by losing an argument to them."

Max told me he'd learned that principle from Ken Donahue, the president of a division of Teledyne, headquartered in Philadelphia. He explained as follows:

> "Ken said a remarkable thing: 'Sometimes I'll have an idea, and the employees will raise issues. And sometimes the facts are with the employees. And I change my mind, drop my sword, and support them. Once you do that, they know it's okay. If you ignore them, and bully through, they think, 'Why should I disagree and end up with emotional scars?' But if they see you admit you're wrong, they learn that it's worthwhile to challenge you. And if they see you change, they'll do it too.'
>
> "In other words, being wrong—and admitting it—becomes just another way the gifted boss develops and motivates great employees.
>
> "And all of this can lead to the possibility that an employee who doesn't start 'great' can be challenged to greatness by a skilled leader."

This took us to the last item on Max's list.

The ordinary boss: seeks team players.
The gifted boss: seeks allies.

"I propose," said Max, pointing to a restaurant, "that we delay the last item till after dinner. Once we talk about great employees, and the alliances they create with gifted bosses, you'll know what you have to do." He turned to me, and I nodded.

"So it's dinner and a discussion of what it takes to be a great employee—both so you can spot them, and so you can be one."

It felt odd to think of myself as an employee. As soon as I'd risen into management, I'd thought of myself as a manager, as a leader. I never gave any thought to what it took to be a better employee, a better follower. But I didn't have time to contemplate this because Max had stopped just outside the entrance to ask me, "So did anything we've talked about strike you as helpful, or have you just been humoring the old guy?"

"Max," I said earnestly, "yesterday I didn't even know it was there, but now I can feel that glass rut closing in on me. Without meaning to, I devoted all my leadership skills and creativity to accomplishing this: an above-average environment for average employees." Max applauded. "And now," I added over his clapping, "I'm determined to go back and create the best place for the best people to work."

The Ordinary Versus
the Great Employee

We ate dinner at Sam's Café, which is on the ground floor of the Arizona Center, one of those giant complexes of offices and retail. Max asked for a quiet spot, and we were seated off to one side of the outdoor dining, looking out on a tree arbor that seemed out of place but tranquil all the same.

When he got around to describing his research on bosses and employees, he told me that he had gone in search of gifted bosses, and then asked them what they looked for in their best employees. "So," he concluded, "my sample was only of gifted bosses. I'm not saying that these are the qualities that every boss craves—then again, who cares what the 'average boss' wants?—these are the traits you need if you are to attract the attention of a great boss. And, by the way, as we shall see in the next phase, that great bosses don't hire employees; they 'talent-hunt' those 'Wild Brains' I was telling you about."

I wanted to hear more about the "talent-hunting," but Max wouldn't be dissuaded: "No, no, no. You mustn't get in a hurry on this one. First, you must be great and then you shall be sought after. Which reminds me of a television executive, Grant Tinker, who had just taken over one of the networks and was asked how he planned to make his network number one. He said simply, 'First we will be best, and then we will be first.' Isn't that marvelous?"

I agreed. But I was eager to move on, so I asked Max, "So what does it take to be 'best' among employees?"

"First, there is the obvious quality—the great ones are exceptionally productive. Which doesn't necessarily mean they work the longest hours. They aren't always the coffee-makers, first one in, but they produce results."

"No surprise there."

"Exactly, and that's why I'm not going to waste a lot of time talking about it. Being a great employee isn't about 'grinding' as much as it is about 'soaring.' We've already said that a great boss and a great employee want the same things—one, freedom; two, a change; and three, a chance. And by defining the great bosses, we have already defined the great employee. In fact, one of the joys of an alliance between two talented people is that the status distinctions fall away, the two merge."

Max gave me a look, and said, "Well, I can see I'm boring you with philosophy—what you want are specifics. And specifics you'll get. First, let's talk about *freedom*—that is, the no-management employee."

Max turned earnest as he said, "The first freedom is trust, knowing that the work will get done and done at least as well as if you had done it yourself. Look at these comments." And he showed me the first list of remarks he had written down, quotes taken verbatim from gifted bosses describing their best employees.

The great ones never let themselves do second-rate work.

If you're in a bind, there they are, jumping in and helping.
You don't even have to ask, *they just know.*

The best employees are their own worst critics—you never have to criticize them, only congratulate.

They dream your dream—you know they have the same agenda you do.

Great employees aren't like children—Did you make your bed? No, with great employees you know that *you are always being helped.*

With them, you don't have to watch your back—they're watching it for you.

Max continued: "The second freedom is handing over parts of your job. The great employees have at least one skill superior to the boss's, and/or serve as a check on the boss's work."

The best employees tap you on the shoulder and ask what you can hand off to them.

My best employee was everything I wasn't, and vice versa.

They tell me what we need, not me telling them.

Great employees have standards that lift us all up. We don't want to disappoint them.

The great ones have a real emotional investment with the customers and understand the customers better than anyone else in the organization.

"It takes a gifted boss to have employees like these, because they are themselves leaders. Other employees look to them and go to them. A boss can feel irrelevant, unless that boss is doing gifted work, creating the magnetic workplace. Agreed?"

I nodded, although inside I was shaking my head, thinking of how far my current employees were from these ideals.

"The next thing," Max said, "that great employees want, and that great bosses love to see, is *change*. They are *'what's next?'* people who are eager for morning. But they don't just sit back in the audience to change, they are onstage. Here are some of the comments I wrote down."

> The best employees seem to perform best in the midst of problems or chaos. They bring a calm to the group. Their self-confidence is contagious.

> The best ones "crystallize" information. They don't talk in technical lingo, they present the options.

> My best employees were the ones who would *show me the possibilities*.

Max tapped the page and said, "Don't you love that one about 'show me the possibilities?' It reminds me of that phrase from some movie: 'Show me the money.'"

"Jerry Maguire."

"Yes. That's the one. And when an employee shows you the possibilities, it's the same thing. That comment came from John Genzale, our poetry reading lion. And after he said that about 'possibilities,' I remember he went on to compare a great employee to an architect who you hire to build your new warehouse. You specify a big box, but a good architect will come back and say, 'This is what you want me to do, but I could also do this ... or this.' The best will open you up."

I added, "When I read the ones about adversity, I thought of a quote you told me, one from Golda Meir: 'A new problem is as good as a vacation.'"

"Wouldn't it be great for you to do a role reversal on your staff. You were telling me how your employees line up outside your door, bringing you their problems. Imagine walking into the office of a great employee and saying, 'We've got a problem' and hearing, 'I'll take care of it. Don't worry.' And you wouldn't worry. It would be like those great P. G. Wodehouse novels, the ones where Bertie is always getting into a jam and running to his butler, Jeeves, for a solution. Jeeves is the quintessential great employee."

I had no idea what he was talking about, but I nodded.

Max then took us back to his list of quotes. "And the last set is about wanting a *chance*. We covered this pretty thoroughly in the gifted bosses section, but here are a few of the sentiments directly from bosses."

> They want to be tested, to almost defy you to give them something they can't handle.

> The great employees are confident employees—they seek out measurement, and want to be paid accordingly.

> The very best are always entrepreneurial. You have to come up with new projects just to keep them interested.

This last section disappointed me because it seemed so distant from my situation as to be irrelevant. I told my companion, "I know you talked about this earlier, but I'm still unclear on how I can get—or give—chunks of responsibility within an organization."

"The best employees," Max began, "are show-offs. They know they're good and want a chance to prove it. They want to get into the game. It's not easy figuring out how to give employees that chance. You somehow have to figure out how to harness entrepreneurial energy without them leaving the company. It's not uncommon to hear a manager say, 'Hire good people and get out of their way.' But many who mouth that cliché only pretend to hand over authority. They continue to make all the decisions while pretending not to, saying to employees, 'It's up to you, *but what I'd do is . . .*'"

I jumped in to relate an instance where a boss had said just that to me, and I had decided to go against his advice. After all, I figured, he said it was up to me. He never forgave me. Never trusted me again. And I soon left.

Max said, "I wish you could work for Larry Tree, a gifted boss who runs EMS—Equipment Maintenance Services—a company that cares for giant industrial equipment in several western states. He literally got out of the way." Max then told me this about Larry Tree:

"While EMS has hundreds of employees, they work in various facilities scattered throughout the West, and Tree has decentralized his business to the point where the headquarters staff consists of just four people. And one of his facilities kicked him out of their building. He had his corporate office in one of the regional facilities, and when they needed more space, he moved his staff into a trailer.

"And, truly having gotten out of the way, Tree is free to devote his time to strategy, acquisitions and to what he calls 'culture development.' He says, 'We are always working on the culture. It's better to be consciously incompetent than unconsciously competent.' And then he laughed and asked me, 'Does that make sense?' Now that's my kind of boss.

"Part of that culture is Tree telling the employees 'Live your dream.' He wants to know the personal dreams of employees and then tries to find a place where they align with the company goals.

"He has harnessed the energies of the entrepreneurial employees by dividing the company into pieces, and regarding the employees who run them as 'CEOs.' One of them, who runs the Wyoming facility, started the company as an hourly employee. Tree says, 'He was a machinist, hired by someone who left the company long ago. I saw his talents, and I encouraged him to dream. I kept finding new assignments for him, to test him, because I wanted to see just how good he could be. He's now CEO of a ten-million-dollar facility and brings twenty percent to the bottom line. I don't think I could do that.' Now that's a great employee, allowed to blossom working with a gifted boss."

But I was back to my old concern, that the example he'd given had little relation to my situation, working inside a company where I had little latitude. Max laughed, saying, "You have a latitude attitude." And he gave my knee another of his viselike grips. The poor thing was starting to be a tad tender.

"So here's an example you'll have to like," Max said. "David Wing spent most of his career managing retail stores and now runs Retail Advisors, a consulting business for retailers. This is what he tells store owners . . . I'm quoting Wing:

"'Treat people as "employees" and that's what you get. And they leave as soon as they can get fifty cents an hour more somewhere else. But treat them as coworkers and everything changes. Make them part of the business, not just employees. You do that by giving them a part of the operation to run. For instance, you put one employee in charge of displays, or men's shirts, or the check-in process. And you get them to learn by teaching. I'd have weekly meetings with discussion topics. I'd say to an employee, "I want to have a meeting on displays, and I want you to run it." Once I had an employee who had a gift for turning returns into new sales. If someone wanted to return an item, they'd always walk out with even more than they brought back. So I told her I wanted her to teach everyone else to do it. She had to figure out just what she was doing in order to teach it. She made us all better.' "

Max waited for my reaction, and I admitted that it *did* apply to my situation. So Max elaborated: "In fact, Wing argues that giving employees 'ownership,' and the chance to prove themselves, is so potent a motivator that withdrawing it becomes the only 'punishment' necessary. He says, 'Say "Jane" screws up to the point that you have to do something. Move her out of her area. She'll come in to work and she'll keep looking over at "John" in her area, thinking, My God, he's touching my merchandise. He's messing up my displays. She'll never make that mistake again.' "

Then Max concluded by saying, "Most employees want more responsibility and more authority—that is, they want a promotion and a raise. But the great employees want literal or figurative ownership. They know they're good, and want the chance to prove it."

During the conversation, we had eaten a first-rate dinner, and we were having coffee when Max recalled for me one of his familiar themes. He said, "Most workplaces are like grade school. A few are like college." He added, "One is about rules and about prodding; the other is about freedom and discovery, about pulling . . .

or at least it should be. Don't get me started on the fact that most universities are not much more than job training centers. Which reminds me of an example that involved a literal college."

Max's example was of Norm Brinker, who created and built the Steak & Ale chain, next presided over the turnaround at Burger King, then built Brinker International (Chili's restaurants, plus Cozymel's, On the Border, and Macaroni Grill). This is how Max told his story:

"Brinker only looked for a job once—when he was graduating from San Diego State. He was every recruiter's dream—a personable young man who on one hand had been on the Olympic equestrian team, but on the other hand worked his way through school selling Cutco knives. So Brinker had plenty of job prospects, including offers from P&G and Bethlehem Steel. Day after day he came to his wife and said, 'Well, honey, they offered me a job but it just didn't sound like fun—so I said, "Probably not."'

"Instead of going with a major corporation, Brinker chose a local chain of coffee shops. I asked him why. He smiled as he recalled the man who would become his mentor. He said, 'All the other people from the big companies were formal, very well dressed. I went to meet with Bob Peterson, and he was wearing a brown plaid shirt and brown slacks, no tie. And he asked me, "Why should I invite you to share my dream?" Then we went into the kitchens where the employees were experimenting with new recipes, and you could feel the energy in the room. They were laughing, having fun.'

"And Brinker found himself trying to talk Peterson into hiring him—at a salary well below what he'd been offered by the major companies.

"I asked how his wife had reacted to the decision to go with laughter instead of income. 'She understood that I never worried about money. My family was poor, poor . . . but happy. And so I've always made career decisions by asking myself, Is this going to make me happier?'"

Max bounced in his seat, expanding on "happier" as the critical job search criterion. Then he continued:

"And it was a profitable decision for Brinker, as it turned out. The dreamer in plaid was also starting a hamburger chain, Jack in the Box, and he eventually let Brinker buy a piece of the new company.

"With the profits from that piece of Jack in the Box, Brinker decided to try going into business for himself. So he opened a standard coffee shop and thereby made the typical mistake of creating a typical business. And, not surprisingly, he soon grew bored. So he tried real estate, and then decided to open a new restaurant. This time he was adamant that it would be fun—for him, the employees and the customers.

"Brinker decided that if he wanted to create a new atmosphere, he'd try a new kind of employee. Until then, restaurants were mostly staffed by middle-aged men and women with low expectations and tired feet. Brinker decided he wanted younger employees, with enough style to pull off wearing Old English costumes, and enough vigor to create a new atmosphere. So he called the nearest college, Southern Methodist University, and told the placement office that he planned to hire fifteen students. The woman at the placement office was cooperative until he mentioned the name, Steak & Ale. When she learned there was liquor

THE GIFTED BOSS ★ 55

involved, she backed out. That's when Brinker got in his car and drove to a fraternity house. He showed pictures of the restaurant and shared his dreams, and got his staff.

"By seeking to create an environment that appealed to him, Norm Brinker invented a new segment of the restaurant business that came to be known as 'casual dining.' And he created a lively work environment where the great employees of the future—kids still in college—could be current great employees. What he had done, without intending to, was to tap into the needs of the best employees. They know they can always get a job and make money. So what do they look for when choosing a workplace? Exceptional employees are drawn to exceptional environments."

Max let me contemplate that story while he drank his coffee. Then he added one more observation about Brinker's restaurant: "Notice that even with part-time restaurant employees, the gifted boss went out in search of great employees instead of sitting back and hoping they'd turn up. This is a case of a great boss figuring out where to go to find employees with the talents he wanted and then courting them, romancing a lively work environment."

Max stretched and said he was ready to head back to the house. "Speaking of romance," he added, "tomorrow we will explore all the amazing ways that gifted bosses find and court highly talented employees."

I saw a chance to provoke him and I took it. "Hold on. What's this 'find and court'? I thought if you created a magnetic workplace then great employees come to you."

"Ah, you've been listening after all. I'm flattered. And on the morrow you will come to understand that, yes, if you create a magnetic workplace, *some* great employees will come to you. Some just appear, usually when some idiot boss has not known how to handle real talent. But there are plenty of great employees who never even think of changing jobs. Literally. It just doesn't occur to them. Some of the best of the best are like that. You have to seek them out. And the only chance you have with them is a workplace suited to them, aka the Best Place for the Best People to Work."

The Courtship Rituals

The next morning I came downstairs and found Max cooking breakfast. He was talking on a portable phone, laughing and cursing and dicing fruit at the same time. He had waffles going, and eggs. He saw me and effortlessly brought me into the work and then into his conversation, telling the person on the other end about our evening, quoting me and making me sound profound.

We sat in a breakfast room worthy of a magazine feature—colors everywhere, indoors and out, windows on two sides, beveled glass insets sending light shafts coming in to cross at angles like swords of musketeers. Later, when I said as much, Max laughed and showed me where the homeowner had a copy of a homes magazine on display, and there was our room. And that morning, as I sat down with Max, I felt as if we were worthy of photo documentation, and silently wished they'd come back to take pictures of us.

But it wasn't long before Max was back to workplaces. He said that in order to understand how gifted bosses and great employees come together, we would need to consider three of the "Six Realities" simultaneously. He gave me another of his worksheets, with these principles:

2. Gifted bosses don't just hire employees, they acquire allies.

3. Great employees don't have jobs, they have talents. They enter the job market once (if at all), and thereafter their talents are spotted, courted and won over.

4. Great bosses and employees often reverse the typical job search: instead of the employee doing the "hunting," it's the boss. The process more resembles a "talent search" than a "job market."

THE ALLIANCE

"I suppose I should begin," Max began, "by explaining why I use the term 'allies.' Given the fact that gifted bosses and great employees want the same thing from the workplace, it might seem that they should be called a workplace 'team.'

"You can, of course, call any group of people who report to one person a 'team'—for instance, the president's cabinet is given that label, although the members of that 'team' rarely work together; instead, they often come together to compete for resources. Likewise, the team image does not fit many of the great bosses or employees that I met. There aren't many 'group decisions,' because the gifted boss is more like an enlightened monarch than a team leader. And while gracious, helpful and cooperative, the great employees are individualists with unique talents. They are not interchangeable. And they grow impatient with committee members—and let's face it, the majority of workplace teams are just committees.

"Instead of 'teams,' the 'alliances' I observed were something other than mere employment. And it wasn't 'mentoring' because it wasn't that one-sided. It's more like a new and improved form of kinship."

He stopped to frown at me, then shook his head, acting hurt and disappointed. "Every time I get the least bit philosophical, you just tune out."

"No. Absolutely not. New form of kinship. I'm right with you."

"Well, let me give you an example, one of my favorites. And it comes from a large corporation, larger than yours, so you can't fall into your 'latitude attitude.' It's one example of a man with the fortune and skill to have worked for a great boss and with a great employee. It's a long story, so enjoy your waffle.

"In the early eighties, when he was a manager in the communications group for the videotape division of 3M, Don Linehan met his first—and only—great boss, an Italian executive who was an assistant to a high-level executive. The Italian, Edoardo Pieruzzi, had been brought in to work at 3M's St. Paul headquarters as part of an informal 'grooming' process. And that's where Pieruzzi discovered Linehan, an energetic employee who wanted to bring new life to the division, and who had ideas about how to do it. And so Pieruzzi made Linehan an ally—not by asking for help, but by giving it.

"Linehan described their early relationship: 'He was very political. He charmed the CEO and all the other top executives. His wife stayed in Italy, so he was free to work twenty-four hours, and to socialize with the executives. He was always available if an executive wanted to talk. And he would plan vacations to Europe for them— arrange every detail. So he got to know everything going on with the executives. And he would apply his political craftiness to my projects. He took my ideas and moved them to the bank.'

"In other words, the role of the gifted boss in this alliance was to be an *idea salesman.* He didn't manage the idea process, he was the agent for the department. Imagine the energy that is unleashed simply from knowing that good ideas are going to be sold to the head of the division. What better way to reinforce creativity than to see ideas blossom into innovations.

"Eventually, Pieruzzi became the VP of the video division and promoted Linehan to be the head of the communications department. One of Linehan's ideas that Pieruzzi sold to upper management was that 3M become a major Olympic sponsor. This would be a fateful project, for it was where Linehan would encounter his own great employee.

"But I'm getting ahead of myself. First, Pieruzzi was promoted again, this time to a job back in Europe. He soon had Linehan come over on business, and once there, took him to dinner at his private club in Brussels. It was there he told Linehan, 'I want you to be head of communications for Europe.'

"Linehan eagerly agreed, and with his wife and son soon moved to Brussels. What followed was what Linehan calls 'the richest years of our lives. My son went to an international school, and his class would travel by train all over Europe. When his class studied the art of Florence, they went to Florence. When my son gave his class report on Michelangelo's *David*, he gave it standing in front of the statue. My son cried when we came back. We all did.'

"What brought Linehan back was a promotion, and a

job back at headquarters in St. Paul. And while he no longer reported to Pieruzzi, they remained allies. Linehan says of him, 'I still thought of him as my surrogate boss. I'd call and tell him a problem and he'd say, "Here's what's going on, and here's what you must do." He knew everything about upper management and was more valuable as a non-boss than a boss. He was my biggest supporter of global projects, and I was his biggest supporter anytime he wanted my help.'

"Pieruzzi was a mentor to Linehan, and coach and father figure and brother and friend. Instead of 'blood brothers' they are 'talent brothers'—committed not just to the other, but also to the other's potential and fulfillment.

"But let's back up to how Linehan found his own great employee.

"When Linehan put together 3M's Olympic sponsorship, there were sixty-five countries involved. Each country had its own program—advertising, promotional tie-ins and using the Games for relationship building with major customers or suppliers. Out of these sixty-five programs, one was special. It was the Canadian program, run by a young 3M employee named Bruce Moorhouse. What impressed Linehan was this: 'Not only that he used his resources wisely and creatively, but he was able to track changes in numbers. He was able to measure what the program actually accomplished. His became the model for the world.'

"And when Linehan returned from Europe, he wanted to put together a new worldwide image campaign. And so he created a task force of eight countries, and included Canada just so he could see more of Bruce Moorhouse's work. 'I had this major program in mind,' Linehan said, 'and I wanted him to be the cornerstone. It took almost a year to bring him in.' And as we shall see, the statement 'bring him in' is the sort of language that a gifted boss uses to describe the hiring of a great employee. The metaphors often involved 'searching' or 'hunting': the great employees were far more often the hunted than the hunters.

"And what made the young Canadian a great employee? In Linehan's words, 'You gave him a project—or okayed one he suggested—and *knew* that it would be on time, on budget, and top quality. And always with a twist, something original, a mark of individuality that made it his. That was his *brand.*'

"Interesting that Linehan, a man who made a career out of building brands for one of the most admired companies in the world, would speak of an employee's talents as a 'brand.' We often hear the advice that every employee thinks of his or her career as a 'business,' but I prefer Linehan's notion of a brand, because it suggests being one of many, and thus calling out for differentiation and image building.

"Besides the now-familiar theme of self-reliance, there is the other theme of kinship: Linehan says that he worried about Moorhouse, and often pleaded with him to work fewer hours—'mothering' him, in a sense.

"But there is another employee trait that is less often remarked upon, and it's important here because it suggests an awareness of the importance of the relationship. Don Linehan, perhaps thinking of his own dinner in Brussels, took Moorhouse to dinner at the Waldorf to offer him the position at headquarters. Linehan knows the date: September seventeenth. He says, 'I know the date because he never let me forget it. He would tell me, "I honor that date. Thank you for hiring me. I can't believe I have this job." And he would also say, "I'll never leave, not as long as you're here."' Isn't that great? No wonder Linehan says of his great employee, 'He was a joy. A jewel.'"

Max nodded to indicate that he was finished. The story had quite an impact on me because it was just the sort of "only connect" relationship that was missing from my own work life. I could only imagine the powerful emotions of aligning myself with someone above and below, knowing that all three of us were looking out for one another. I said, "I hope that sort of thing is possible where I work. I'm afraid we aren't 3M."

"Don't worry. Yes, the quality of people at 3M is extraordinarily high. But with that in mind, I think that there's one more lesson in Don Linehan's story. In his decades at 3M, he had dozens of good employees and one great one. And he counted them up for me, and he had fourteen bosses, but formed an alliance with just one. One. Of course, maybe his standards were raised by being at such a magnetic place. Even so, the point is that alliances are too rare. But you will find them if you believe in them, if you long for them, and devote yourself to being worthy of them."

"You make it sound almost mystical."

"Not mystical, at least not to me. Maybe a 'high calling.' A different class . . . a 'noblesse oblige'? Those musketeers you mentioned would understand the rare combination of solemn duty and playfulness that grows out of a deep professional kinship. I once tried to write a family motto and came up with this: 'To live with honor and dignity, and not be too damn sanctimonious about it.' That's the same sort of feeling you get from these alliances."

"I want one . . . or two or three," I insisted.

"Well, the easiest place to start is with finding a great employee you can practice being gifted on. You told me before that the changes you intend to make will scare off some of your current employees. Let's talk about how you'll replace them."

THE SPOTTING AND COURTING

Max began by quoting the great coach Don Shula when he was asked about the role of "luck" in his victories. Shula had replied, "Sure, luck means a lot. Not having a good quarterback is bad luck."

Max explained: "Gifted bosses are not content to sit back and hope that great employees are sent over by Human Resources. They are masters of spotting and courting talent." And then he gave me some examples.

The "Mole"

"There's an architect named Randy Chamberlain—fascinating man—who runs Habitat, a company that operates throughout the country, designing retail stores, restaurants, sales offices, signs, model homes."

Max was in ecstasy, describing the creativity of Habitat's projects. Then he said, "A few years back, one of the company's major clients was a homebuilder whose marketing director was a former accountant, Paul Brunoforte. Working on Brunoforte's projects, Randy Chamberlain had a feeling about him. As he told me, 'You have to develop the ability to look into a second level, to see people at another level of reality.' And he came to believe that he'd spotted the ideal person to bring financial structure to Habitat."

Grabbing my forearm, he added, "But he also knew that Brunoforte had no interest in leaving his employer, which was twenty times larger than Habitat. So Randy Chamberlain undertook a talent courtship. For instance, when Habitat fell behind schedule on one of Brunoforte's projects, Chamberlain and his staff worked through the weekend, installing signs in time for the opening of a new model home complex. Not only did they work through the weekend, but through a storm. Chamberlain took photos of his exhausted team and gave them to Brunoforte. 'I wanted him to see the pride we had in the company,' Chamberlain said. 'I wasn't trying to show him what we went through, but who we were. I was courting him.' He's the only executive I've met who actually used the word *courting*—and it fits perfectly."

Max continued: "Anyway, Chamberlain held off on speaking to Brunoforte about working together. For two years, he held off. He told me, 'I was waiting for the right timing. I knew other people who knew Paul. I even had a spy in the company. He was to advise me when the time was right to approach him. And one day I got a call: "You ought to talk to Paul today." And I did.'

Max ended his story theatrically, poking the air. "Paul Brunoforte is now president of Habitat."

As I listened to Max, I could see how the word *courtship* applied. I'd met a few people in my life who'd told me romantic stories along the lines of, "I saw her across the park one day and knew she was the one for me. Three years later we married." Not having experienced such a revelation, I suspected it was some sort of hormonal coincidence, a chemical version of a lunar eclipse. But here was a business leader following the courtship model. Taken together with the 3M guys, I was beginning to see that Max was right when he accused me of going into the game with a team of "walk-ons." And at that instant it hit me, a cold fear: What if some of the other division heads in the company were finding employees the way Max was describing? What if comparable divisions at competitors were out "courting" the best talent? If so, what was I getting? Leftovers? The best employees never got to the labor pool where I went for employees. No wonder that despite all my efforts to bring innovation to our division, we still didn't "dazzle" the way I hoped we would. Max had my full attention.

The "Warehouse"

"This is another of my favorite examples," Max said. "Bobette Gorden now runs a speakers bureau called NewInformation Presentations. Before starting her company, she was a sales rep for radio stations, and she recalled for me how it was she came to work for a gifted boss.

> "'He was the manager for a radio station, one of the biggest in town. And I went to talk to him about a job, although he didn't have an opening. He called the head of another station—his best friend—and said he was sending me over. And I started working there. Later, I found out that he knew his best friend was looking for work and would be leaving, sooner or later. And so he put me there, let me get some experience and watched to see if he was right about me. He followed my progress, stayed in touch. Then, a year later, hired me—right after his friend resigned. He let someone else train me, and at the same time, he warehoused me, till he could bring me over.'

"Isn't that great?" Max said. "First we have one boss who spends two years bringing someone in, using a 'mole' to choose the right time. And now we have another boss who 'warehouses' an employee for a year. This is not your ordinary job market, is it?"

And with that Max slapped the table, saying, "Oh, I just remembered another good one. This has the record for the longest courtship I've encountered. Have you heard of a company called Solectron?"

"Sounds familiar. Didn't they win a Baldridge Award?"

"Good. Yes. Two of them, in fact. It's a five-billion-dollar-a-year business, but few people have heard of Solectron because they don't have their own brands; they manufacture products for other companies. But here's the story: A man named Winston Chen worked at IBM for many years, and got to be close to his boss, Ko Nishimura. Well, Chen takes the job running Solectron, at the time a small company. But after he leaves IBM, he still maintains his friendship with his old boss. The two of them frequently have lunch or dinner, and Chen keeps pulling his old boss in—maybe I should say 'reeling him in.' Here is how Ko Nishimura described to me his relationship with Chen during the ten years they did not work together:

"'He started out by asking me for my advice—"Gee, what do you think?" or "Gee, what should I do about this—any suggestions?" Like he needed my advice. And somewhere during the ten years, his question changed to "Gee, why don't you help me run the company?"

"'But IBM had been good to me. They paid for me to get a doctorate at Stanford, something I never could have done otherwise. And I continued to learn. I had commitments. But by the mid-eighties, I felt I couldn't contribute any more . . . structure issues. I began to feel that I could help most by leaving. And so when Winston brought up again about me helping him run the company, I showed an interest. He said, "Come over and we'll figure out who'll do what." And I did. He was the boss and I was chief operating officer, and that was fine with me.'"

Max tapped my arm, adding, "Do you see how Chen kept involved with his old boss? How Chen educated Nishimura about

Solectron, not by pushing information on him, but by asking for advice? That's how the best salespeople sell, by the way—with questions. And notice how Chen kept the job offer open for ten years, till Ko was ready to take it? And how he custom fit the job to this old friend? Eventually Chen retired, and Nishimura replaced him as CEO and then chairman. In the years since Nishimura came, the company has grown from less than a hundred million dollars in revenues, to over five billion. And yet Nishimura remains modest, giving credit to his old employee/boss, saying, 'I just continued what he started.'"

I appreciated the story but wasn't eager to get involved in decade-long courtships. "Does it always take so long?" I asked, trying not to sound pleading.

Max smiled. "My impatient young friend. Well, yes and no. The idea is that you are always looking for talent. Your job as a gifted boss is to be a talent scout. And once you spot talent, you start to build a relationship. So it might take years to spot the right person and years to build a relationship. Once you have the process going, it's going—there's a 'pipeline' of job candidates you're watching. And then it just happens naturally. For instance Dave Ridley, the VP of marketing for Southwest Airlines, told me that he'd been very impressed by one of the interns that worked in his department one summer. But, no openings that summer. Ridley kept in touch with the kid. Two years later, he had a perfect fit and finally brought him in. It can happen overnight, or it can take a decade."

I told Max that I could picture myself creating a file on every talented person in my industry. That I was not just a scout, but the Director of Player Personnel.

Max replied, "You just reminded me of a great conversation I had with Lou Holtz, the football coach. Let me digress a second to tell you about the gifted boss in his own career: Woody Hayes.

Holtz told me a number of stories about being an assistant to Hayes, but the most striking was that the whole time he knew him, Hayes turned down every raise he was offered, saying, 'Give it to the assistants, they have families to raise.' Can you imagine?"

"No," I said simply.

Max smiled. "We have miles to go. Anyway, back to hiring. Holtz told me this:

"'You can't just wait till there's an opening and say, "Who can we hire?" That's how you end up with a group of second-stringers. Say you hire ten guys. If you're lucky, five are good. So all the responsibility gravitates to the five. They resent it. And they are also the ones who are attractive to other schools. So you end up replacing them with five more. And, say, two of those are good. Over time, you end up with all second-stringers.'"

"So," I asked, "what did Holtz recommend? Do you hire twenty?"

"No," Max countered quickly, then pulled a face, reconsidering. "Well, in a way, I guess it was a bigger number than that. What Holtz did was keep a hiring list. On it were prospects who would fit every job he had. For someone to make the list was like being halfway to hired—although nobody knew about the existence of that list. Remember, these jobs weren't even open; but he kept the list, just in case. Whenever he'd hear about a good assistant, he'd keep an eye on the guy, try to get to know him well enough to know if he wanted to work with him, and to know how to win him over. So when an opening appeared, Holtz knew the man he wanted and how to court him. He knew who wanted to be a head coach and who wanted to go to the NFL and so on. He didn't say, 'Come and help me,' but 'Here's how I can help you get what you want.' And he established a track record of doing just that. Holtz has former assistants all over the NCAA and NFL."

My first reaction was to think that it would be a mistake to let a great assistant go, but then it occurred to me that it would be a lot easier to help employees move on if you had a list of replacements.

"By the way," I asked Max, "did Holtz ever tell you what he looked for in an assistant?"

"He told me he looked for a 'natural teacher' and then said with real intensity, "The great coaches are fun to be around... they *laugh!*'" Which, naturally, set Max to laughing.

I was eager to get my scouting under way, although I voiced one concern: "It sounds like it could take years to run across these prospects for great employees. Any way to speed things up?"

"Not years. I suspect that if you look at all the people you come in contact with, you'll have some prospects immediately. You won't be surprised to hear that I have a story on that subject."

The Reversal

Max then told me of Erik Saltvold:

"He's just thirty-three, but he's been in business for twenty years. As a high school student, he started a bike sales and repair business for a work-study project. Growing up, Saltwold lived with his family in an old farmhouse, and it had an unused barn, which he converted into a showroom. He bought used bikes, fixed then resold them. Soon—he was just fourteen, at this point—he decided to stock new bikes. So he went to a wholesaler to make his first buy. The fellow asked his name. 'Erik,' he replied.

"'Not *your* name, the company name.'

"'I don't have one.'

"'Well, I need to put down something. How about Erik's Bike Shop?'

"And by age fifteen Eric had a real bike shop in the barn,

and was having his mom drive him into Minneapolis to the wholesaler where he would order thousands of dollars of merchandise.

"The company name hasn't changed, but Erik's Bike Shop now has six locations in the Twin Cities and a hundred and fifty employees. And those employees have come from Erik's recruiting of salespeople.

"It makes sense. The best salespeople are heavily involved with bikes. Saltvold says, 'It's a "techie" sport and there are people who love to tinker with bikes. And it's not a get-rich industry, so you have to love bikes to work in it. There is a fairly small pool of individuals with the interests and background. Where do you find potential employees with those characteristics? They come in the store all day long.' Saltvold told me, 'I've hired so many customers that all the managers know to look at customers as potential employees. When they get to know one that would fit into our company, they ask, "How would you like to work with us?" In other words, the customers become salespeople, and the salespeople become managers.'"

This story did not seem as relevant to my situation, because I don't have customers in the same sense as a retail operation. But by this point, I could tumble to Max's broader point: in this case, look at everyone you come in contact with. I found myself thinking of one young woman who worked for one of our consultants . . . a great employee.

"Did I lose you?" Max asked.

"I just started thinking of a possible candidate. She definitely qualifies as a Wild Brain. A true innovator. She'd be fabulous in my department, but she's got a good job now. I doubt I could even match her salary, much less beat it."

Max made a show of tearing a piece of paper off his pad and then wadding it up and pitching it at my head. "There you go, back into the glass rut, thinking in the average way about the average hiring process. First, they all have good jobs, the great employees. Almost all, anyway. But get to know this prospect. Find out what she really wants to work on. She may be dreaming of a project that would revolutionize how you work. Remember: freedom, a change and a chance. The old school is to hire someone you need by offering twenty percent more money. Well, try offering a hundred percent more freedom or a hundred percent more excitement. Remember Norm Brinker being hired by the 'dreamer in brown plaid.' You need to get yourself free to dream and then find a dream to share."

He was right. As soon as I'd pictured myself with this prize catch of an employee, my excitement had caused me to fall back on familiar thinking. Now I was thinking of what I could accomplish with an alliance.

The Antibureaucrat Goes Hiring

With his eyes twitching in anticipation, Max declared, "Now I'm going to tell you a story that will shake up your thinking. You cannot be in a glass rut and do what Ron Walters did. He was running a sales office for a national printing company. He'd met a person at another firm whom he really wanted to hire and had worked at getting to know. One day she told him she was ready to change jobs . . . immediately. He did not have an opening, or any money in the budget. But he hired her anyway. For the first month he paid her out of his own pocket. Now there's someone working in a bureaucracy who refused to think like a bureaucrat."

I confess I found myself refusing to consider doing something comparable.

Max saw my consternation, and added, "Ron Walters was building a team and he knew that a great employee would return wealths to him. Not just wealth, but wealths. And, by the way, I should tell you a little more about this guy. He eventually left the big firm and started his own company, Freedom Printing, and built it to a multi-million-dollar operation in just a few years. He created a magnetic workplace, and one way he insured that it was the best place to work was that he would encourage his employees to look for other jobs and to come back and tell him what they found out there. Over the years, many took him up on that suggestion. He learned a lot—it was 'competitive intelligence'—but the goal was to be certain that they weren't offering a better workplace. And he never once lost an employee in the process."

Max stopped himself. "But I'm digressing. I wanted to tell you about his other hiring strategy. Besides just spotting people he came in contact with, he would ask his customers who they would like to work with. You could do the same. I know, I know. You don't have the same kind of customers."

He stopped again, this time to narrow his eyes and say, "Don't make me wad up another piece of paper."

I held up my hands. "No need. I'm not thinking like a bureaucrat. What I'm going to do is go to the people in our company in other departments and ask them about people they've worked with at previous employers. I'm thinking of a brand manager who recently came over from Intel. There might be a great employee at Intel in a department comparable to mine, whom I could contact. Maybe arrange to meet at one of the conventions or somewhere. Start tracking that person. Maybe we don't pay more than Intel, but in my department, at least, we're going to have more freedom, energy and excitement."

Max stood and gave me a bow.

"Okay. You've got it," Max said, delighted. "You are now an

official talent scout. I loved your idea of having a file on every great prospect in the country, or maybe the world. So, let me ask you now a question I asked you on the phone when we first started all this. What's your philosophy of hiring?"

I had an answer: "My department will be—no, make that 'is becoming'—the best place for the best people to work. And it's my job to let the best people know. Hiring isn't something you do when an employee quits. And it happens mostly outside the job market. A lot of great employees never look for jobs. So I need to spot them and court them. And since I'll be freed from most managing chores, I can devote myself to scouting, to networking."

"Very good. I have just one quibble. I wish you'd ended that statement two words sooner. To me, 'scouting' and 'networking' are different. You could go to a thousand luncheons and never come away with a great employee, or a great boss, either. You could have five thousand names on a Rolodex, and all it would accomplish is to keep you too busy to seek out great employees. I'm not interested in cultivating contacts, in being able to pick up the phone and get tickets to some Broadway show. That's fine if you want to do it. But the scouting process isn't just getting to know a lot of people, it's getting to know the work of highly talented people."

Seeing a Lot of Games

"And to continue the analogy a bit further," Max said, "the best talent scout is going to see a lot of games, see a lot of prospects. One way to do that is to have worked with a lot of people. So this is one instance where older is better ... *if* the person has been spotting talent all along, and keeping in touch. We'll talk later about how talented people keep recycling one another.

"But there are ways for someone in your position to start spotting talent. And you might want to emphasize young talent, because great employees rise so quickly that it's hard to get them later on. So you can hire interns. Or teach a college class. I've known several professionals who do this not just to be stimulated by young minds but also to spot the best young talent. That was another of the tricks of John Genzale, our poetry man. He's recruited so many rising journalists that the publisher of the main paper in town went to the dean and complained that they were 'tired of getting Genzale's leftovers.'

"And speaking of colleges—they went one step further at Marketplace Ministries in Dallas. This is a fascinating company—they place corporate chaplains in companies around the country. They have about five hundred of them."

I expressed my doubts about religion being mixed in with corporate life. Max countered, saying, "I know what you mean. But it's not like that. The founder, Gil Stricklin, was an air force chaplain, and it's all nondenominational. The idea is to have someone around the office or factory that you can *really* talk to. The idea is so powerful that one of the key employees is a man who left a New York ad agency and took a cut in pay of over one hundred grand. Talk about a magnetic workplace!

"Anyway, don't let me digress. My point is that Gil—the founder—did more than teach a class. He helped a big seminary in Dallas create a master of corporate chaplaincy—the first in the world, as far as I know. His goal was to boost the concept, but there was a marvelous unintended consequence: He has created a flow of talent. He helped create a graduate program that finds and trains potential employees. And all the students do an internship with Gil's firm. So he gets to see them all in action. In effect, he grows his own talent, and the crop pays to be grown."

My lack of immediate response was enough to get Max to jump in and say, "Okay, okay, you're going to tell me that it's not in your power to create a new graduate program. I'm not sure that's true, but let's go with the assumption. How's this: College profes-sors love their students to work on real-world projects. You get some work done for free, or almost free, and you get to work with potential recruits. You see their minds at work."

"That I could do with a phone call. A professor approached me last year, and I put him off."

"Remind me to give you a quarter for the call," he said, play-ing at sarcasm. But then he was going on: "Or, you might try temps. There are executive temps now, so you can 'try out' employees. But you can also use lower-level temps as a source of trainees for higher-level positions. I've known executives—for instance, Bryan Stauning of Information Management Systems in Minneapolis—who prefer to use a lot of temps in the clerical roles, not because they don't have enough work for full-timers, but because they want a chance to spot great employees, ones they'll hire and train for other positions.

"Oh, one more," Max said, reinvigorating himself with a rec-ollection. "I have got to tell you about Susan and Barry Brooks, who own a mail-order gift business called Cookies from Home. Barry was interviewing for a part-time supervisor, and in comes an older man that Susan describes as looking as if he were wearing one of those Groucho masks. Turns out that he's a retired execu-tive, looking for something to get him out of the house. His name is Vince Ciccarelli, and he was a turnaround specialist in New York. Instead of giving him the job he was applying for—production supervisor—they hire him to review their operations. And soon Barry and Susan fall in love with the guy's business wisdom. So Barry offers him a permanent job, but Ciccarelli turns it down, saying that he has decided to go back into retirement. And then he goes into Susan's office to tell her of his decision and to say good-bye. Well, Susan Brooks is not the sort of person you say no to. As he's talking, she walks over and closes her office door, then, standing in front of it, arms out, she announces, 'You can't leave. I don't care if you work an hour a day or ten, but you're not leaving till you agree to work for us. We need you.' Ciccarelli's reaction was to throw back his head and laugh. Susan described that moment, that laugh, by saying, 'I knew then that I could give him what he needed—to be needed.'"

Max continued: "And here's where the story gets even more interesting. She told him that he could set his own conditions of employment—whatever he wanted. And he came back and said that he wanted to leave every day at three o'clock, and on Fridays at noon. And then he told the owners of the company that he wanted them to report to him. He said, 'You can fire me any time you want, but you work for me.' And Susan and Barry agreed, which tells you something about them as gifted bosses. That decision paid off—their revenues had been stagnant before Ciccarelli joined them; it's doubled in the three years since."

As Max spoke I was struck by how far my own attempts at hiring had been from those of Susan Brooks or Lou Holtz or the others. My efforts were, by comparison, cold—not just impersonal but self-centered. I'd never taken the time to figure out what employees wanted from life, just how much I could offer. And by using the traditional methods, I would never ever have seen a retired gem of an employee, much less tried to put together a work relationship suited to such a person.

The Discounters

Max stopped and stared at me. "What?" I said, waiting to be accused of something less than full attention. But he was lost in his own recollections. "Oh, just that there was one other source I wanted to suggest." He grimaced and then said, "Oh, yes. I like this one. And if you're ready to take a few chances, you might like it too. It's the 'damaged goods' approach. Sometimes you can pick up a great employee who would normally be unavailable, someone who should be at a much higher level. I hired one guy who had been fired from another company after his wife left him and he'd gone into a depression. A drinking problem. I told him, 'If you beat it, I'll hire you.' That was the ray of hope he needed. And he recovered and has worked for me ever since. Brilliant and completely loyal to our alliance.

"And I met a man who worked within a big corporation who had a collection of Wild Brains he had assembled. He confided in me that it was easy. What he did was hire troublemakers, people other managers were about to give up on because they were difficult to manage. He established his department as a place for 'difficult people.' They weren't difficult for him, because he set them loose instead of trying to manage them, and they turned out amazing work. Another case of a person in the middle of a big bureaucracy who managed to turn the disadvantages of size to his favor."

The Old Methods Made New

We discussed how I could apply these strategies to my hiring. When I thought we were finished with the subject, Max announced that he wanted to cover one last point.

"It was important to break through your glass rut and get you thinking like a talent scout. Mostly you'll search out talent; occasionally it will drop on you. Either way, you keep the pipeline flowing. But there are situations where you don't have anyone in the pipeline and you need to do some instant scouting/hiring."

Max then told me of John Kilcullen, the CEO of IDG Books, the folks who've had the incredible success of the *For Dummies* series of books.

"After the company's early success, John wanted to hire a financial genius. So instead of bringing in a search firm, he calls the head of the biggest industry convention and asks, 'Who's the best financial mind in publishing?' And his answer was 'Steve Berkowitz.' Then Kilcullen gets the convention guy to tell Berkowitz, 'You should meet each other.' Then, when the convention comes along, Kilcullen arranges to take an afternoon off to play golf with Berkowitz. Kilcullen is no golfer—in fact, he showed up in blue jeans, which aren't allowed in the course's dress code, so he ended up playing in linen dress pants, which he ruined. But Kilcullen was willing to make a fool of himself, trying to play, just to have four or five hours to get to know the guy, to interview him without his knowing it. They hit it off, and then it was time for Kilcullen to begin the courtship.

"Turns out the biggest obstacle was getting Berkowitz, and his wife—especially his wife—to leave Long Island. So Kilcullen flies cross-country to New York, rents a car and drives to their home, so he can sit down with them both and persuade them to come to California to take a look. And they did, and were hooked."

Max stopped himself to smile at me, reading in my face that I'd profited from that example. I asked him for more examples, and he told me of Leroy Cook, who heads a national referral network for private investigators. He needed to hire someone quickly and decided to run a newspaper ad. But, being a gifted boss, he didn't run an ordinary ad. He had tried those in the past and was disappointed with the quality of people who applied. So he decided to run an ad that began WANTED: SUPERMAN OR WONDER

WOMAN and described a great employee. He didn't get many responses but did tap into a whole new level of interesting candidates. In fact, readers of the classifieds were tearing out the ad to give to people they thought were great employees.

Max jumped ahead: "Another, related case was from a guy I mentioned earlier, Ron Walters and his printing company. He's the one who paid a new employee out of his own pocket. Well, he needed a 'temp.' But when he calls the agency, he says, 'Don't send the usual person. Send someone special.' And they did. It's remarkable what you can get just by asking. It turns out that the temp was a woman who had just moved to town. She's a great employee and knows it. And so she was working as a temp in order to 'try out' companies. She spots Ron as a great boss and goes to him and says, 'What would it take to get hired here?' That's a great example of a great employee taking the initiative, and it's also an example of how, every once in a while, a great employee falls from the heavens."

I responded by saying, "I suppose that the trick is to recognize them when they fall."

Max nodded and said, "Sometimes you get just a glimpse. Which takes us to Gary Lannigan. When he was marketing director for a shipbuilding company, he was walking past the front desk and overheard a woman talking to the receptionist. The woman was explaining that she had just read a newspaper article about the company and how fast it was growing, so she thought they might have a job for her. The receptionist turns her down like a bedspread."

I laughed at that image, and Max gave credit for the line to P. G. Wodehouse. "Anyway, the receptionist sends this woman away. But Lannigan recognizes the initiative. He sees someone who didn't rely on typical techniques, and he's wise enough to know that the best employees are not typical. So he stops her as she's leaving and learns that she's been out of the job market for twenty years, raising a family, and now she's ready to work again. The upshot is that Lannigan hires her and gives her the receptionist's job."

Max stopped and said, "So there it is. You learn to be a scout, you plan your employee 'mergers and acquisitions' and then you keep your mind open, hoping to get the occasional gift from the old methods."

I nodded, eager to get started. I was looking forward to Monday, when I would be back in the office and I could start designing my magnetic workplace and start my prospect files.

"There are two more subjects," Max said, "and then we'll stop talking about business and do some sight-seeing. And the next topic is"—at this he leaned in and spoke in a hammy whisper—"the secret skill. Shhhh."

The Secret Skill

We stopped long enough to clean up the kitchen and to move back onto the patio. Sparrows flitted in the branches of Palo Verde trees, and the sun was skittering through the lacy branches, warming us as we sat. Max passed over another sheet of paper with one of his principles.

> 5. **While many gifted bosses have created such special work environments that they have virtually no turnover, many others embrace substantial turnover and become masters of "the secret skill" of firing.**

Sounding unusually somber, he said, "Nowhere in my research did I find such a dichotomy among gifted bosses as in their attitudes toward employee turnover and firings. More than half of the gifted bosses have substantial turnover and don't mind. Indeed, they welcome it, causing much of it themselves, by "letting go" a substantial proportion of their staffs. However, many others—at least one-third of the bosses—have virtually no turnover."

I offered this observation: "It seems to me that a gifted boss would fit the latter case. After all, a wise boss selects employees wisely and then creates a marvelous work environment that people don't want to leave."

"Yes. True. But there is a competing logic. A great boss sets high standards and isn't afraid to admit that employees often fall short. Also, it can be exhausting working at such a high level, and employees often opt for a softer environment. Result: substantial turnover."

"Or," I added, "maybe they didn't do such a good job of talent scouting."

Max grinned and nodded. "You're right. If you hire people on hunches, rather than seeing their work over time, you'll make mistakes.

"Either way," he continued, "there are two ways to think about turnover. Some companies merely focus on the cost of hiring and training employees and assume that the less turnover the better. But the right kind of turnover can actually be quite healthy. If a company sets high standards and rewards excellence, and the result is that twenty percent of the employees leave each year, that company will grow mighty—they will be like the title of the book Joe Namath wrote many years ago, *I Can't Wait Until Tomorrow... 'Cause I Get Better Looking Every Day.*"

Max digressed a while about Namath but then resumed, saying, "On the other hand, if the company is inept or has a dreadful work environment, it's the best employees who can most easily move on, and so even a small turnover becomes disastrous because it is from the top, a 'brain drain.' The upshot is that the company with twenty percent turnover can be much healthier than the one with ten percent turnover."

I asked Max if that really happened.

"There is research on healthy turnover under the rubric 'functional turnover,'" he replied. "But the best way to understand the concept is to look at some of the most admired companies in the country. For example, while Southwest Airlines is famous for its hiring practices, no one says much about its firing practices—but you should know that they consider the first six months a trial period in which any employee can be fired at will, and that includes union employees. And Nordstrom loses nearly a quarter of its salespeople each year. The leaders of the company accept such turnover—maybe even welcome it—regarding it as a natural selection process."

Here I stopped Max to question him about the wisdom of that approach.

He responded, "One of the sayings at Nordstrom is 'Your performance is your review.' Given that much of the employee's income is from commissions, and that expectations for hard work are very high, the employees tend to select themselves out. In fact, one of the advantages of having a great employee or two around is that they can make firing irrelevant. Remember the executive with the shipbuilder, Gary Lannigan? One day he went into the company facilities on a Sunday, the day before they were planning to take some boats to a major trade show. And while walking through, Lannigan came across a lone employee—a young man, a recent immigrant, who was finishing work on a boat. As they talked, Lannigan realized that this kid had exceptional personal standards, that he was doing work beyond the company's usual level of preparation. And so the next day Lannigan tells the president, 'Take care of this kid.'"

I found myself wondering how often it happens that a young kid who doesn't speak English very well has two key executives watching over him. Max concluded the story by saying, "So the kid gets promoted and promoted and finally goes off to join a major shipbuilder. But the story doesn't end there. The kid—now middle-aged—started his own company. And the big company he left missed him so much, they went to him and bought his company just to get him back. Now that's a great employee. When I asked Lannigan just what traits this guy had, his answers were all about high standards. And then he said something I hadn't heard from anyone else but I suspect is true elsewhere. He said, 'I never had to fire anybody after he came to work for us. He would scare off all the people who didn't aspire to being the best.'"

He gave me time to contemplate that.

"Still," he continued, "despite the high standards and the presence of other great employees as role models or scarecrows, a large number of gifted bosses do a lot of firing. What surprised me was, when I was able to get some of them to open up about their firing practices, that they are masters of shedding unwanted employees, often doing it so gracefully that the ex-employee remains an ally of the firm, and sometimes even returns. Here's another example from John Genzale:

> "John told me of the time when he was leaving the *Miami News* and the staff had a going-away party for him. *Seven of the people he had fired* showed up. When I asked if they had come to 'dance on his grave,' he laughed. 'No, they wanted to wish me well. They all knew that I had always wished them well and that I tried to help them. I never sacrificed a person's dignity, and never fired a person who deep down didn't know it wasn't working out.'
>
> "I asked for an example. He told me of a woman who had consistently violated one of the company policies. He talked, then pleaded, then threatened. Finally, he told her, 'The next time, I'm going to have to fire you.' And when the next time came, he told her sadly, 'I love you, but it's over.' The event was so expected, so de-emotionalized, that she reacted by asking to use Genzale's phone. She proceeded to use his phone to postpone an appointment

with her hairdresser. And he then helped her think through her career options, and helped her find another job.

"But Genzale also gave me an example of a person he did *not* fire. 'We had an older guy, a real gentleman, who was nearing seventy, and the company had no mandatory retirement age. He was over the hill. I knew I should replace him with a better person. But he had no family, just a dog. The paper and the dog, that was his whole life. I couldn't fire him. Would we be better off replacing him? Yes. Would we be better people? No.'"

Max added, "That story illustrates the role of firings in the culture of the company. I've known companies to keep on employees who are struggling—health, family, drinking, drugs—the company holding off, trying to help. I once told the story about the paper and the dog to a writer in Albuquerque, Tony Lesce. And he told me he'd worked for a newspaper publisher, a great boss, who had an employee with a drinking problem. 'Occasionally, this guy would pass out. We would step over him, there on the floor. But the publisher wouldn't fire him because he felt the employee would turn around. It was one reason we all loved this publisher—he cared that much about his people.'"

Max stopped to shrug, a gesture that didn't fit him. He added, "This was years ago. I'm not certain that someone would do the same today. And, once again, there is logic on the other side. Larry Tree, the CEO who moved the headquarters staff into a trailer, told me, 'One way to reward a performer is to admonish a non-performer. The employees think, Hey, management notices. They care. When you ignore mediocrity, the bar is lowered. Then it's okay to do less.'"

Max quietly continued: "And Ken Donahue of Teledyne admitted to me sadly that firing can be 'an important management tool.' What he means is that you use firing and hiring to set new standards, to demonstrate to other employees what you are looking for. After three years without sales growth, he replaced his head of sales, and sales went up sixty percent. He says, 'People are smart, they pick up on it. Employees look at that and think, "I understand—here's the performance and work ethic that's rewarded." And they look at the person who left and think, "And there's the performance and work ethic that is unacceptable." It's part of the process of getting people to understand what the company wants. You see people who are out, and know what they would have done. And you see people who are new, and know what they are doing. Before long you don't have to ask: You know it, feel it—this is what the company would want me to do.'

"So," Max said, leaning in, "these bosses accept the need to fire people. But that doesn't mean they jump to it. As Ken Donahue put it, 'If it's easy to fire someone, it's probably the wrong decision.' What he meant was that if it's easy, you're not caring enough. He also argued that treating people with dignity sends another type of message: 'Employees want to know that if they have to leave, they'll be able to feed their families, have the time to find a new job.'"

With this, Max returned to his old self, bouncing in his seat and saying, "Angelo Petrilli is one of the gifted bosses who does more than give departing employees time, he gives them his help. 'I tell them, "I know you've done your best, but you haven't found what you were meant to do." And then I help them focus on their strengths and weaknesses, and then try to use my network to help them find a new job.' He also admitted, 'Sometimes I feel like I'm a headhunter.' But time and caring comes back to gifted bosses— instead of making enemies, they actually make allies with those they've fired. Norm Brinker told me this, 'If you care, you attract quality people. Winners attract winners and leaders attract leaders.

But sometimes people aren't performing and they've got to go. You deal with it kindly and with compassion. You help them to do better in the next job. At one point, I had so many people I had fired who became regular customers, that one of the managers told me, "You've got to fire more people; it's good for sales."'"

Max told me several stories of fired employees who ended up being hired back. He recounted cases of gifted bosses who had employees who have left two or three times. They leave and try something new, and come back grateful and recharged. Here I interrupted long enough to add a personal example. While I'm not trying to horn in on the "gifted boss" category, on this one occasion I got it right. When I ran a division of a market research company, I had a young Colombian woman working for me. Suddenly, she lost interest in her work, became absentminded, missed deadlines, and so on. She had fallen in love. I told myself that I'd "lost her to Cupid," which was charming . . . at first. Months passed and she never regained her interest. After many discussion sessions, I had to fire her. I could only console myself with the knowledge that it was best for the company and maybe for her too, that the change might reinvigorate her. Through mutual friends, I followed her progress. Half a year later, I hired her back, and she was once again a joy to me and the company.

Max responded by saying that gifted bosses confirm what I learned from that experience: "The expression 'I had to fire her' is the right one. When there is *no other option*, and everybody knows it—boss, employee and coworkers—that's the right time. And when it's that time, the gifted boss–great employee alliances need not be ended, just suspended, a kind of workplace 'rain delay.' As we shall see in a minute, boss-employee alliances have a way of realigning, often lasting a lifetime."

Interconnected Careers

"Now, as you may recall," Max said gently, "I'm not a fan of lifetime employment, or the old corporate pyramid. Still, it saddens me to see the decline of the old corporate loyalty, mostly because of what came next. What replaced it?"

It took me a minute to realize he was waiting for an answer. "Greed, self-interest, politics."

"Yes, instead of replacing lifetime employment with the joy of discovery, we got instead the fear of obsolescence. That's why alliances can be so soul satisfying. You make a permanent connection. Companies may come and go, but alliances endure." And he handed me the next principle.

> 6. **An alliance between a gifted boss and a great employee is a kinship of talent, often creating a bond that can last a lifetime.**

"A computer engineer named Dick Ruth," Max began, "who worked on a series of groundbreaking technical projects, like the Atlas missile guidance system and the Honeywell 6000, reflected back on his long career and how he kept intersecting the same individuals and said, 'There's a national—no, international—brotherhood of mavericks, and they find and refind each other.' Those are his words—the 'brotherhood of mavericks.' Sounds like a union for nonjoiners. And it will also sound familiar to gifted bosses and great employees, who without ever signing up, have become part of a talent union."

Max leaned in, gathering his intensity. "A computer systems engineer, Arno Rite, gave me an example of interconnected careers that I have in my memory. . . . Did I tell you that I have a photographic memory?"

"No more same-day service," I said, chuckling. "Yes."

He winked at me. There aren't too many people who can wink and make it seem natural, but Max was one. "Anyway, it went something like this." He took out a piece of paper and wrote the process. I've added some notes to replace his running commentary. It isn't important to follow the convolutions, just to accept the fact that such convolutions exist.

STEP ONE

- Rite takes a job at AMERCO (parent company for U-Haul and some smaller companies). New to management, he starts to build a department.

- He inherits Employee A.

- Then he hires Employee B (at urging of Employee A).

- Then he hires Employee C (via internal hire).

STEP TWO

- Employee B gets a new job at MicroAge (a Fortune 500 computer sales company), a promotion to department head.

- Soon after starting, Employee B convinces MicroAge to bring in Rite as head of a different department.

- Rite joins the company, and soon after, he brings over Employee C.

STEP THREE

- Employee C leaves to work for a MicroAge client.

STEP FOUR

- Rite and Employee C both leave their jobs in order to join together and create a new start-up, Dolphin Systems.

After finishing, Max said, "Let me pause to give you a sub-story that is very relevant to your situation. Rite should never have hired the person I've been calling 'Employee C.' Rite had a job opening at AMERCO and had several internal candidates who wanted to fill it. One of these was the obvious choice—highly qualified, technically superior to the others, and due for a promotion. Internal politics left no other option. But Rite had spotted a great employee, another internal candidate, one with far less technical knowledge and less tenure, but who had more personality, creativity and zest."

Max held up both index fingers, saying, "Corporate politics demanded the first candidate; Rite wanted the second one. So Rite decided that if he didn't like the results of the hiring process, he should change the process. He added a new step and had the two 'finalists' come back to take a 'what if?' test of various difficulties that could be encountered on the job. Selecting the scenarios carefully, he was able to weight them to the talents of the great employee, rather than to the skills of the more experienced candidate. And so he gathered 'proof' that the great employee was also the better candidate."

Max then explained that many of the most thoroughly intertwined careers were in technical fields, where the available pool of employees is limited. But alliances exist in every field and often result in careers that reunite. He told me of the career of a lawyer we've discussed earlier, Nancy Loftin. When she was working for the Securities Division of the Arizona Corporation Commission she hired a new staff member right out of law school. Her instincts were correct about him, and when she resigned to spend time with her new baby, he was promoted to her old job.

Later, when she was ready to restart her career, he hired her to work for him.

Both eventually left the Corporation Commission: he to join a large law firm in San Francisco; she to become the chief legal counsel for a large utility company, APS. When he later visited her, he admitted that the law firm life was a disappointment. As soon as she had an opening, she offered him a job, and he accepted.

Max gave me other examples, most so Byzantine that I won't attempt to recreate them here. Listening to him, I realized that I had encountered such alliances in my own work, I'd just never stopped to analyze them. For instance, I'd met an ad agency creative director named Richard Calvelli (whose credits include "I love what you do for me ... Toyota" and "How do you spell relief?"). He spoke to me of working with a mutual friend, Steve Patchen. On three occasions Calvelli got a new job and each time started a campaign for the new company to hire Steve, not only to have a pal around but also because he knew he could count on his old friend to create the environment for truly creative advertising to take place.

Max summed up the examples by saying, "What these stories of interlocking careers make clear is that the selection of a boss is significant, often more significant than the choice of an employer company, perhaps more important than the choice of a career.

"I've been working for over fifty years, and one thing hasn't changed: the way most employees think about 'opportunities.' They tend to think almost exclusively of the job—and they evaluate that job mostly on the salary, maybe the title, maybe the benefits. Occasionally an employee will move up a level and consider the company or industry. Even so, this tends to be a surface analysis, thoughts such as 'It's working for a Fortune 500 company' or 'It's a chance to get out of banking.' Rarely is the boss a factor in the job decision, unless the person has experienced a great one. That made sense in the postwar hierarchical corporation, in which an employee would move within the organization and have many bosses, often more than one in a year. But it no longer makes sense, especially for talented employees. By choosing a gifted boss, they assure that their talents will be developed, and they gain an ally who may figure in their careers for a lifetime."

And then Max made some comments that struck me as particularly helpful. He said, "When employees hear about the latest panacea—networking, networking, networking—they naturally tend to think of the dreary business card exchanges at professional organizations and service clubs. But if the same amount of energy were devoted to maintaining relationships with former employers and coworkers, it would yield far more opportunities. There is a tendency for everyone at companies to forget those who leave. The departed person first gets blamed, and then gets forgotten. And someone who leaves a company will rarely see those left behind. But the gifted boss never forgets a great employee and maintains contact."

I thought of Max's earlier example, Dave Ridley, the VP of marketing for Southwest Airlines who hired a young intern two years after the internship ended.

"This also suggests," Max said, "that the wise employee will take every opportunity to display his or her talents within the company and the industry, especially where gifted bosses might see them. The alliances often start long before the actual boss-employee relationship. And, as we have seen, often continue after it. They exist on a separate plane, a kind of family—connected not by blood but talent."

And Max concluded with a quote from Dan Schweiker, the CEO of China Mist Tea. Commenting on the "family" relationship with his employees, he offered a different metaphor: "With the disintegration of families, people join companies like ours for the same reason that inner-city kids join gangs. They want to belong. It's that same feeling here, but you live longer. We have retirement benefits."

Conclusions

Max rummaged around in his leather portfolio and handed me a sheet of paper. It was the "Six Realities of Gifted Bosses and Great Employees." And he handed me a couple of other pages, saying as he did, "These 'realities' suggest new leadership methods as well as new career strategies. So I couldn't resist writing up a few suggestions on applying those principles."

Here's what those pages contained:

- The hiring process is not passive—the employer isn't engaged in "sorting" but "spotting." Then, once spotted, the talented employee must be courted. (After all, these are *great* employees—they are likely to be treated well and paid well.) The gifted boss creates an exceptional environment and uses it to romance the great employee.

- Hiring is rarely based on just a job interview or referral— both sides understand that these are artificial. They want to see the other person's work, and the person at work, to see if they are talent "kin."

- Given the benefits of the alliance, having the right boss may be more important than the right company or even the right job.

- Given the importance of a gifted boss/great employee alliance, and the fact that such alliances begin outside the job market, new methods are demanded of individuals who want to emulate the success of talented individuals.
  —For bosses, the findings suggest that they deemphasize the traditional job market and instead increase opportunities to see talent in action.
  —Once talent is identified, great bosses learn the skills of bringing it inside—sometimes taking years, sometimes involving the creation of special projects, occasionally requiring "warehousing," "moles" or other unusual tactics.
  —As for employees, the talent-mating approach would suggest that they seek to broaden the number of people with whom they work, inside and outside the company, putting their talents on display in personal "product demonstrations." And whereas managers have traditionally done "empire building," the employee undertakes a similar strategy of "audience building."

I looked up from reading his summaries. "And with that," Max said, slumping back in his chair, feigning exhaustion, "you have sucked my brain dry. I don't have another thought left. Do not ask me any more questions."

I grinned and asked a question: "What should I do first?"

He flopped around, trying to reslump. "More, more, more. That's all I hear from you."

"I guess I'll just have to go back and fire the entire staff and start over," I said to tweak him.

But he was already working his way up, drawn irresistibly to my question.

"Okay, okay. Here's what I'd do. I would *not* start firing people, at least not yet. You haven't worked at being a gifted boss, so don't expect to have employees suited to a gifted boss. But I'd say you ought to let them know they are about to experience a dramatic break from the past."

"A set of experiments," I added, knowing that concept was important to Max.

"Yes, you might pick a dozen things that will make your division exceptional, make it magnetic. I don't know your kind of work well enough to tell you just what to do, but the list would surely include these:

- "You'd start by replacing rules with standards. For your department, you'd have to figure out what makes a great report or a great presentation—quality, creativity, speed, whatever. Your best becomes your norm. If you had a list of the five traits of a great presentation, and scored each one, that alone would change the way everyone works.

- "You insist that your employees stop coming to you for solutions, but that they become experts on options. I'd make a motto out of 'Show me the possibilities.'

- "You might also work with each employee to develop a personal 'brand.' Insist that each one have a specialty. The typical performance review dwells on weaknesses, and the result is that everyone moves toward average on all traits. But a performer becomes great by having a great strength. Dwell on those.

- "And, most important, 'give 'em something to talk about.' You need a departmental strength to dwell on. Remember the poetry readings. You need to find your poetry. Maybe you collect reports from outside your industry and analyze them together. Or maybe you take the department on field trips to other corporations to learn what they do, and you adapt the best ideas. Maybe you bring in an acting coach to work with your employees on presentation skills. I'm not sure what it is for you, but find your poetry.

- "And through all these experiments, remember the goal is to make your group into **The Best Place for the Best People to Work.**"

There was a long silence as Max waited for me and my note taking to catch up. As I wrote out those suggestions, I realized that I could implement them and some other experiments within a week or two. And I could predict which of the employees would embrace these experiments and which would be heel draggers. In fact, I was already looking forward to scaring off a couple of the slackers. I said to Max, "By the time I get off the plane this evening, I'll have the list ready. And I know who I'll need to get rid of too."

"Don't be too sure," Max warned. "Some will surprise you. And I hope you'll have learned something about 'outplacement,' about graceful departures."

"Absolutely. Our corporation has good internal job movement. And thinking of myself as an 'outplacer' will remove some of my guilt feeling and make it easier to raise my standards and not keep putting off the need to get rid of the lackluster employees."

"Good. And then there's the hiring."

"I am now a talent scout. I am going to track every great employee in my field and even some outside it. I'm not going to wait for employees to hunt for a job with me, I'm going to get out and hunt them."

"Perfect. And I'd like to see you start to pay attention to new role models—agents, football coaches, heads of sales operations. For example, last time I visited my stockbroker I stopped to meet the man who heads the office, and I asked how he hires the top-producing brokers, something for which he is famous. He said this: 'I make it my business to know every top broker in town.' And then he said, 'The best ones, the ones I'd like to hire, I "drip on."' He explained what he meant by saying that he calls them once every month or two, or sends them an article. He said, 'I don't talk them into moving to my office, but I want *them* to talk to *me* if they start to think about moving.'"

Max added, "At first I disliked that notion of 'dripping,' but it's stuck with me. Here's the lesson: It's not enough to know who they are, but they have to know who you are. You might occasionally invite them to one of the events you put on, whatever your version of the poetry reading ends up being."

I was still writing furiously. Max laughed, and said, "Look at how serious we've gotten. Speaking of role models, take the coach of the University of Colorado football team, Rick Neuheisel, who is creating a self-perpetuating flow of recruits. Neuheisel was criticized for taking his team on ski trips, and thus risking injuries. His response was, 'My fear isn't that players get hurt. My fear is that players don't have fun, don't have a great time here. I want everyone who plays for me to want his son to play for me.'" Max grabbed my knee, and I realized it was still sore from yesterday.

"I don't know about your employee's offspring working for you," Max said, "but it's got to be fun. If you don't walk through your department and hear laughter, then you're not doing it right. When people are doing what they do best, they feel a special energy that comes close to giddiness. That could be one standard you put on yourself—you walk the halls and count how many laughs you hear."

I wasn't sure if Max was kidding or not, but I wrote it down, thinking that maybe I'd get a collection of quote books and joke books for the department and start making humor a part of our presentations. And I wondered aloud if I'd have the guts to create a standard for laughs-per-hour for presentations.

He beamed at me and said, "The hardest part is over. You've broken that glass rut. Instead of thinking about what you have to do, you're thinking about all you could do."

"One thing more," I said. "What about finding a gifted boss?"

"Ah, yes. We mustn't overlook the other side of our coin. All that you're doing here is going to make you visible. Remember: The gifted bosses are hunters. You're going to be a much bigger target after today."

"I understand," I replied, "but shouldn't I do more than wait?"

"Well, you're hardly waiting. We just talked about how you can help your current employees be great, and you need to do the same for yourself—you'll be working on your strength, finding your poetry, and you'll be known for your creative options. But you'll also be searching the company, the city, the country, maybe the world, for ideas on how to improve your work. And that means you'll meet some gifted bosses. And then you can make yourself available."

"Available?"

"Don't be coy. In fact, I bet there's a gifted boss somewhere in your corporation that you know."

"There is one man I'd love to work for."

"And I imagine that everyone in the company says dreamily, 'I'd love to work for him.' And maybe one in a hundred will actually make it happen."

He could see the puzzled look I had on my face.

"See what I've done," Max moaned. "I've done just what I've told you not to do in your department. I'm handing you answers instead of forcing you to create options. So you tell me: How could you get him to hire you?"

"First, I suppose I would need to get to know him. But, no, not just *know* him. I would need for him to see my work. And so I could find what companywide projects he's working on and try to represent our division."

"And?"

"I could ask him to speak to our group. I know he does 'brown bag lunches' for his employees and has speakers, maybe he'd come visit us. And he could learn about all our experiments."

"You've got it. Once you start to look, the ways present themselves. And then, when you develop some sort of ongoing relationship, you 'drip' on him. And eventually you get invited in. I met a man who wanted to work for a boss he admired. They had both worked in the same corporation, but she had moved on and eventually got to be the president. He had kept in touch, and so it was perfectly natural that he called to congratulate her on the new job. She says, 'I wish you were going to be there.' And he says, 'Maybe we could make that happen.' And two weeks later, he's the vice president."

"That's all. I'm finished. You're on your own."

Max fell back in his seat, a kid in an aging body, fizzing with the wisdom of nearly eight decades of curiosity. I thought of where we had begun this conversation, how heavy my heart had been, wondering if I could find meaning in my work, and if I couldn't, how could I find meaning in my life? And here I sat, knowing that I was no longer working for my salary but working on finding my poetry. I was no longer just shoring up my little weaknesses, I was evolving my strengths. And I no longer felt lonely in the postloyalty world, because I knew that I was going to develop alliances. I already had a great employee and gifted boss—Wild Brains— waiting to be courted.

I sat staring off up toward the tall cactuses, thinking these thoughts. When I glanced over at Max, I saw him staring at me paternally, and then a suspicion came over me: He was a gifted boss who was bringing me along, who was turning me into a great employee, worthy of his company.

I smiled, and he did a couple of Groucho eyebrow raises and said, "I'll get the car. There's one last stop before we're done."

The chairs were deep and angled back, so Max reached out a hand, saying, "Help me up." I took his hand with both of mine, and then he added his other hand around mine. After he rose, I held on for a moment in this four-hand shake, and he winked his wink and he laughed that laugh and we stood a minute, only connecting.

Epilogue

My return flight was scheduled for midday, twenty-four hours after I'd landed, just as Max had suggested. As we drove, I realized I was eager to return to the office. It had been a while since I'd had that feeling.

But Max had one last surprise for me, one last lesson about what I might strive to create in a workplace.

We drove to a newly built industrial area not far from the airport. Max was in Phoenix on business for one of the companies he owned, but he had promised some friends at a company called Insight that he would come by. When he picked Phoenix as the spot for our rendezvous, this was the event that he had wanted me to see.

We started with a tour of the building, the one Max had described for me the day before that is shaped like a giant X, which forces employees to converge in a pedestrian roundabout in the middle. But there were few employees converging, not that morning. We went back to the entrance we'd come through half an hour earlier. Before it had been mostly empty, but now we joined a crowd of hundreds of employees. And there we found two barbers, shaving heads.

It turns out that one of the key employees, Jon Moss, had battled Hodgkin's disease and won, and was ready to get back to work. When his return had been scheduled a couple of weeks back, one of Moss's coworkers went to the company's young CEO, Eric Crown, and explained that his department wanted to do something special for the return. And since Moss had lost his hair, thanks to the chemotherapy, some of them were planning to shave their heads, assuming Eric didn't mind. Not only didn't he mind, he suggested that the company donate a hundred dollars to the American Cancer Society for each shaved head. And Eric said that he would join in, on the condition that his would be the hundredth head shaved.

I chatted with one young man who was putting his name on a list for the barbers, and he commented, "I'm signing away my hair . . . and my social life." Nearby, a thoughtful soul was handing out packets of sunblock, to prevent those pale scalps from getting sunburned after work.

It took a while, but when the head count reached one hundred, a chant went up for the CEO's head: "ER-IC, ER-IC, ER-IC." And when he took his turn, the crowd, turning giddy by then, hooted and cheered for him at a startling volume. And even after his head was glistening, still the line continued. The final count was 192, including four women.

Then the word came that Moss was going to address us. I imagined how strange this would be for him, to return to work after many weeks, and to come into this room and see the banners and all those shaved heads.

He went to the front, a slender man of perhaps thirty years, with dark eyes, wearing an Insight shirt and a shy grin, and as he reached the front, a great cheer rose up from the crowd. He was stunned and moved—you could see the emotions pass over him— knocked back and pulled forward.

He eventually said a few words of thanks, all but speechless, and then he passed among them, feeling their bald heads, and they feeling his, every eye wet.

Max and I stood to the side, silent. Then he put his arm around my shoulder and whispered, "Oh, my . . . This is . . . No Ordinary Workplace."

We were quiet on the way back to the airport, minds and hearts full. When he dropped me off, his rental car idling at the departures ramp, Max got out to give me one last hug and a final shoulder squeeze. Just before he turned to go, he promised to come visit later in the year. Then, as he ducked inside the car he called back to me, "I'll know where to find you—out where the Wild Brains roam." And he laughed his barking laugh. I watched him pull away, vowing to myself to make it true.

Acknowledgments and Sources

This book is a collection of the wisdom of gifted bosses, and I thank them for their generosity, their kindnesses and ready laughter. Never has my research been such a joy.

As I sat down to write a bibliography, I realized that I didn't need one—with the exception of a few short quotations, all of the stories and examples were told to me by gifted bosses, either specifically for this book or during interviews for one of my newspaper columns. Instead, what is called for is an explanation. My task was to organize gifted boss stories, striving to create a book worthy of their wisdom. The best way to do so, I decided (thanks to the tough-love counsel of Kim Sauer of the Margret McBride Literary Agency), was to put them in the form of a conversation. If I wrote it well, perhaps you will be a bit disappointed to learn that it did not happen in just one day. Yes, there is a Max—his personality is that of my friend Roger Axford, a retired college professor and full-time eccentric. I used Roger's personality as a conduit to express what I'd learned. The book's other character is me, and also (I hope) you—Everymanager. All the stories within the story are true and merely rearranged to fit into a conversation.

In addition to all the gifted bosses who appear in this book, my thanks to Norm Stoehr, Steve Brown, Bob Nelson, Steve Patchen, Jim Fickess, Richard Gooding, Roger Axford and many Dautens: Jeri, Sandy, Hilary, Trevor and both Joels. Also, I am grateful to my agent, Margret McBride, and her team; and to my editor, Henry Ferris, and the folks at William Morrow.

A QUICK START

on the Journey to Being a Gifted Boss

1. ASK: "DO YOU WANT TO BE GREAT?"

My favorite story in the book is the one about the artillery battalion voted best in the world (page 32). The transformation began when the officer in charge created a list of standards of excellence whereby he was able to say to his troops, in effect, "This is what it takes to be great. Do you want to be great?"

Create that list and you shift the group mind. Instead of just meeting internal goals, you start the conversation about making your team special.

2. START WINNING

"Great employees don't have jobs, they have talents." Do a team talent inventory. You not only need to define what it takes to be a great team, but what could allow each person to be a star. If you aren't keeping score, you can't win.

3. START EXPERIMENTING

As you invite employees to develop their own specialties, insist on experiments. Include time in each staff meeting

for reports on experiments. Start the applause. Be delight-
able.

4. ENCOURAGE THE GRACEFUL DEPARTURE OF MEDIOCRITY

Assume the best, but know that not every employee is
willing or able to be on a high-performance team. Give everyone a chance and plan to be surprised, but, odds are, you'll
have to say farewell to some sweet, content mediocrities.
Don't start firing, just make clear your high standards (and
tie rewards to those standards) and second-rate employees
will seek to move to where they are more welcome. Help
them go.

(When you start to falter—and you will—picture this:
What will it be like when you've taken the worst employees
on your team and replaced them with new talent as good, in
their own way, as your best-ever employee? How much more
could you accomplish?)

5. START FILLING THE TALENT PIPELINE

One of the most striking differences between ordinary
bosses and great ones is the time spent on hiring. Gifted
bosses are talent hunters. If you're going to be a gifted boss,
you'll need a talent pipeline. Start a list of people you'd like
to hire. Keep in touch in ways that keep them interested in
working with you. ("Drip on them," as one manager put it.)

6. REFUSE TO BE ORDINARY

You aren't just making your numbers, you're writing
your story. Make it a good one. We started this list with
"here's what it takes to be great." But you also need a specialty, which is simply being able to tell anyone how you and

your team are special. "Our team is different because we
_____." And it doesn't count to fill in that blank with
"really care" or some other generic, smiley-face crap that anybody can say—it has to be important and interesting. Do
that, and your group will take pride in being different.
That's when great employees will seek you out and you'll be
riding the spiral of talent.

DISCUSSION GUIDE
for Manager Meetings

1. This is a great way to lead a group into a Gifted Boss conversation: "I want you to take a minute and picture the best employee you've ever had, in any job."

You can then ask each manager to describe that best-ever employee and what made each one special. (Note: We want to get past the usual adjectives—"loyal," "hardworking" and the like—to get to the employee's uniqueness. Don't settle for generic comments; insist on examples. Don't stop till you've brought these "best-evers" to life—the memory of great employees should inspire and guide future hiring.)

Follow up by asking those with good examples of high-level employees, "How did you find that person?"

After getting examples of best employees and where those employees were found, invite a discussion of lessons that can be learned about hiring.

2. Remind the group of Max's contention that the best employees are rarely in the job market. Consider offering provocative suggestions for discussion, such as "Should we stop posting jobs?" and "Should we be asking ourselves with

every hiring decision, 'Does this potential new hire have a shot at being in the best-ever pantheon of great employees?'"

Other follow-up questions:

"Where/how can we spot talent?"

"Once we spot talent, how can we 'court' great employees?"

3. Max argues, "Gifted bosses don't hire employees, they acquire allies."

How would the "ally" metaphor change how you view the team you manage? (Compare "allies" to "family.")

How does it change your view of your other team, the one your boss leads?

4. Max proclaims that gifted bosses and great employees both want the same thing: "Freedom from management, mediocrity and morons." Said another way, they want to be free to do great work.

How can we free ourselves from useless management chores? What can we get rid of?

As for "mediocrity and morons," a frequent complaint by schoolteachers is their need to devote so much time to struggling or trouble-making students that they largely ignore the most capable ones. Do you see a parallel in working with difficult employees?

What can we start doing to become "the best place for the best people"?

5. One of the surprising facts about great bosses is that many of them have substantial employee turnover. (They hire employees of such high caliber that they get hired away, and, on the other end of the talent spectrum, ease out

mediocre employees.) Discuss "ideal turnover." Ask, "Could we pull off a 'be great or be gone' policy?"

How do we think of those high-level employees who've left the team, the ones we were sorry to see leave? Are they "traitors" or "graduates"? Are there any former employees we should work to keep in a "lifelong alliance of talent"?

FUTURE MEETINGS: Assign each manager to make use of the "Quick Start" implementation guide that precedes this outline. Schedule a meeting to discuss initial efforts, especially each manager's list of what it takes to be a great team/department.

Also schedule follow-up discussions for once or twice each month. (Putting them on the calendar for six months or a year sends the unmistakable message that you mean to make changes stick.)

In those follow-through meetings, insist that each manager report on actual changes made—not just plans, but actual progress—especially experiments underway, employee turnarounds or departures, and the talent pipeline. You want reports on what is *different* about each team; after all, "Different isn't always better, but better is always different."